Oracle WebLogic Server 12c Advanced Administration Cookbook

Over 60 advanced recipes to configure, troubleshoot, and tune Oracle WebLogic Server

Dalton Iwazaki

[PACKT] enterprise
PUBLISHING
professional expertise distilled

BIRMINGHAM - MUMBAI

Oracle WebLogic Server 12c Advanced Administration Cookbook

First published: June 2013

Production Reference: 1110613

Published by Packt Publishing Ltd.
Livery Place
35 Livery Street
Birmingham B3 2PB, UK.

ISBN 978-1-84968-684-6

www.packtpub.com

Cover Image by Abhishek Pandey (abhishek.pandey1210@gmail.com)

Credits

Author
Dalton Iwazaki

Reviewers
Vivek Acharya
Daniel Amadei
Wickes Potgieter

Acquisition Editor
Martin Bell

Lead Technical Editor
Azharuddin Sheikh

Technical Editors
Vrinda Nitesh Bhosale
Saijul Shah

Copy Editors
Brandt D'Mello
Insiya Morbiwala
Laxmi Subramanian

Project Coordinator
Anurag Banerjee

Proofreaders
Cecere Mario
Lindsey Thomas

Indexer
Monica Ajmera Mehta

Production Coordinator
Melwyn D'sa

Cover Work
Melwyn D'sa

About the Author

Dalton Iwazaki lives in Sao Paulo, Brazil and started working with technology in 1994 in a school lab, at the age of 17. As a system administrator, Dalton configured and maintained the network (Novel 3.12), the computers (Window 3.11, Windows NT 4.0, Windows 95), and the Internet. He also took his first steps in programming by building the school website in ASP and a computer voting system to simulate the election process in Delphi.

In 1999, Dalton moved to a new company and started working with Java development. During this period, he worked on many Java server-side applications and dug deep to understand the use of JDBC, JMS, JMX, XML, and multithreaded applications. He built some frameworks from scratch to help the development, and started working on the Application Server world with IBM Websphere, Resin, Tomcat, JBoss, and BEA WebLogic. Until 2004, Dalton moved around to other companies working either as a Java developer or Java Architect.

In 2004 and 2005, Dalton worked as a Software Development Manager; he lead 10 developers to build the entire website, provisioning and back office operations of a new ISP Provider with a variety of integrations and languages, such as Java, VB, C#, Perl, and PHP. Dalton then moved to a large international bank to work as a project manager in 2005 and 2006. His role was to manage the Internet Banking and Credit Card portals and integrate the business clients and the development team. From 2006 to 2008, Dalton started and worked on his own company, a design agency focused on the delivery of web solutions.

In 2008, Dalton started working in partnership with Oracle Consulting on the infrastructure level of the WebLogic Server. In the following year, Dalton started a new company named VN Tecnologia, an IT professional services provider and Oracle Partner Network member. Working together with Oracle's clients and projects, Dalton's solid expertise in infrastructure and Java development are a rare combination used in his specializations - WebLogic Server configuration, administration, troubleshooting, and tuning. You can reach Dalton Iwazaki at `dalton.iwazaki@gmail.com`.

I want to thank my family for their support and patience. To my lovely wife Cibele, my son Ian, and my daughter Lia.

About the Reviewers

Vivek Acharya is an Oracle Consultant working as a professional freelancer. He has been a part of the design, development, consulting, and architect world for approximately 7 years, working in Oracle Practice at GE, IBM, HP. He is an Oracle Certified Expert as Oracle Fusion—SOA 11g Implementation Specialist and Oracle BPM 11g Implementation Specialist. He has experience and expertise in Oracle Fusion—SOA, BPM, BAM, Mediator, B2B, BI, AIA, WebLogic, workflow, Rules, WebCenter, ECM, IDM, Oracle fusion applications, SaaS, On Demand, and so on. He loves all things to do with Oracle Fusion Applications, Oracle SOA, Oracle BPM, cloud computing, salesforce, SaaS, and BSM.

He has authored a couple of books on distributed systems, Oracle BPM, and many others. He likes to play Synthesizer and loves travelling. You can add him to your LinkedIn list by going to the link `http://www.linkedin.com/pub/vivek-acharya/15/377/26a`, write to him on `vivek.oraclesoa@gmail.com`, and read about him and his works at `http://acharyavivek.wordpress.com/`.

Daniel Amadei is a Senior Principal Consultant working for Oracle Consulting Services in Brazil and has more than 10 years of experience in IT market being a specialized consultant and solutions architect for SOA and Enterprise Applications. He has strong analytical and problem-solving abilities with solid experience in development and architecture of applications.

He is a specialist in SOA and EAI Oracle middleware products, web services and related technologies and the Java Platform, especially Java EE. He has been working with Java since 1999 and SOA/EAI since 2007 and has, at the time of this book's writing, 8 certifications related to his specialties, including Oracle Certified SOA Architect, Oracle SOA Foundation Practitioner and Sun Certified Enterprise Architect for J2EE.

You can write to him on `daniel.amadei@gmail.com`, and read about his works at `http://www.amadei.com.br`.

I'd like to thank the author, Dalton, for writing this great book and for giving me the chance to learn a lot by reviewing it. I'm mainly a developer, and getting my hands in this infrastructure book gave me lots of valuable information.

Wickes Potgieter has worked as a product specialist for over 12 years. His main focus was on the BEA WebLogic suite of products, and after the Oracle acquisition of BEA Systems, focused on the Oracle Fusion Middleware suite of products. His experience ranges from Solution Architecture, Infrastructure Design, administration, development, presales, and training to performance tuning of the Oracle Fusion Middleware products, JVM, and custom applications. He specializes in Oracle WebLogic Server, JRockit, Service Bus, SOA, AIA, BPM, BAM, Enterprise Manager 11g/12c, WebCenter, Identity and Access Management, and Application Performance Management.

He formed a specialized consulting company in 2003 with offices in the United Kingdom and South Africa, covering customers in the EMEA region. His company is an Oracle Gold partner and has a team of specialized Oracle Fusion Middleware consultants servicing customers both onsite and offsite.

You can visit the TSI-Systems website at `www.tsisystems.co.uk`, and Wickes can be contacted on `wickes@tsisystems.co.uk`.

I would like to thank my wife Mary Jane for her patience and for assisting me through all the late nights. Thank you to all my friends and family for their constant encouragement.

www.PacktPub.com

Support files, eBooks, discount offers and more

You might want to visit www.PacktPub.com for support files and downloads related to your book.

Did you know that Packt offers eBook versions of every book published, with PDF and ePub files available? You can upgrade to the eBook version at www.PacktPub.com and as a print book customer, you are entitled to a discount on the eBook copy. Get in touch with us at service@ packtpub.com for more details.

At www.PacktPub.com, you can also read a collection of free technical articles, sign up for a range of free newsletters and receive exclusive discounts and offers on Packt books and eBooks.

http://PacktLib.PacktPub.com

Do you need instant solutions to your IT questions? PacktLib is Packt's online digital book library. Here, you can access, read, and search across Packt's entire library of books.

Why Subscribe?

- ▶ Fully searchable across every book published by Packt
- ▶ Copy and paste, print and bookmark content
- ▶ On demand and accessible via web browser

Free Access for Packt account holders

If you have an account with Packt at www.PacktPub.com, you can use this to access PacktLib today and view nine entirely free books. Simply use your login credentials for immediate access.

Instant Updates on New Packt Books

Get notified! Find out when new books are published by following @PacktEnterprise on Twitter, or the *Packt Enterprise* Facebook page.

Table of Contents

Preface

Oracle WebLogic Server 12c Advanced Administration Cookbook guides you through over 60 recipes covering right from the basics of the WebLogic Server 12c installation to JDBC, JMS, cluster configuration, and tuning. This book covers the day-to-day tasks of a WebLogic administrator, and is enhanced with a lot of tips to build a WebLogic production environment focused on stability, high availability, and performance.

What this book covers

Chapter 1, Install, Configure, and Run, covers the first steps to installing and configuring WebLogic Server 12c.

Chapter 2, High Availability with WebLogic Clusters, explains how to set up a WebLogic Cluster.

Chapter 3, Configuring JDBC Resources for High Availability, teaches how to configure and tune the JDBC resources focused on high availability.

Chapter 4, Configuring JMS Resources for Clustering and High Availability, teaches how to set up JMS resources with WebLogic Clustering.

Chapter 5, Monitoring WebLogic Server 12c, explains how to monitor WebLogic Server 12c with the included tools.

Chapter 6, Troubleshooting WebLogic Server 12c, teaches how to find solutions to the most common problems.

Chapter 7, Stability and Performance, teaches how to tune the configuration for a production environment with resilience, stability, and performance.

Chapter 8, Security, teaches how to configure security, including SSL and authentication.

What you need for this book

You'll need the following:

- **Oracle WebLogic Server 12*c***: http://www.oracle.com/technetwork/middleware/weblogic/downloads/index.html

- **Oracle JRockit 6 R28**: http://www.oracle.com/technetwork/middleware/jrockit/downloads/index.html

- **Apache HTTP Server 2.2**: http://httpd.apache.org

Who this book is for

The book is targeted at the datacenter operator, system administrator, or Java developer who already knows the basics of WebLogic Server installation and configuration, but wants to go deeper into more advanced topics and concepts, such as monitoring, configuration for high availability, and tuning to achieve a stable and resilient environment.

Conventions

In this book, you will find a number of styles of text that distinguish between different kinds of information. Here are some examples of these styles, and an explanation of their meaning.

Code words in text, database table names, folder names, filenames, file extensions, pathnames, dummy URLs, user input, and Twitter handles are shown as follows: "The filename is jrockit-jdk1.6.0_XXX-linux-x64.bin, where XXX stands for the JRockit release and JDK version."

A block of code is set as follows:

```
<Location /app01>
SetHandler weblogic-handler
WebLogicCluster prodsrv01.domain.local:8001,prodsrv02.domain.
local:8002,prodsrv03.domain.local:8003,prodsrv04.domain.local:8004
</Location>
```

Any command-line input or output is written as follows:

```
[wls@prod01]$ cd $WL_HOME/common/bin
```

New terms and **important words** are shown in bold. Words that you see on the screen, in menus or dialog boxes for example, appear in the text like this: "Follow the onscreen instructions and type /oracle/Middleware for the **"Middleware Home" = [Enter new value or use default]** screen".

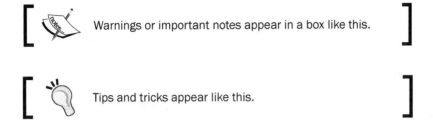

[Warnings or important notes appear in a box like this.]

[Tips and tricks appear like this.]

Reader feedback

Feedback from our readers is always welcome. Let us know what you think about this book—what you liked or may have disliked. Reader feedback is important for us to develop titles that you really get the most out of.

To send us general feedback, simply send an e-mail to feedback@packtpub.com, and mention the book title via the subject of your message.

If there is a topic that you have expertise in and you are interested in either writing or contributing to a book, see our author guide on www.packtpub.com/authors.

Customer support

Now that you are the proud owner of a Packt book, we have a number of things to help you to get the most from your purchase.

Errata

Although we have taken every care to ensure the accuracy of our content, mistakes do happen. If you find a mistake in one of our books—maybe a mistake in the text or the code—we would be grateful if you would report this to us. By doing so, you can save other readers from frustration and help us improve subsequent versions of this book. If you find any errata, please report them by visiting http://www.packtpub.com/submit-errata, selecting your book, clicking on the **errata submission form** link, and entering the details of your errata. Once your errata are verified, your submission will be accepted and the errata will be uploaded on our website, or added to any list of existing errata, under the Errata section of that title. Any existing errata can be viewed by selecting your title from http://www.packtpub.com/support.

Piracy

Piracy of copyright material on the Internet is an ongoing problem across all media. At Packt, we take the protection of our copyright and licenses very seriously. If you come across any illegal copies of our works, in any form, on the Internet, please provide us with the location address or website name immediately so that we can pursue a remedy.

Please contact us at `copyright@packtpub.com` with a link to the suspected pirated material.

We appreciate your help in protecting our authors, and our ability to bring you valuable content.

Questions

You can contact us at `questions@packtpub.com` if you are having a problem with any aspect of the book, and we will do our best to address it.

1
Install, Configure, and Run

In this chapter, we will cover the following recipes:

- ▸ Installing WebLogic Server 12c
- ▸ Creating the WebLogic domain
- ▸ Distributing the domain files to remote machines
- ▸ Starting the Node Manager
- ▸ Starting the Administration Server
- ▸ Saving and activating changes in the Administration Console
- ▸ Protecting changes in the Administration Console
- ▸ Extending and customizing the Administration Console
- ▸ Enabling RESTful Management Services
- ▸ Starting/Stopping the WebLogic Managed Server
- ▸ Deploying applications

Introduction

WebLogic Server is Oracle's flagship J2EE application server and is the foundation of the Oracle Fusion Middleware range of products, such as Oracle SOA Suite, Oracle WebCenter, and Oracle Service Bus. The new 12c version is being fully integrated with Oracle's Middleware products, and the system administrators who are already familiar with the core WebLogic administration tasks will be one step ahead of the market demand.

Oracle WebLogic Server 12c applications and systems deployed in production environments normally require performance, scalability, and high availability; these are usually not needed in a development environment. The recipes in this book focus on achieving these objectives.

This chapter condenses the core tasks a WebLogic administrator should know, such as downloading the correct package, installing it, and creating a WebLogic domain, configuring it, and managing it.

Installing WebLogic Server 12c

You should already be familiar with basic WebLogic installation, so this recipe covers the steps to a quick installation of WebLogic Server 12c in production environments.

This recipe will focus on a new install rather than upgrades or migrations.

Getting ready

It is important to navigate through Oracle's website and check if the chosen hardware and operational system architectures are supported in Certification Matrix before installing WebLogic Server. You should look for system requirements and supported platforms for WebLogic Server 12c. This is crucial for a production environment since Oracle Support verifies if you are running a supported configuration when an issue appears.

The book assumes the following hardware and software architectures for WebLogic Server 12c installations:

- X86-64 processor (such as Intel Xeon or AMD Opteron)
- Linux x86-64 architecture (such as Red Hat Enterprise Linux or Oracle Linux)

Operational systems based on Linux x86-64 (64-bit) are the most commonly used in production environments, and these instructions should cover other Unix architectures as well.

 The use of WebLogic Server in Microsoft Windows for production environments will not be considered in this book.

Oracle JRockit 6 for Linux x86-64 is the **Java Virtual Machine** (**JVM**) that has been used through the rest of this book. Download it at `http://www.oracle.com/technetwork/middleware/jrockit/downloads`. The filename is `jrockit-jdk1.6.0_XXX-linux-x64.bin`, where XXX stands for the JRockit release and JDK version.

The package **WebLogic Server 12c (12.1.1) generic installer (997 MB) for use with 64-bit JVMs** should also be downloaded at `http://www.oracle.com/technetwork/middleware/weblogic/downloads`. The filename is `wls1211_generic.jar`.

To simplify the reading, we'll use the following terms when referring to the directories:

- ► $JAVA_HOME to JRockit/Java Home directory: /oracle/jvm
- ► $MW_HOME to Middleware Home: /oracle/Middleware
- ► $WL_HOME to WebLogic Home: /oracle/Middleware/wlserver_12.1

How to do it...

Carry out the following steps to install WebLogic Server 12c:

1. Create a dedicated user to host and run WebLogic Server 12c in Linux. Log in as the root user and create the user and the group named wls, and define a new password for it:

   ```
   [root@prod01]# groupadd wls

   [root@prod01]# useradd -g wls wls

   [root@prod01]# passwd wls

   Changing password for user wls.

   New UNIX password: <new password>

   Retype new UNIX password: <new password>
   ```

2. Log in as the wls user and set the correct file permissions:

   ```
   [wls@prod01]$ umask 027
   ```

3. Run the JRockit installer in console mode and install JRockit:

   ```
   [wls@prod01]$ ./jrockit-jdk1.6_xxx-linux-x64.bin -mode=console
   ```

4. Follow the onscreen instructions and type /oracle/jvm in the Product Installation directory. You can just press *Enter* for all the other options. JRockit will be installed without the demos and with no source code.

5. Run WebLogic Server 12c Generic Installer in console mode:

   ```
   [wls@prod01]$ /oracle/jvm/bin/java -jar wls1211_generic.jar -mode=console
   ```

6. Follow the onscreen instructions and type /oracle/Middleware for the **"Middleware Home" = [Enter new value or use default]** screen. Press *Enter* to move forward.

7. Skip the **Register for Security Updates** screen by typing *3* to navigate to **3 | Receive Security Update:[Yes]**, then type No and then Yes. Press *Enter* to move forward.

8. Type *1* to select the **1 | Typical** option on the **Install Type** screen.

9.   The freshly installed /oracle/jvm JDK should be selected. If not, add it by typing *1* for **1|Add Local Jdk**.

10. Press *Enter* to confirm all the other screens.

How it works...

These install instructions will provide a clean and fresh WebLogic Server 12c installation in the prod01 hostname.

It also covers some basic user administration in Linux that can be skipped if you already have an operational system user.

 Don't forget to set the correct file permissions with umask before installing WebLogic Server 12c.

Both JRockit and WebLogic Server were installed in the console mode option without any graphical interface. Production environments are more restricted, and console mode requires only a **terminal**; it is faster and does not need an X11 Server.

Generic installer is used to install WebLogic since it is the one that contains the native library for x86-64. The native library is important because it enables the use of a native socket reader that is much faster than the pure Java socket reader. This library enables what is called the performance pack on WebLogic and is mandatory in a production environment.

The installation process is very straightforward and only copies the files to their directories. The next step is to create a new WebLogic domain.

See also

  ▶   *Creating the WebLogic domain*

Creating the WebLogic domain

With WebLogic Server 12c installed, you can now create a new WebLogic domain.

The WebLogic domain is the central configuration entity of WebLogic Server. The domain should have at least one WebLogic Server instance with the role of the Administration Server. The Administration Server is the access point used for configuration, deployment, and monitoring.

More WebLogic Server instances can be created to be part of the domain. All other WebLogic Server instances of the domain that are not the Administration Server are called the Managed Servers. They should host the deployed applications and resources.

A WebLogic cluster can also be added to the domain. The cluster consists of one or more Managed Servers acting as one single entity. A single WebLogic Server installation is not restricted to one WebLogic domain, and more domains can be created using the same installation.

Getting ready

Before creating a new WebLogic domain, you have to plan and define its architecture. For production environments, it is mandatory to use WebLogic clusters with a minimum architecture of at least two WebLogic Server instances (the Managed Servers) in two different machines. The objective is to avoid having a single point of failure.

We will create a new WebLogic domain called PROD_DOMAIN with an administration instance (AdminServer) named PROD_AdminServer and a WebLogic cluster PROD_Cluster with the two Managed Servers PROD_Server01 and PROD_Server02. The two machines hosts are called prod01 and prod02. Since you have already installed WebLogic Server 12c in prod01, install it in prod02 as well. We will assume these names throughout the entire book.

The machines prod01 and prod02 should also have IP addresses assigned and be visible through the network. It's recommended to use the **fully qualified domain name** (**FQDN**) of the servers. In this recipe, and the rest of the book, prod01 is prod01.domain.local and the hostname of the prod02 machine is prod02.domain.local.

 To simplify the reading, we'll use the following term when referring to the directories:

$DOMAIN_HOME to the created WebLogic Domain directory—/oracle/Middleware/user_projects/domains/PROD_DOMAIN.

How to do it...

To create a new WebLogic domain, follow the ensuing steps:

1. Log in as a wls user on the first machine prod01 and navigate to the following folder:

    [wls@prod01]$ cd $WL_HOME/common/bin

2. Start WebLogic Configuration Wizard in console mode:

    [wls@prod01]$ ./config.sh -mode=console

3. Follow the onscreen instructions and type *1*, and press *Enter* to select the **Create a new WebLogic domain** option on the **Welcome** screen.

4. Type *1* and press *Enter* to select the **Choose WebLogic Platform components** option on the **Select Domain Source** screen.

5. Press *Enter* again to continue with the **Basic WebLogic Server Domain - 12.1.1.0 [wlserver_12.1]** template.

6. On the **Edit Domain Information** screen, type the domain name `PROD_DOMAIN` and press *Enter* twice.

7. Leave `/oracle/Middleware/user_projects/domains` unchanged on the **Select the target domain directory for this domain** screen and press *Enter*.

8. On the **Configure Administrator User Name and Password** screen, set the WebLogic administrator username and password. Type the username as `wlsadmin` and type *2* to set the password and *3* to type the password again and confirm it. Press *Enter* to move forward.

9. The **Domain Mode Configuration** screen is where you set the **production mode**. Type *2* and press *Enter*.

10. The installed JRockit should already be selected as `/oracle/jvm` on the **Java SDK Selection** screen. Press *Enter* to continue.

11. On the **Select Optional Configuration** screen, type *1* for **the Administration Server** and *2* for the **Managed Servers, clusters, and machines**.

12. On the **Configure the Administration Server** screen, type *1* to set the Administration Server name as `PROD_AdminServer`. Leave the other options in their default values and press *Enter* to move to the next screen.

13. Then add the two Managed Server instances on the **Configure Managed Servers** screen.

14. Type `PROD_Server01` to add the first server, then type *2* to modify the listen address to `prod01.domain.local`. Type *3* to modify the port to `8001`, press *Enter*, and then type *5* to finish this server.

15. Do the same for the second server and type *1* to add, type `PROD_Server02` as the name, and type *2* to modify the listen address to `prod02.domain.local`. Type *3* to modify the port to `8002`. Press *Enter* to continue.

16. Add the cluster on the **Configure Clusters** screen. Type `PROD_Cluster` and press *Enter* to create it. Type *3* and modify the **Cluster Address** field to `prod01.domain.local:8001,prod02.domain.local:8002`.

17. The next screen is the **Assign Servers to Clusters** screen. Type *1* to select `PROD_Cluster`. Then type *2* to **Select All** and press *Enter*. Confirm it by pressing *Enter* again.

18. Configure the two machines on the **Configure Machine** screen. Type `prod01` and press *Enter*. Type *2* to change the listen address to `prod01.domain.local` as well. Type *4* when done.

19. Add the second machine typing *1* and name it as `prod02`. Press *Enter* and press *Enter* again to skip the **Unix Machine** screen.

20. You will now assign the Managed Servers to their respective machines on the **Assign Servers to Machines** screen.

21. Type 1.1 to choose prod01 and type *1* and press *Enter*. Now type 1-2 and press *Enter* assigning the PROD_AdminServer and PROD_Server01 servers. Press *Enter* again to return.

22. Type 1.2 to choose prod02, then type *1* and *1* again, and press *Enter* to finish.

How it works...

A new domain was created in the console mode using the Configuration Wizard. Console mode was used instead of graphical interface mode due to the usual restrictions of a production environment.

The PROD_DOMAIN domain was created with one the Administration Server named PROD_AdminServer and one cluster PROD_Cluster containing the two Managed Servers PROD_Server01 and PROD_Server02.

The WebLogic domains can work in two different modes: production and development. The development mode is only recommended to be used in single WebLogic instance domains, normally at the developer desktop. The PROD_DOMAIN domain was created in Production mode, which deactivates some features such as auto-deployment.

 It's good practice to use a prefix such as PROD when naming the domain, the cluster, and the servers. It can be hard to find WebLogic Server when working with a production farm that contains hundreds of WebLogic instances.

The domain contains what is considered to be a minimum architecture for a production environment. With the two Managed Servers of the cluster hosted by different machines, the platform avoids a single point of failure in the case of a machine crash.

There's more...

You can create the domain using the Configuration Wizard in graphical mode with all the same options if you have a functional X11 Server.

See also

▶ *Distributing the domain files to remote machines*

Distributing the domain files to remote machines

A new domain is installed and configured in one machine (prod01). Since the architecture includes another machine (prod02), the domain files now have to be distributed in all the machines of the domain.

This recipe contains the steps to distribute the files either by using the built-in WebLogic tools pack and unpack or by copying them manually in the command line of the shell.

Getting ready

Create a new template of the domain using the pack command in the prod01 machine. With the template created in prod01, use the unpack command to distribute the files to the machine prod02 (and to all machines used by the WebLogic cluster).

How to do it...

Carry out the following steps to distribute the domain files:

1. Log in as a wls user on the first machine prod01 and navigate to the folder:

   ```
   [wls@prod01]$ cd $WL_HOME/common/bin
   ```

2. Run the following command:

   ```
   [wls@prod01]$ ./pack.sh -domain=$DOMAIN_HOME-template=$WL_HOME/
   common/templates/domains/PROD_DOMAIN_template.jar -template_
   name=PROD_DOMAIN -managed=true
   ```

   A file $WL_HOME/common/templates/domains/PROD_DOMAIN_template.jar
   will be created.

3. Log in as a wls user on the second machine prod02 and copy the template from prod01 to prod02:

   ```
   [wls@prod02]$ scp wls@prod01:$WL_HOME/common/templates/domains/
   PROD_DOMAIN_template.jar $WL_HOME/common/templates/domains/
   ```

4. Run the following commands to unpack the template:

   ```
   [wls@prod02]$ cd $WL_HOME/common/bin
   ```

   ```
   [wls@prod02]$ ./unpack.sh -template=$WL_HOME/common/templates/
   domains/PROD_DOMAIN_template.jar -domain=$DOMAIN_HOME
   ```

How it works...

The `unpack` command will create the necessary files to host the WebLogic domain `PROD_DOMAIN` on the `prod02` machine based on the template created with the `pack` command on `prod01`.

An entry to the `PROD_DOMAIN` domain will automatically be added to the `nodemanager. properties` file.

There's more...

We can also distribute the WebLogic domain files manually. In this section, we will see how this can be achieved.

Distributing WebLogic domain files manually

You can simply copy the domain files manually too; just don't forget to edit the `nodemanager.domains` file and add the domain entry.

As in the prior chapter and the rest of the book, the `$DOMAIN_HOME` environment variable points to the `/oracle/Middleware/user_projects/domains/PROD_DOMAIN` directory.

1. Log in as a `wls` user on the machine `prod02` and copy the domain from `prod01`:

    ```
    [wls@prod02]$ mkdir -p $DOMAIN_HOME
    [wls@prod02]$ scp -rp wls@prod01:$DOMAIN_HOME $DOMAIN_HOME/..
    ```

2. Edit the `nodemanager.domains` file:

    ```
    [wls@prod01]$ vi $WL_HOME/common/nodemanager/nodemanager.domains
    ```

3. Add the following entry if it doesn't exist:

    ```
    PROD_DOMAIN=/oracle/Middleware/user_projects/domains/PROD_DOMAIN/
    ```

See also

> ▸   *Starting the Node Manager*

Starting the Node Manager

The Node Manager is the WebLogic Server utility to control the lifecycle—start, stop, restart—of the WebLogic Managed Server instances and the Administration Server.

In production environments, the Node Manager is needed to meet the high availability requirements.

In this recipe, the system administrator will learn how to start and stop the Node Manager.

Getting ready

The Node Manager is already installed with WebLogic Server 12c. There are two versions of the Node Manager: a Java version and a script version. This recipe will cover the Java version. The Java version is the most commonly used version, and it is more complete and more secure than the script version.

How to do it...

1. Log in as a `wls` user on the first machine `prod01` and navigate to the folder:

    `[wls@prod01]$ cd $WL_HOME/server/bin`

2. Start the Node Manager in the background. Since it's the first time you are starting it, the `$WL_HOME/common/nodemanager/nodemanager.properties` file will be created.

    `[wls@prod01]$ nohup ./startNodeManager.sh &`

    `[1] <PID>`

    ``nohup: appending output to `nohup.out'``

3. Do the same on the `prod02` machine and on all the machines of the WebLogic domain.

How it works...

You can leave the default values created for `nodemanager.properties`.

The Node Manager has started and is listening to port `5556`. The `<PID>` value is the number of the newly created process.

Since the `prod01` and `prod02` machines were configured when you created the WebLogic domain `PROD_DOMAIN`, the Node Manager should be reachable and able to receive start and stop commands from the Administration Console.

There's more...

In this section, we will see how to shut down the Node Manager:

Shutting down the Node Manager

There is no formal command to shut down the Node Manager, so you'll have to do it manually, killing the process:

1. Find the `<PID>`value of the Node Manager process:

   ```
   [wls@prod01]$ ps aux | grep weblogic.NodeManager | grep -v grep |
   awk '{print $2} '
   <PID>
   ```

2. Issue a `kill` command to `PID` to finish it:

   ```
   [wls@prod01]$ kill <PID>
   ```

   Or, force the process to finish:

   ```
   [wls@prod01]$ kill -9 <PID>
   ```

See also

▸ *Starting the Administration Server*

▸ *Starting/Stopping the WebLogic Managed Server*

Starting the Administration Server

Administration Server is a WebLogic Server instance specific to administering a WebLogic domain through the Administration Console application at the `/console` URI.

It's a common task to deploy runtime applications to the Administration Server in development environments, but you should avoid doing it in production. Leave the Administration Server only to the administrative tasks of the console.

Getting ready

Since there is only one Administration Server per WebLogic domain, you have to start the Administration Server only in `prod01`.

How to do it...

To start the Administration Server, follow the ensuing steps:

1. Log in as the `wls` user on the first machine `prod01` and navigate to the folder:

   ```
   [wls@prod01]$ cd $DOMAIN_HOME/bin
   ```

2. Start the Administration Server:

   ```
   [wls@prod01]$ ./startWebLogic.sh
   ```

3. The server will initiate the startup process and ask for the WebLogic Administrator username and password:

   ```
   Enter username to boot WebLogic server: wlsadmin

   Enter password to boot WebLogic server:
   ```

4. Type `wlsadmin` as the username and the `<password>` value you previously specified during domain creation.

5. WebLogic Administration Server will start.

How it works...

The Administration Server is now running and waiting for connections in the host and port that are specified during domain creation at `http://prod01.domain.local:7001/console`.

```
<Started the WebLogic Server Administration Server "PROD_AdminServer" for
domain "PROD_DOMAIN" running in production mode.>
```

There's more...

The system administrator should also create a `boot.properties` file to avoid entering the boot username and password in every WebLogic Server startup.

Creating the boot.properties file

Specify a `boot.properties` file so the Administration Server doesn't ask for the username and password at startup.

1. Go to the Administration Server root folder:

   ```
   [wls@prod01]$ cd $DOMAIN_HOME/servers/PROD_AdminServer
   ```

2. Create and enter a new directory:

   ```
   [wls@prod01]$ mkdir security

   [wls@prod01]$ cd security
   ```

3. Create a new file called `boot.properties` with `wlsadmin` as the username and the `<password>` value you specified:

   ```
   [wls@prod01]$ echo -ne "username=wlsadmin\npassword=<password>" >
   boot.properties

   [wls@prod01]$ cat boot.properties
   username=wlsadmin
   password=<password>
   ```

4. The next time you start WebLogic Administration Server, it will use the credentials from the `boot.properties` file. The file will also be encrypted:

```
[wls@prod01]$ cat boot.properties
password={AES}If68A2GSiO6Fa8w4j0giDJGR0FATHnfPsoZvpmF/Ipc\=
username={AES}UYyIQYkN6z5o8PsS/IccG3VgZv6LP1zj+Ro1JBDb2ZE\=
```

Starting the Administration Server in the background

You usually start the Administration Server as a background process in Linux.

1. Go to the WebLogic domain's `bin` directory:

   ```
   [wls@prod01]$ cd $DOMAIN_HOME/bin
   ```

2. Start the Administration Server in the background:

   ```
   [wls@prod01]$ nohup ./startWebLogic.sh &
   [1] <PID>
   ```

The `<PID>` value is the process ID of the Administration Server.

The standard output (`stdout`) and standard error (`stderr`) of the process will be appended to a file called `$DOMAIN_HOME/bin/nohup.out`.

Accessing the Administration Console

The Administration Console application is running in the Administration Server. To access it, follow the ensuing steps:

1. Open your web browser and navigate to `http://prod01.domain.local:7001/console`:

2. Type the `wlsadmin` username and the password that was specified earlier.

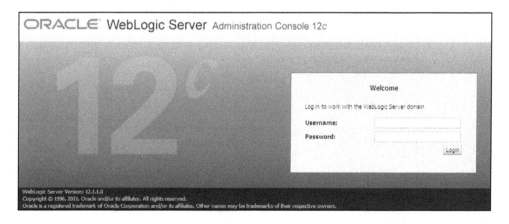

▸ *Starting the Node Manager*

▸ *Starting/Stopping the WebLogic Managed Server*

Saving and activating changes in the Administration Console

The Administration Console is the central application for administering your WebLogic domain. The WebLogic domain PROD_DOMAIN was configured to start in production mode; this means you'll have to obtain the domain configuration lock before saving and activating changes. This protection is to prevent changes from other users during your edit session.

Getting ready

WebLogic Administration Server must be up and running.

How to do it...

Carry out the following steps to save and activate changes:

1. Access the Administration Console with your web browser at http://prod01. domain.local:7001/console.

2. Obtain the configuration lock by clicking on **Lock & Edit**:

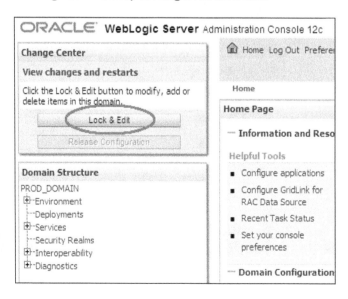

3. Make the necessary changes and click on the **Save** button to save it.

4. If there are any configuration changes pending, the **Lock & Edit** button should be labeled now as **Activate Changes**:

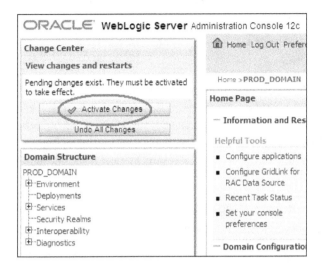

5. Click on the **Activate Changes** button to confirm the changes.

How it works...

All saved changes made before activating the session are saved in the $DOMAIN_HOME/ pending directory. It contains the new version of the configuration files (config.xml). As soon as the **Activate Changes** option is clicked on, the Administration Server issues a command to all the WebLogic Managed Server instances to update the configuration. If any of the Managed Servers do not accept the new configuration, the changes are rolled back and the Administration Console will show a message. If the new configuration is accepted by the Managed Servers, the changes will be activated and the configuration files will be updated by all the servers and one very machine belonging to the domain.

There's more...

The system administrator can also make configuration changes through WLST.

Making changes using the WLST

Under the hood, WebLogic Server uses a JMX framework that exposes WebLogic MBeans to manage its configuration. The Administration Console issues JMX commands as you make changes to Configuration Manager MBean. MBeans can be accessed through WLST.

Edit, save, and activate the changes through WLST:

1. Log in as a `wls` user to shell and start WLST:

    ```
    [wls@prod01]$ $WL_HOME/common/bin/wlst.sh
    Welcome to WebLogic Server Administration Scripting Shell
    Type help() for help on available commands
    wls:/offline>
    ```

2. Connect to the Administration Server using `wlsadmin` as the user, `<pwd>` as the password, and `t3://prod01.domain.local:7001` as the server URL:

    ```
    wls:/offline>connect("wlsadmin","<pwd>","t3://prod01.domain.
    local:7001")
    Connecting to t3://prod01.domain.local:7001 with userid wlsadmin
    ...
    Successfully connected to Admin Server 'PROD_AdminServer' that
    belongs to domain 'PROD_DOMAIN'.
    wls:/PROD_DOMAIN/serverConfig>
    ```

3. Start the editing, make the necessary changes, and activate it in the end:

    ```
    wls:/PROD_DOMAIN/serverConfig>edit()
    Location changed to edit tree. This is a writable tree with
    DomainMBean as the root. To make changes you will need to start
    an edit session via startEdit().

    For more help, use help(edit)
    You already have an edit session in progress and hence WLST will
    continue with your edit session.

    wls:/PROD_DOMAIN/edit !>startEdit()
    Starting an edit session ...
    Started edit session, please be sure to save and activate your
    changes once you are done.

    wls:/PROD_DOMAIN/edit !>< make necessary changes >

    wls:/PROD_DOMAIN/edit !> save()
    Saving all your changes ...
    Saved all your changes successfully.
    ```

```
wls:/PROD_DOMAIN/edit !>activate()
Activating all your changes, this may take a while ...
The edit lock associated with this edit session is released
once the activation is completed.


Activation completed


wls:/PROD_DOMAIN/edit> exit()
Exiting WebLogic Scripting Tool
```

See also

▸ *Starting the Administration Server*

Protecting changes in the Administration Console

Change management in a production environment is critical and has to be done with careful preparation and planning. WebLogic provides a way to save and later track all the changes made in its configuration.

This recipe focuses on how to enable the embedded configuration backup, how to enable the configuration changes audit, and how to automatically record a Jython script to all the changes made in the Administration Console that can be used later with WLST.

Getting ready

WebLogic Administration Server must be up and running.

How to do it...

Carry out the following steps to protect the configuration changes:

1. Access the Administration Console with your web browser at `http://prod01.domain.local:7001/console`.

2. Click on the **Preferences** link.

3. Enable the following checkboxes:

   Show Advanced Sections

   Warn If User Holds Lock

   Warn User Before Taking Lock

4. Click on the **Save** button.

5. Open the **WLST Script Recording** tab.

6. Enable the following checkboxes:

   Append to File

   Automatic Recording

7. Click on the **Save** button.

8. Obtain the configuration lock by clicking on **Lock & Edit**.

9. Click the PROD_DOMAIN link on the **Domain Structure** on the left.

10. Choose **Change Log and Audit** in the **Configuration Audit Type** drop-down menu.

11. Enable the **Configuration Archive Enabled** checkbox.

12. Set the number of back files in the **Archive Configuration Count** text field. Type 250 as the value. The default value is 50.

13. Click on the **Save** button.

14. Activate the changes by clicking on the **Activate Changes** button.

15. You will have to restart the Administration Server for the changes to take effect.

How it works...

The **Preferences** section changes will enable some messages in the Administration Console that will warn the user when the edit lock is already being used in another browser session. This is important in a production environment to avoid the changes being made by other administrators at the same time.

The WLST Script Recording changes will enable a Jython script to be recorded to every change made in the Administration Console. The script is recorded by default in the $DOMAIN_HOME root directory with a filename Script*.py.

With the backup configuration enabled, every time the domain configuration is modified, a JAR file containing the old configuration ($DOMAIN_HOME/config/*) will be archived until the limit of 250 archives as you defined in **Archive Configuration Count**. Change the value so it suits your needs. JAR will be saved in the directory $DOMAIN_HOME/configArchive/ config-XXX.jar. The lesser the XXX number, the older the configuration archive is.

The audit configuration registers every step and change made in the Administration Server log file (.log). The following example shows the `wlsadmin` user changing the JTA timeout from 30 to 300:

```
<BEA-159904><USER wlsadmin MODIFIED com.bea:Name=PROD_DOMAIN,Type=JTA
ATTRIBUTE TimeoutSeconds FROM 30 TO 300>
```

There's more...

Enabling the protection changes can also be done through WLST.

Protecting changes using WLST

You can use WLST to make the exact same configuration changes. The exception is the **Preferences** section, which is a bunch of parameters from the Administration Console application and not from the WebLogic domain:

1. Log in as a `wls` user to shell and start WLST:

   ```
   [wls@prod01]$ $WL_HOME/common/bin/wlst.sh
   ```

2. Connect to the Administration Server using `wlsadmin` as the user, `<pwd>` as the password, and `t3://prod01.domain.local:7001` as the server URL:

   ```
   wls:/offline>connect("wlsadmin","<pwd>","t3://prod01.domain.
   local:7001")
   ```

3. Run the following WLST commands:

   ```
   edit()
   startEdit()
   cmo.setConfigurationAuditType('logaudit')
   cmo.setConfigBackupEnabled(true)
   cmo.setArchiveConfigurationCount(250)
   save()
   activate()
   exit()
   ```

See also

- *Starting the Administration Server*
- *Saving and activating changes in the Administration Console*

Extending and customizing the Administration Console

The Administration Console is a Java web application based on the WebLogic portal that can be modified and extended. These console extensions can be used to customize the Administration Console layout, style, logos, and images, and also to add extra pages, and extra functionalities to monitor and manage WebLogic Server and deployed applications.

This recipe will focus on creating a simple console extension to change a few text elements of the PROD_DOMAIN the Administration Console.

Getting ready

This task requires you to have ANT installed. It can be downloaded at http://ant.apache.org. Download the latest stable build and install it. The filename should be apache-ant-XXX-bin.zip where XXX stands for the ANT version.

 All necessary work will be done in a Linux environment. You can assume the use of the prod01 machine in this recipe.

How to do it...

Carry out the following steps to customize and extend the Administration Console:

1. Log in as a wls user to the first machine prod01 and unzip ANT:

    ```
    [wls@prod01]$ cd /oracle
    [wls@prod01]$ unzip apache-ant-XXX-bin.zip
    ```

2. Create a symbolic link ant pointing to the apache-ant-XXX directory:

    ```
    [wls@prod01]$ ln -s apache-ant-XXX ant
    [wls@prod01]$ ls -l
    lrwxrwxrwx 1 wlswls   16 Aug  9 10:37 ant -> apache-ant-XXX
    drwxr-xr-x 6 wlswls 4096 May 22 06:24 apache-ant-XXX
    ```

3. Export the environment variables:

    ```
    [wls@prod01]$ export JAVA_HOME=/oracle/jvm
    [wls@prod01]$ export ANT_HOME=/oracle/ant
    [wls@prod01]$ export MW_HOME=/oracle/Middleware
    [wls@prod01]$ export WL_HOME=/oracle/Middleware/wlserver_12.1
    [wls@prod01]$ export PATH=$ANT_HOME/bin:$JAVA_HOME/bin:$PATH
    ```

4. Change to the console extension templates directory:

   ```
   [wls@prod01]$ cd $WL_HOME/server/lib/console-ext/templates
   ```

5. Run ANT to expand the Look and Feel Template (`laf`):

   ```
   [wls@prod01]$ ant -f build-new-laf.xml -Dname=myConsoleExt -Ddir=/
   oracle/myConsoleExt

   Buildfile: /oracle/Middleware/wlserver_12.1/server/lib/console-
   ext/templates/build-new-laf.xml


   all:
        [mkdir] Created dir: /oracle/myConsoleExt

        [unzip] Expanding: /oracle/Middleware/wlserver_12.1/
   server/lib/console-ext/templates/laftemplate.zip into /oracle/
   myConsoleExt

         [move] Moving 1 file to /oracle/myConsoleExt/framework/
   markup/lookandfeel


   BUILD SUCCESSFUL

   Total time: 1 second
   ```

6. Extract and copy the default message bundle `global.properties` to the project from the `console.jar` file:

   ```
   [wls@prod01]$ cd /oracle/myConsoleExt/WEB-INF

   [wls@prod01]$ mkdir classes

   [wls@prod01]$ cd classes

   [wls@prod01]$ $JAVA_HOME/bin/jar -xf $WL_HOME/server/lib/
   consoleapp/webapp/WEB-INF/lib/console.jar global.properties
   ```

7. Edit `global.properties`:

   ```
   [wls@prod01]$ vi global.properties
   ```

8. Change the `window.title` and `login.title` values from:

   ```
   window.title=Oracle WebLogic Server Administration Console

   login.title=Welcome
   ```

   To:

   ```
   window.title=My Company-Oracle WebLogic Server Administration
   Console

   login.title=Welcome to "My Company"
   ```

9. Archive the `myConsoleExt` extension and move the package to the `PROD_DOMAIN` console extensions directory:

    ```
    [wls@prod01]$ cd /oracle/myConsoleExt
    [wls@prod01]$ $JAVA_HOME/bin/jar -cf myConsoleExt.war *
    [wls@prod01]$ mv myConsoleExt.war $DOMAIN_HOME/console-ext/
    ```

10. Restart the Administration Server.

11. Access the Administration Console login page and check the text changes.

12. Before the changes are made, it should look like the following screenshot:

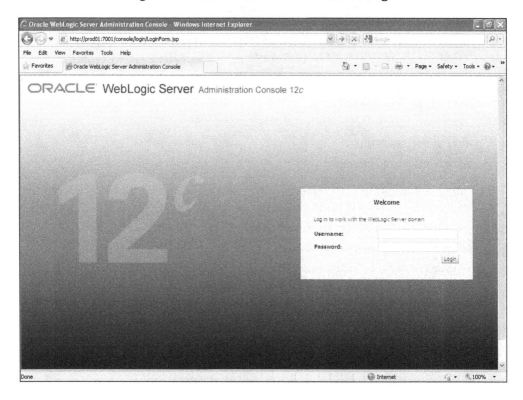

And afterwards, you will notice the changes highlighted in the following image:

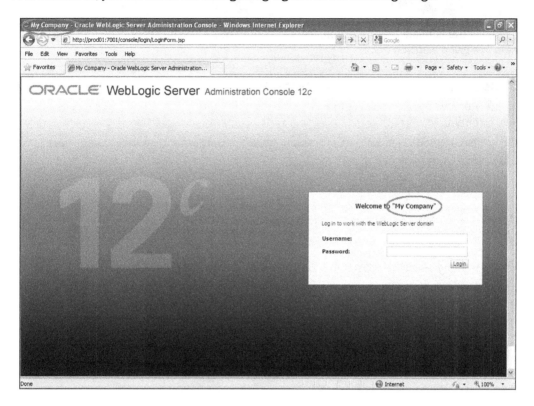

How it works...

You created a `myConsoleExt.war` console extension application that changes some of the text of the Administration Console.

Other modifications can be made to the following resources to suit your customization needs:

▶ Images:`/oracle/myConsoleExt/images/*/oracle/myConsoleExt/framework/skins/myConsoleExt/images/*`

▶ Stylesheet:`/oracle/myConsoleExt/css/*/oracle/myConsoleExt/framework/skins/myConsoleExt/css/*`

▶ JSP:`/oracle/myConsoleExt/framework/skeletons/myConsoleExt/*`

▶ Text:`/oracle/myConsoleExt/WEB-INF/classes/global.properties`

The `global.properties` file is the generic resource bundle that holds the text messages. Depending on the internationalization needs, you may create the appropriate files for each language. More details can be found at `http://docs.oracle.com/cd/E24329_01/web.1211/e24966/bundles.htm#g1076214`.

There's more...

To remove the Administration Console extension or to add more pages and content to it, follow the given instructions.

Removing the console extension from the Administration Console

1. Remove the `myConsoleExt.war` file from the `PROD_DOMAIN` console extensions directory:

   [wls@prod01]$ rm -rf $DOMAIN_HOME/console-ext/myConsoleExt.war

2. Restart the Administration Console.

 Clean your browser cache before accessing the Administration Console again.

Adding pages and content to the Administration Console

Adding other content to Console involves developing a WebLogic portal web application, using NetUI, portlets, JSP, and other J2EE technology. It is a Java programming task, which is beyond the scope of this book.

You can check Oracle's documentation at `http://docs.oracle.com/cd/E24329_01/web.1211/e24966/addcontrols.htm#CNSLX159`.

See also

- ▸ *Starting the Administration Server*
- ▸ *Saving and activating changes in the Administration Console*

Enabling RESTful Management Services

WebLogic Server 12c introduces the possibility of monitoring WebLogic Server using RESTful Web Services with new **RESTful Management Services**.

RESTful Management Services is disabled by default. This recipe will enable it.

Getting ready

WebLogic Administration Server must be up and running.

To enable WebLogic RESTful Management Services, you have to access the Administration Console at `http://prod01.domain.local:7001/console`.

How to do it...

Carry out the following steps to enable RESTful Management Services:

1. Access the Administration Console with your web browser at `http://prod01.domain.local:7001/console`.

2. Click on the **Lock & Edit** button to create a new change session.

3. Navigate to **Settings for Domain | General** by clicking **Home** and then **Domain** or by clicking the `PROD_DOMAIN` link.

4. Check the **Enable RESTful Management Services** checkbox, as shown in the following screenshot:

5. Restart WebLogic Administration Server and all Servers of the domain.

How it works...

RESTful Management Services exposes WebLogic Server instances and WebLogic clusters, applications, and data sources to be monitored using the HTTP GET method and RESTful formats, such as XML, JSON, and HTML.

The following table displays the resources to be monitored and the corresponding URIs to be accessed.

Resource	URI
Servers	`http://prod01.domain.local:7001/management/tenant-monitoring/servers`
Specific Server	`http://prod01.domain.local:7001/management/tenant-monitoring/servers/<servername>`
Clusters	`http://prod01.domain.local:7001/management/tenant-monitoring/clusters`
Specific Cluster	`http://prod01.domain.local:7001/management/tenant-monitoring/clusters/<clustername>`
Applications	`http://prod01.domain.local:7001/management/tenant-monitoring/applications`

Resource	URI
Specific Application	`http://prod01.domain.local:7001/management/tenant-monitoring/ applications/<applicationname>`
Data Sources	`http://prod01.domain.local:7001/management/tenant-monitoring/datasources`
Specific Data Source	`http://prod01.domain.local:7001/management/tenant-monitoring/datasources/<datasourcename>`

 To access the full response format of each resource, add `"?format=full"` at the end of the URI.

The following image illustrates a RESTful request to monitor all servers of the domain. It contains the name, state, and health of the Administration Server instance `PROD_AdminServer`. It also contains the WebLogic version, the machine that this server is running, open sockets, the Java version, the operational system, the Java heap size, and the Java heap in use. The `PROD_Server01` and `PROD_Server02` instances are down, and their state is also displayed as **SHUTDOWN**:

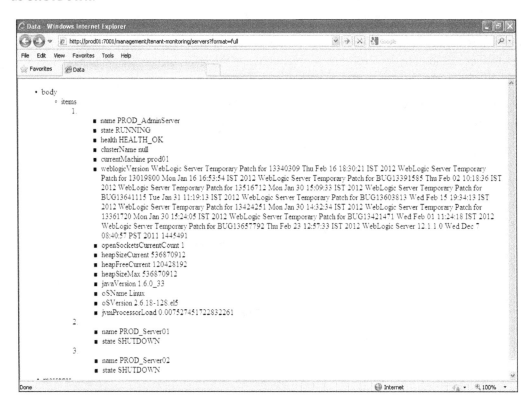

There's more...

RESTful Management Services can also be enabled through WLST.

Enabling RESTful using WLST

1. Log in as a `wls` user to shell and start WLST:

   ```
   [wls@prod01]$ $WL_HOME/common/bin/wlst.sh
   ```

2. Connect to the Administration Server using `wlsadmin` as the user, `<pwd>` as the password, and `t3://prod01.domain.local:7001` as the server URL:

   ```
   wls:/offline>connect("wlsadmin","<pwd>","t3://prod01.domain.
   local:7001")
   ```

3. Run the following WLST commands:

   ```
   edit()

   startEdit()

   cd('/RestfulManagementServices/PROD_DOMAIN')

   cmo.setEnabled(true)

   save()

   activate()

   exit()
   ```

4. Restart WebLogic Administration Server and all servers of the domain.

See also

- *Starting the Administration Server*
- *Saving and activating changes in the Administration Console*

Starting/Stopping the WebLogic Managed Server

This recipe will show how to start and stop the WebLogic Managed Server from the Administration Console.

Getting ready

The Node Manager must be up and running in each of the computers of the WebLogic domain.

How to do it...

Carry out the following steps to start and stop the WebLogic Managed Server:

1. Access the Administration Console with your web browser at `http://prod01.domain.local:7001/console`.

2. Navigate to the **Settings for Domain** page by clicking on **Home** and then **Domain** or by clicking the `PROD_DOMAIN` link.

3. Click on the **Control** tab.

4. Select the checkbox to the left of the WebLogic Server name, and click on the **Start** button to start the servers or the **Shutdown** button to shutdown. The **Shutdown** button has two options: **When work completes** or **Force Shutdown Now**. Select **Force Shutdown Now**.

5. Confirm the operation by clicking on the **Yes** button on the **Server Life Cycle Assistant** page.

How it works...

When a start/stop operation is invoked for Managed Server, the Administration Console issues this command to the Node Manager. The Node Manager receives the startup parameters and credentials from the Administration Console and starts the Managed Server.

The Managed Server then contacts the Administration Server and checks for configuration changes and if necessary, updates it. If the Administration Server is not reachable, the Managed Server uses the local copy of the configuration from the `$DOMAIN_HOME/config/*` directory.

It's possible to start the WebLogic Server instances without the Node Manager; but unless you have your own monitoring and high availability method to the WebLogic domain, it is recommended to use the Node Manager in production environments.

There's more...

The Managed Server can also be started and stopped using WLST.

Starting/stopping the Managed Servers with WLST and the Node Manager

Carry out the following steps:

1. Log in as a `wls` user to shell and start WLST:

   ```
   [wls@prod01]$ $WL_HOME/common/bin/wlst.sh
   ```

2. Connect to the Administration Server using `wlsadmin` as the user, `<pwd>` as the password, and `t3://prod01.domain.local:7001` as the server URL:

   ```
   wls:/offline>connect("wlsadmin","<pwd>","t3://prod01.domain.
   local:7001")
   ```

3. Run the following WLST command to start `PROD_Server01`:

   ```
   start('PROD_Server01','Server')
   ```

4. To stop the Managed Server, type the following command:

   ```
   shutdown('PROD_Server01','Server')
   ```

The WLST method works the same way as the Administration Console. The Administration Console and WLST are both clients accessing the Node Manager, and both invoke start/stop operations on it.

Starting/stopping with the provided shell script

You can use the `startManagedWebLogic.sh` and `stopManagedWebLogic.sh` script located at the `$DOMAIN_HOME/bin` directory:

1. Go to the WebLogic domain's `bin` directory:

   ```
   [wls@prod01]$ cd $DOMAIN_HOME/bin
   ```

2. Start the Managed Server `PROD_Server01` typing:

   ```
   [wls@prod01]$ ./startManagedWebLogic.sh PROD_Server01 t3://prod01.
   domain.local:7001
   ```

3. The server will initiate the startup process and ask for a WebLogic administrator username and password:

   ```
   Enter username to boot WebLogic server: wlsadmin

   Enter password to boot WebLogic server:
   ```

4. Type `wlsadmin` as the username and `<password>` you previously specified at the domain creation as the password.

5. The WebLogic Managed Server will start.

6. To stop the `PROD_Server01` Managed Server, provide the credentials `wlsadmin/<password>`:

   ```
   [wls@prod01]$ ./stopManagedWebLogic.sh PROD_Server01 t3://prod01.
   domain.local:7001

   Stopping Weblogic Server...


   Initializing WebLogic Scripting Tool (WLST) ...


   Welcome to WebLogic Server Administration Scripting Shell
   ```

```
Type help() for help on available commands

Please enter your username :wlsadmin
Please enter your password :<password>
Connecting to t3://prod01.domain.local:7001 with userid wlsadmin
...
Successfully connected to Admin Server 'PROD_AdminServer' that
belongs to domain 'PROD_DOMAIN'.

Warning: An insecure protocol was used to connect to the
server. To ensure on-the-wire security, the SSL port or
Admin port should be used instead.

Shutting down the server PROD_Server01 with force=false while
connected to PROD_AdminServer ...

Exiting WebLogic Scripting Tool.

Done
```

Scripts usage

```
startManagedWebLogic.sh <serverName> <admin_url>
stopManagedWebLogic.sh <serverName> <admin_url>
stopManagedWebLogic.sh <serverName> <admin_url>
<user> <password>
```

The `boot.properties` file must be created the same way it was created before in order to provide the credentials, otherwise WebLogic will not start.

WebLogic Server will look for the credentials provided in the `boot.properties` file under $DOMAIN_HOME/servers/<servername>/security/ when starting from the script.

On the other hand, the credentials will be stored automatically in $DOMAIN_HOME/servers/<servername>/data/nodemanager/boot.properties if the startup command is issued to the Node Manager. WebLogic Server will not ask for the username/password.

See also

▸ *Starting the Node Manager*

▸ *Starting the Administration Server*

Deploying applications

This recipe will cover the deployment of a J2EE **Application archived file** (**EAR**), but it also applies to **Web Application** (**WAR**), **Resource Adapters(RAR)**, and other JAR archived files, such as libraries, EJBs, and Java classes.

The following steps will walk you through the process to deploy the application. The WebLogic administrator usually assumes the deployer role in a production environment, so make sure to define a well-structured procedure to deploy the applications and follow it.

Getting ready

This recipe will deploy an archived application file called `myApp.ear`. The application will be target of the `PROD_Cluster` cluster instead of the individual Managed Servers.

How to do it...

Carry out the following steps:

1. Create a new directory to be the application installation directory using the syntax/ oracle/applications/<environment>/<application>/<version>:

    ```
    [wls@prod01]$ mkdir -p /oracle/applications/prod/myApp/v1
    [wls@prod01]$ cd /oracle/applications/prod/myApp/v1
    ```

2. Create two directories:

    ```
    [wls@prod01]$ mkdir app
    [wls@prod01]$ mkdir plan
    ```

3. Copy the `myApp.ear` file to the `app` directory.

4. Access the Administration Console with your web browser at `http://prod01.domain.local:7001/console`.

5. Click on the **Lock & Edit** button to start a new edit session.

6. Navigate to the **Deployments** page by clicking on the link in the domain structure.

7. Click on the **Install** button to install a new application.

8. Type the path `/oracle/applications/prod/myApp/v1/app` and click on **Next**.

9. Select `myApp.ear` from the list and click on **Next**.

10. Select **Install this deployment as an application** and click on **Next**.

11. Select the **All servers from the cluster** radio button from the `PROD_Cluster` cluster and click on **Next**.

12. Leave the default options and click on the **Finish** button.

13. A new deployment plan file will automatically be created in `/oracle/applications/prod/myApp/v1/plan/Plan.xml`.

14. Click on the **Activate Changes** button to apply the changes.

15. The application should be in a **Prepared** state. Start the application by selecting the `myApp` checkbox and clicking on the **Start** button with the **Servicing all requests** option.

How it works...

This procedure installs a simple enterprise application named `myApp` to the cluster `PROD_Cluster` in the WebLogic domain.

The application is distributed to the cluster using the default deployment option stage mode. In the stage mode deployment, the Administration Server prepares the `myApp.ear` file to be copied to the stages directory of each of the Managed Servers of the cluster `PROD_Cluster`. The directory is `$DOMAIN_HOME/servers/<servername>/stage/<application>`.

WebLogic will use this local copy until a new redeployment is made.

There's more...

There are many options to achieve the same results when deploying.

Deploying using the weblogic.Deployer tool

You can use the command-line tool `weblogic.Deployer` to make deployment changes in a WebLogic domain.

To perform the same deployment of `myApp.ear` to the `PROD_Cluster` cluster, do the following:

1. Go to the WebLogic domain's `bin` directory:

    ```
    [wls@prod01]$ cd $DOMAIN_HOME/bin
    ```

2. Set the environment variables:

    ```
    [wls@prod01]$ . ./setDomainEnv.sh
    ```

3. Run the `weblogic.Deployer` command line with the parameters:

    ```
    [wls@prod01]$ java weblogic.Deployer -adminurl t3://prod01.domain.
    local:7001 -username wlsadmin -password <pwd> -deploy -targets
    PROD_Cluster /oracle/applications/prod/myApp/v1/app/myApp.ear
    ```

4. The following should be the output:

    ```
    weblogic.Deployer invoked with options:  -adminurl t3://prod01.
    domain.local:7001 -username wlsadmin -deploy -targets PROD_Cluster
    /oracle/applications/prod/myApp/v1/app/myApp.ear

    <Info><J2EE Deployment SPI><BEA-260121><Initiating deploy
    operation for application, myApp [archive: /oracle/applications/
    prod/myApp/v1/app/myApp.ear], to PROD_Cluster .>
    ```

5. The `myApp` application should be deployed to the `PROD_Cluster` cluster.

Deploying applications using WLST

Now let's deploy the application through WLST using the following steps:

1. Log in as a `wls` user to shell and start WLST:

    ```
    [wls@prod01]$ $WL_HOME/common/bin/wlst.sh
    ```

2. Connect to the Administration Server using `wlsadmin` as the user, `<pwd>` as the password, and `t3://prod01.domain.local:7001` as the server URL:

    ```
    wls:/offline>connect("wlsadmin","<pwd>","t3://prod01.domain.
    local:7001")
    ```

3. Run the following WLST command to deploy the `myApp.ear` application to the `PROD_Cluster` cluster:

    ```
    deploy("myApp", "/oracle/applications/prod/myApp/v1/app/myApp.
    ear","PROD_Cluster")
    ```

4. The following should be the output:

```
Deploying application from /oracle/applications/prod/myApp/v1/app/
myApp.ear to targets PROD_Cluster (upload=false) ...
```

```
<Apr 6, 2013 11:02:24 PM BRT><Info><J2EE Deployment SPI><BEA-
260121><Initiating deploy operation for application, myApp
[archive: /oracle/applications/prod/myApp/v1/app/myApp.ear], to
PROD_Cluster .>
```

```
.Completed the deployment of Application with status completed
```

```
Current Status of your Deployment:
```

```
Deployment command type: deploy
```

```
Deployment State      : completed
```

2
High Availability with WebLogic Clusters

In this chapter we will cover the following recipes:

- ▶ Creating a WebLogic cluster
- ▶ Defining a Hostname/Alias for the Listen Address value
- ▶ Configuring HA WebLogic cluster parameters
- ▶ Using Unicast for cluster communications
- ▶ Using Multicast for cluster communications
- ▶ Installing Apache HTTP Server for the Web tier
- ▶ Using the Web Server Plug-in to load balance HTTP Requests to WebLogic cluster
- ▶ Defining a network channel for cluster communications
- ▶ Configuring high availability for Administration Server

Introduction

WebLogic clustering is a highly recommended configuration for production environments. The WebLogic cluster provides reliability and high availability by distributing the requests and the load to the WebLogic Server instance members of the cluster.

Using WebLogic cluster also facilitates the administration tasks because WebLogic Server automatically distributes the configuration and deployment changes to all WebLogic Server instances, including the distribution of the deploy file to all machines.

Clustering can also avoid a single point of failure. If a machine crashes, the system can still operate with the WebLogic Manager Servers of the other machines. The architecture can grow and scale horizontally by adding more WebLogic Server instances to the cluster and distributing them to new machines.

Creating a WebLogic cluster

A WebLogic cluster is normally created with the domain using the Configuration Wizard tool. The cluster can also be created and added to an existing domain by using the Administration Console. This recipe will cover adding a new cluster to the existing PROD_DOMAIN domain.

A WebLogic cluster was previously created using Configuration Wizard earlier in this book. The same cluster will be created this time, but with four Manager Server instances instead of two. So remove the original cluster before creating the new cluster.

The new cluster will be called PROD_Cluster with four WebLogic Server instances PROD_Server01, PROD_Server02, PROD_Server03, and PROD_Server04. Machine prod01 will host the instances PROD_Server01 and PROD_Server02 and machine prod02 will host the instances PROD_Server03 and PROD_Server04.

PROD_DOMAIN Topology:

```
PROD_DOMAIN
   |___ PROD_AdminServer
   |
   |___ PROD_Cluster
        |___ PROD_Server01
        |___ PROD_Server02
        |___ PROD_Server03
        |___ PROD_Server04
```

Machine distribution, WebLogic Server instances, and listen ports Topology:

```
Machine
   |___ prod01
   |    |_____ PROD_AdminServer  (7001)
   |    |_____ PROD_Server01     (8001)
   |    |_____ PROD_Server02     (8002)
   |
   |___ prod02
        |_____ PROD_Server03     (8003)
        |_____ PROD_Server04     (8004)
```

Getting ready

Make sure the Administration Server is up and Node Manager is running on all machines in the domain.

If the cluster PROD_Cluster was created previously, delete it from the domain before creating the new one:

1. Log in as a wls user to shell and start WLST:

    ```
    [wls@prod01]$ $WL_HOME/common/bin/wlst.sh
    ```

2. Connect to the Administration Server using wlsadmin as the user, <pwd> as the password and t3://prod01.domain.local:7001 as the server URL:

    ```
    wls:/offline> connect("wlsadmin","<pwd>","t3://prod01.domain.
    local:7001")
    ```

3. Run the following WLST commands to delete the original PROD_Cluster cluster and the Managed Server instances:

    ```
    edit()
    startEdit()


    editService.getConfigurationManager().removeReferencesToBean(getMB
    ean('/Clusters/PROD_Cluster'))


    cd('/')
    cmo.destroyCluster(getMBean('/Clusters/PROD_Cluster'))


    cd('/Servers/PROD_Server01')
    cmo.setCluster(None)
    cmo.setMachine(None)


    editService.getConfigurationManager().removeReferencesToBean(getMB
    ean('/Servers/PROD_Server01'))


    cd('/')
    cmo.destroyServer(getMBean('/Servers/PROD_Server01'))


    cd('/Servers/PROD_Server02')
    cmo.setCluster(None)
    cmo.setMachine(None)
    ```

```
editService.getConfigurationManager().removeReferencesToBean(getMB
ean('/Servers/PROD_Server02'))

cd('/')
cmo.destroyServer(getMBean('/Servers/PROD_Server02'))
activate()
```

The old cluster has now been removed and the new cluster is ready to be created.

How to do it...

To create the new cluster PROD_Cluster:

1. Access Administration Console with your web browser at http://prod01.domain. local:7001/console.

2. Click on the **Lock & Edit** button to start a new edit session.

3. Expand the **Environment** tree on the left and click on **Clusters**.

4. Click on the **New** button to start creating a new cluster.

5. Type PROD_Cluster on the **Name** field. Leave the **Messaging Mode** in the Unicast mode and the rest of the parameters at their default values. Click on the **OK** button.

6. The PROD_Cluster cluster will be displayed in the **Clusters** table list. Click on the PROD_Cluster cluster to navigate to **Configuration | General**. Click on the **Servers** tab to navigate to **Configuration | Servers**. Click on the **Add** button, as shown in the following screenshot:

7. Type PROD_Server01 in the **Server Name** field and 8001 in the **Listen Port** field. Click on **Finish**.

8. Repeat the steps to add the three remaining WebLogic Server Instances to the PROD_ Cluster according to the topology: PROD_Server02 port 8002, PROD_Server03 port 8003, and PROD_Server04 port 8004.

9. Assign the newly created Managed Server instances to their respective machines. On the navigation tree to the left, navigate to **Environment | Machines** and click on the prod01 machine. Now, go to **Configuration | General** and click on the **Servers** tab to go to **Configuration | Servers**, (as shown in the following screenshot):

10. Click on the **Select an existing server** option, **the and associate it with this machine** radio button, select PROD_Server01 from the **Select a server** drop-down menu and click on the **Finish** button. Now do the same for PROD_Server02.

11. Go back to the **Machines** page and click on the PROD_Cluster cluster to navigate to **Configuration | Servers**. Add the Server instances PROD_Server03 and PROD_Server04 to the prod02 machine. Click on the **Finish** button.

12. Click on the **Activate Changes** button to finish.

How it works...

You have just created the four new WebLogic Managed Server instances, assigned them to the machines prod01 and prod02, and added them to the new cluster PROD_Cluster.

In the next few recipes, you'll configure other recommended cluster parameters, which are essential for the cluster to run properly in a production environment.

There's more...

The same cluster can also be created using the following WLST.

Creating a WebLogic cluster using WLST

1. Log in as `wls` user to shell and start WLST:

   ```
   [wls@prod01]$ $WL_HOME/common/bin/wlst.sh
   ```

2. Connect to the Administration Server using `wlsadmin` as the user, `<pwd>` as the password, and `t3://prod01.domain.local:7001` as the server URL:

   ```
   wls:/offline> connect("wlsadmin","<pwd>","t3://prod01.domain.local:7001")
   ```

3. Run the following WLST commands to create the cluster and server instances:

   ```
   edit()
   startEdit()

   cd('/')
   cmo.createCluster('PROD_Cluster')
   cd('/Clusters/PROD_Cluster')
   cmo.setClusterMessagingMode('unicast')

   cd('/')
   cmo.createServer('PROD_Server01')
   cd('/Servers/PROD_Server01')
   cmo.setListenPort(8001)
   cmo.setCluster(getMBean('/Clusters/PROD_Cluster'))
   cmo.setMachine(getMBean('/Machines/prod01'))

   cd('/')
   cmo.createServer('PROD_Server02')
   cd('/Servers/PROD_Server02')
   cmo.setListenPort(8002)
   cmo.setCluster(getMBean('/Clusters/PROD_Cluster'))
   cmo.setMachine(getMBean('/Machines/prod01'))

   cd('/')
   cmo.createServer('PROD_Server03')
   ```

```
cd('/Servers/PROD_Server03')
cmo.setListenPort(8003)
cmo.setCluster(getMBean('/Clusters/PROD_Cluster'))
cmo.setMachine(getMBean('/Machines/prod02'))

cd('/')
cmo.createServer('PROD_Server04')
cd('/Servers/PROD_Server04')
cmo.setListenPort(8004)
cmo.setCluster(getMBean('/Clusters/PROD_Cluster'))
cmo.setMachine(getMBean('/Machines/prod02'))

activate()
exit()
```

See also

▸ *Configuring HA WebLogic cluster parameters*

▸ *Using Unicast for cluster communications*

▸ *Using Multicast for cluster communications*

Defining a Hostname/Alias for the Listen Address value

The WebLogic Managed Server instances of the cluster were created in the previous recipe but a **Listen Address** value was not assigned to any of it.

The objective of this recipe is to assign a unique hostname or alias as the Listen Address value for each of the Managed Servers instead of assigning the prod01, prod02 hostnames or the IP address.

Getting ready

For the cluster PROD_Cluster the FQDNs: prodsrv01.domain.local, prodsrv02. domain.local, prodsrv03.domain.local, and prodsrv04.domain.localwill be used as the listen addresses. For example, PROD_Server01, PROD_Server02, PROD_ Server03, and PROD_Server04, will be used respectively.

From the WebLogic configuration perspective, it doesn't make any difference if the addresses `prodsrv01.domain.local`, `prodsrv02.domain.local`, `prodsrv03.domain.local`, and `prodsrv04.domain.local` point to the IP addresses of the machines `prod01` and `prod02` or to **Virtual IP addresses** (**VIP**).

How to do it...

To change and configure the listen addresses of the Managed Servers:

1. Access the Administration Console with your web browser at `http://prod01.domain.local:7001/console`.

2. Click on the **Lock & Edit** button to start a new edit session.

3. Expand the **Environment** tree on the left and click on **Servers**.

4. Click on the `PROD_Server01` server to navigate to the **Configuration | General** tab of the first Managed Server.

5. Type `prodsrv01.domain.local` in the **Listen Address** field, as shown in the following screenshot. Click on the **Save** button.

6. Repeat the previous steps to configure `PROD_Server02`, `PROD_Server03`, and `PROD_Server04` to use `prodsrv02.domain.local`, `prodsrv03.domain.local`, and `prodsrv04.domain.local` in the **Listen Address** field. Click on the **Save** button in each step.

7. Click on the **Activate Changes** button.

How it works...

The uniqueness of the **Listen Address** field is an important configuration as it allows the WebLogic cluster to provide the flexibility needed for high availability, and to use the automatic/manual server and service migration. It also guarantees the independence and decoupling of each of the WebLogic Managed Server configurations.

It's also a good practice to use a different **Listen Port** for the Managed Servers. Using different `hostname:port` combinations should avoid possible port conflicts when two Managed Servers would possibly listen for the same IP address if a migration situation arises.

 As a rule of thumb, use a unique hostname for the **Listen Address** field and a unique port for the **Listen Port** field. Also always use a fully qualified domain name.

There's more...

Setting the **Listen Address** value can also be done using WLST.

Defining the Listen Address value using WLST

Carry out the following steps to change the **Listen Address** value:

1. Log in as a `wls` user to shell and start WLST:

    ```
    [wls@prod01]$ $WL_HOME/common/bin/wlst.sh
    ```

2. Connect to the Administration Server using `wlsadmin` as the user, `<pwd>` as the password and `t3://prod01.domain.local:7001` as the server URL:

    ```
    wls:/offline> connect("wlsadmin","<pwd>","t3://prod01.domain.
    local:7001")
    ```

3. Run the following WLST commands to create the cluster and the server instances:

    ```
    edit()
    startEdit()

    cd('/Servers/PROD_Server01')
    cmo.setListenAddress('prodsrv01.domain.local')
    cd('/Servers/PROD_Server02')
    cmo.setListenAddress('prodsrv02.domain.local')
    cd('/Servers/PROD_Server03')
    cmo.setListenAddress('prodsrv03.domain.local')
    cd('/Servers/PROD_Server04')
    ```

```
cmo.setListenAddress('prodsrv04.domain.local')


activate()
exit()
```

See also

▶ *Defining a network channel for cluster communications*

▶ *Configuring high availability for Administration Server*

Configuring HA WebLogic cluster parameters

This recipe will cover other WebLogic cluster adjustments needed for high availability in production. The parameters are **Failure Action**, **Panic Action**, **Cluster Address**, and **Number of Servers in Cluster Address** for the cluster, and **CrashRecoveryEnabled** for Node Manager.

Getting ready

To change the Node Manager **CrashRecoveryEnabled** parameter, edit the configuration $WL_HOME/common/nodemanager/nodemanager.properties file in all machines.

The cluster parameters are changed using the Administration Console or WLST.

How to do it...

To change the Node Manager's parameter:

1. Log in as a wls user to shell and shutdown Node Manager:

    ```
    [wls@prod01]$ ps aux | grep weblogic.NodeManager | grep -v grep |
    awk '{print $2}'
    <PID>
    [wls@prod01]$ kill -9 <PID>
    ```

2. Edit nodemanager.properties:

    ```
    [wls@prod01]$ vi $WL_HOME/common/nodemanager/nodemanager.
    properties
    ```

3. Locate the CrashRecoveryEnabled parameter and change the line:

    From:

    ```
    CrashRecoveryEnabled=false
    ```

To:

```
CrashRecoveryEnabled=true
```

4. Type `:wq!` to save the file and exit.

5. Start Node Manager:

```
[wls@prod01]$ cd $WL_HOME/server/bin
[wls@prod01]$ nohup ./startNodeManager.sh &
```

6. Repeat the steps on every machine in the domain.

To change the cluster parameters:

1. Access the Administration Console with your web browser at `http://prod01.domain.local:7001/console`.

2. Click on the **Lock & Edit** button to start a new edit session.

3. Expand the **Environment** tree on the left and click on **Clusters.**

4. Click on the `PROD_Cluster` cluster to navigate to **Configuration | General** and type 4 in the **Number Of Servers In Cluster Address** field. Leave the **Cluster Address** field empty and click on the **Save** button.

5. Click on the **Advanced** link to display extra options and then select the **WebLogic Plug-in Enabled** checkbox, as shown in the following screenshot:

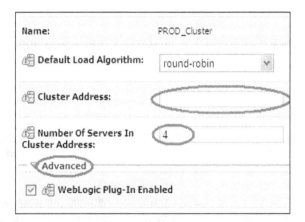

6. Click on the **Save** button.

7. Click on the **Overload** tab to navigate to **Configuration | Overload** of `PROD_Cluster`.

8. Change the **Failure Action** drop-down menu to **Force immediate shutdown of this cluster** and the **Panic Action** field to **Exit the cluster process** (as shown in the following screenshot):

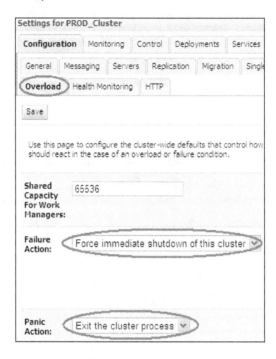

9. Click on the **Save** button and then the **Activate Changes** button.
10. Restart all Managed Servers of the PROD_Cluster cluster.

How it works...

Failure Action and **Panic Action** are the WebLogic overload settings that can shutdown a Managed Server when it reaches a FAIL state or when it throws an **Out of Memory** (**OOM**) PANIC error. Both errors would leave the affected Managed Server in an inconsistent state and would probably hang or return application errors to client requests. The Node Manager monitors the Managed Servers and restarts the failed instance automatically. Unless there is an analysis of the root cause of these errors, it's recommended to enable both parameters.

CrashRecoveryEnabled is the Node Manager parameter that must be enabled so Node Manager can restart a crashed/failed WebLogic Managed Server instance automatically.

The **Cluster Address**, **Number of Servers in Cluster Address**, and **WebLogic Plug-in Enabled** are cluster configurations for the distribution of requests and load balancing.

The **Cluster Address** configuration is used by the **Enterprise JavaBeans (EJB)** and RMI objects deployed in the cluster. Leave the **Cluster Address** configuration empty so the EJBs create the cluster address dynamically based on which network channel the request is received.

If the request is received on the default network channel, the cluster address is created using the default network channel listen address and listen port. If the request is received on a custom network channel, the cluster address is created using the custom network channel listen address and listen port.

There's more...

The cluster settings can also be modified through WLST.

Changing the cluster settings using WLST

1. Log in as a `wls` user to shell and start WLST:

    `[wls@prod01]$ $WL_HOME/common/bin/wlst.sh`

2. Connect to the Administration Server using `wlsadmin` as the user, `<pwd>` as the password and `t3://prod01.domain.local:7001` as the server URL:

    `wls:/offline> connect("wlsadmin","<pwd>","t3://prod01.domain.local:7001")`

3. Run the following WLST commands to create the cluster and the server instances:

    ```
    edit()
    startEdit()

    cd('/Clusters/PROD_Cluster')
    cmo.unSet('clusterAddress')
    cmo.setNumberOfServersInClusterAddress(4)
    cmo.setWeblogicPluginEnabled(true)

    cd('/Clusters/PROD_Cluster/OverloadProtection/PROD_Cluster')
    cmo.setPanicAction('system-exit')
    cmo.setFailureAction('force-shutdown')
    cmo.createServerFailureTrigger()

    cd('/Clusters/PROD_Cluster/OverloadProtection/PROD_Cluster/ServerFailureTrigger/PROD_Cluster')
    cmo.setMaxStuckThreadTime(600)
    ```

```
cmo.setStuckThreadCount(0)
activate()
exit()
```

Using Unicast for cluster communications

The Oracle WebLogic Server 12c can use either **Multicast** or **Unicast** for cluster communications. Since WebLogic version 10, the default cluster communication is the Unicast.

To improve Unicast reliability it's recommended to enable two extra configurations.

Getting ready

The first thing is to add a JVM argument to every WebLogic Managed Server instance of the cluster. The Administration Server must be running to make the changes.

After adding the JVM argument, the `config.xml` configuration file must be manually edited to make the second change. Therefore you will need to make sure every WebLogic Server instance is down, including the Administration Server.

How to do it...

Add the JVM argument:

1. Access the Administration Console with your web browser at `http://prod01.domain.local:7001/console`.

2. Click on the **Lock & Edit** button to start a new edit session.

3. Navigate to **Configuration | Server Start** by clicking on the WebLogic Server name, then on the **Server Start** tab.

4. Add the argument `-Dweblogic.unicast.HttpPing=true` to the **Arguments** field. The argument must be added to all Managed Server instances of `PROD_Cluster`: `PROD_Server01`, `PROD_Server02`, `PROD_Server03`, and `PROD_Server04`. Click on the **Save** button for every change.

5. Click on the **Activate Changes** button.

6. Navigate to **Domain | Control** by clicking on the `PROD_DOMAIN` link to the left and then on the **Control** tab.

7. Select and shut down all servers from the list.

Edit the `config.xml` file:

1. Log in as a `wls` user to the first machine `prod01` and navigate to the folder:

   [wls@prod01]$ cd $DOMAIN_HOME/config

2. Make a backup of the `config.xml` file:

   [wls@prod01]$ cp config.xml config.xml_backup

3. Open `config.xml` to be edited:

   [wls@prod01]$ vi config.xml

4. Find the `<cluster>` definition tag of `PROD_Cluster`:

   ```
   <cluster>
       <name>PROD_Cluster</name>
       <cluster-messaging-mode>unicast</cluster-messaging-
       mode>
   </cluster>
   ```

5. Add the `<message-ordering-enabled` tag:

   ```
   <cluster>
       <name>PROD_Cluster</name>
       <cluster-messaging-mode>unicast</cluster-messaging-
       mode>
       <message-ordering-enabled>true</message-ordering-
       enabled>
   </cluster>
   ```

6. Type `:wq!` to save the file and exit.

7. Copy the file to all machines in the domain:

   [wls@prod01]$ scp config.xml wls@prod02:$DOMAIN_HOME/config

8. Start the Administration Server.

How it works...

The `-Dweblogic.unicast.HttpPing=true` argument enables an internal health check on Unicast communications that improves its reliability.

The `<message-ordering-enabled>` tag forces Unicast communications to be processed in order, avoiding some issues with JNDI updates and JMS Topics.

See also

▶ *Configuring HA WebLogic cluster parameters*

▶ *Using Multicast for cluster communications*

Using Multicast for cluster communications

WebLogic can also use Multicast for cluster communications.

When configured for using Multicast, the Managed Servers of the cluster subscribe to a Multicast address and port and listen for heartbeats and cluster messages. Unlike Unicast, Multicast communication uses UDP and broadcasts the message through the network and therefore does not guarantee that the message is received.

Getting ready

To configure Multicast, the Administration Server must be running.

How to do it...

To configure the Multicast communication for the cluster:

1. Access the Administration Console with your web browser at `http://prod01. domain.local:7001/console`.

2. Click on the **Lock & Edit** button to start a new edit session.

3. Expand the **Environment** tree on the left and click on **Clusters**.

4. Click on the `PROD_Cluster` cluster to navigate to **Configuration | General** and click on the **Messaging** tab to navigate to **Configuration | Messaging**.

5. Change the **Messaging Mode** drop-down menu to **Multicast**. Configure the **Multicast Address** value to `239.192.0.0` and the **Multicast Port** to `7001` (as shown in the following screenshot):

6. Click on the **Save** button and then on the **Activate Changes** button.
7. Restart all Managed Servers of the PROD_Cluster cluster.

How it works...

Multicast includes additional configuration at the networking and operational system level.

Multicast Address 239.192.0.0 and **Multicast Port** 7001 are the default values. The range from 224.0.0.0 to 239.255.255.255 can be used. Do not use an address within the x.0.0.1 range where x is between 0 and 9.

 Don't use two clusters with the same Multicast address in the same network or they will conflict.

There's more...

The Multicast can also be configured through WLST.

Configuring Multicast using WLST

1. Log in as a `wls` user to shell and start WLST:

    `[wls@prod01]$ $WL_HOME/common/bin/wlst.sh`

2. Connect to the Administration Server using `wlsadmin` as the user, `<pwd>` as the password, and `t3://prod01.domain.local:7001` as the server URL:

    ```
    wls:/offline> connect("wlsadmin","<pwd>","t3://prod01.domain.
    local:7001")
    ```

3. Run the following WLST commands to create the cluster and the server instances:

    ```
    edit()
    startEdit()

    cd('/Clusters/PROD_Cluster')
    cmo.setClusterMessagingMode('multicast')
    cmo.setMulticastPort(7001)
    cmo.setMulticastAddress('239.192.0.0')

    activate()
    exit()
    ```

See also

*   ▶ *Configuring HA WebLogic cluster parameters*
*   ▶ *Using Unicast for cluster communications*

Installing Apache HTTP Server for the Web tier

This recipe will describe a quick installation of the Apache HTTP Server because a Web tier is needed to illustrate the use of WebLogic Web Server plug-in.

The plug-in is used for load balancing and the failover of HTTP requests to WebLogic Server, and the next recipe will cover its configuration and usage.

Getting ready

This recipe assumes a Web tier with two dedicated Linux x86-64 machines named `web01` and `web02`. Both machines should have Apache HTTP Server 2.2.x running and listening for HTTP requests on port `80`. The Apache HTTP Server runs under the shell user `webadmin`.

 In production, use a minimum of two machines in all tiers to avoid a single point of failure.

Download Apache HTTP Server 2.2.x at `http://httpd.apache.org/docs/2.2/install.html#download`. Make sure you download the Unix Source and the latest stable version. The filename should be `httpd-2.2.xx.tar.gz` where the `xx` stands for the minor version.

Also, verify if the operational system meets the requirements at `http://httpd.apache.org/docs/2.2/install.html#requirements` to build and install Apache HTTP Server.

 To simplify the reading, we'll use the term `$APACHE_HOME` when referring to to the Apache HTTP Server directory, `/oracle/apache`.

How to do it...

To install Apache HTTP Server, carry out the following steps:

1. Create a dedicated user to host and run Apache HTTP Server 2.2.x in Linux. Log in as the `root` user and create the user and group named `webadmin` and set a new password for it:

   ```
   [root@web01]# groupadd webadmin
   [root@web01]# useradd -g webadmin webadmin
   [root@web01]# passwd webadmin
   Changing password for user webadmin.
   New UNIX password: <new password>
   Retype new UNIX password: <new password>
   ```

2. Log in as a `webadmin` user, create a temporary directory and extract the downloaded file to it. Consider that the `httpd-2.2.xx.tar.gz` file is located in the home directory:

   ```
   [webadmin@web01]$ cd
   [webadmin@web01]$ gunzip -d httpd-2.2.xx.tar.gz
   [webadmin@web01]$ mkdir ~/apache-tmp
   ```

```
[webadmin@web01]$ cd ~/apache-tmp
[webadmin@web01]$ tar xfv ../httpd-2.2.xx.tar
```

3. This recipe will use `/oracle/apache` as the default installation folder for Apache
    HTTP Server. Run the `configure` command from the temporary directory to prepare
    the source files:

```
[webadmin@web01]$ cd ~/apache-tmp/httpd-2-2.xx
[webadmin@web01]$ ./configure --prefix=/oracle/apache --with-
mpm=worker
```

4. Compile and build Apache:

```
[webadmin@web01]$ make
```

5. Install Apache:

```
[webadmin@web01]$ make install
```

6. Apache HTTP Server should be installed at `/oracle/apache` with the following
    directory structure:

```
[webadmin@web01]$ cd $APACHE_HOME
[webadmin@web01]$ tree -d
.
|-- bin
|-- build
|-- cgi-bin
|-- conf
|   |-- extra
|   `-- original
|       `-- extra
|-- error
|   `-- include
|-- htdocs
|-- icons
|   `-- small
|-- include
|-- lib
|   `-- pkgconfig
|-- logs
|-- man
|   |-- man1
```

```
|     `-- man8
|-- manual
|    |-- developer
|    |-- faq
|    |-- howto
|    |-- images
|    |-- misc
|    |-- mod
|    |-- platform
|    |-- programs
|    |-- rewrite
|    |-- ssl
|    |-- style
|    |   |-- css
|    |   |-- lang
|    |   |-- latex
|    |   `-- xsl
|    |       `-- util
|    `-- vhosts
`-- modules
```

38 directories

7. Open and edit the Apache configuration `httpd.conf` file:

   [webadmin@web01]$ vi $APACHE_HOME/conf/httpd.conf

8. Locate the following two lines. They are at different locations of the file:

   Listen 80

   #ServerName www.example.com:80

9. Change the location to:

   Listen web01:80

   ServerName web01:80

10. Type :wq! to save the file and exit the editor.

11. As a `root` user, change `apachectl` and `httpd` file owner to `root` and add the `setuid` file permission so Apache can listen to port `80`:

    ```
    [root@web01]$ cd $APACHE_HOME/bin
    [root@web01]$ chown root:webadmin apachectl httpd
    [root@web01]$ chmod u+s apachectl httpd
    ```

12. Apache HTTP Server is now ready to be started with the `webadmin` user:

    ```
    [webadmin@web01]$ $APACHE_HOME/bin/apachectl start
    ```

13. Test if Apache is running:

    ```
    [webadmin@web01]$ curl http://web01
    <html><body><h1>It works!</h1></body></html>
    ```

14. To shutdown Apache, issue the stop command:

    ```
    [webadmin@web01]$ $APACHE_HOME/bin/apachectl stop
    ```

15. Remove the temporary directory:

    ```
    [webadmin@web01]$ rm -rf ~/apache-tmp
    ```

16. Repeat all the steps on the `web02` machine, using the appropriate `web02` hostname when needed.

How it works...

Apache HTTP Server 2.2.x is now installed with the default options and will be used as a Web Server example in the next recipe.

Other Apache configurations are not within the scope of this book, so the only setting changed so far is the default `127.0.0.1` listen address, which is now configured to use the `web01` and `web02` hostnames.

See also

▶ *Using the Web Server Plug-in to load balance HTTP Requests to WebLogic cluster*

Using the Web Server Plug-in to load balance HTTP Requests to WebLogic cluster

The WebLogic cluster itself does not distribute the incoming HTTP requests across the Managed Servers, so the architecture design should foresee a load balance mechanism.

WebLogic can use either an external load balancer appliance/hardware such as the BIG-IP F5 (`http://www.f5.com/products/big-ip`), a Web Server such as the Apache HTTP Server configured with the WebLogic Web Server plug-in, or the embedded WebLogic `HttpClusterServlet` configuration.

Load balancing options:

- ▸ External load balancer
- ▸ Web Server with plug-in
- ▸ WebLogic `HttpClusterServlet` configuration

For production environments, it is recommended to use a mixed architecture that includes an external load balancer and a Web Server with the proxy plug-in. The HTTP requests will be received and distributed by the external load balancer to the Web Servers, and the Web Servers will then proxy the requests through the plug-in across the WebLogic Managed Servers of the cluster. The WebLogic `HttpClusterServlet` configuration is not recommended for use in production. The HTTP request sequence is as follows:

Client -> External Load Balancer -> Web Server + plug-in -> WebLogic cluster

Consider always including a Web Server tier + WebLogic plug-in to distribute the HTTP requests across the WebLogic cluster.

Although it is possible to use only the external load balancers in the architecture, it's highly recommended to include the Web Server and the plug-in. The plug-in contains all the logic for the load balancing, session stickiness, and in particular the clustering failover with the transparent connection failover.

More importantly, the plug-in is needed when setting up the workload management through work managers, which will be seen later in this book.

Getting ready

The Web server plug-in can be used together with an Apache HTTP Server, Netscape IPlanet, or Microsoft IIS web servers. This recipe will use the Apache installation from the previous recipe.

Unlike previous WebLogic versions, the plug-in is not included in the WebLogic Server 12c installation.

At the time of writing this book, there is no 12c plug-in version released yet and the version 11g should be used.

To download the plug-in, access My Oracle Support at `https://support.oracle.com` and read the note ID: *WebLogic Server Web Server Plug-In Support [ID 1111903.1]*.

 An `Oracle.com` account must be provided to log in to *My Oracle Support*.

Click on the link provided in the note ID to download the WebLogic 11g plug-in. The filename should be of the format `WLSPlugins11g-xxx.zip` and be about 260 MB in size.

How to do it...

To configure the WebLogic plug-in, carry out the following steps:

1. Log in as a `webadmin` user to the `web01` machine, create a temporary directory and extract the downloaded file to it. Consider that the file `WLSPlugins11g-xxx.zip` is located in the home directory. In this example, only the plug-in for Apache 2.2 for Linux 64-bit (`WLSPlugin11g-64bit-Apache2.2-linux64-x86_64.zip`) will be extracted from the `zip` file:

   ```
   [webadmin@web01]$ cd
   ```

```
[webadmin@web01]$ mkdir ~/plugin-tmp

[webadmin@web01]$ cd ~/plugin-tmp

[webadmin@web01]$ unzip ../WLSPlugins11g*.zip WLSPlugin11g-64bit-
Apache2.2-linux64-x86_64.zip

[webadmin@web01]$ unzip WLSPlugin11g-64bit-Apache2.2-
linux64-x86_64.zip
```

2. Stop the Apache HTTP Server if it is already running:

   ```
   [webadmin@web01]$ $APACHE_HOME/bin/apachectl stop
   ```

3. Copy the plug-in files to Apache `lib` directory:

   ```
   [webadmin@web01]$ cp ~/plugin-tmp/lib/* /oracle/apache/lib/
   ```

4. Create and edit a new file named `httpd-weblogic.conf` to hold the plug-in configuration file:

   ```
   [webadmin@web01]$ vi $APACHE_HOME/conf/extra/httpd-weblogic.conf
   ```

5. Add the following lines to the file:

   ```
   LoadModule weblogic_module lib/mod_wl.so
   <Location />
     SetHandler weblogic-handler
     WebLogicCluster prodsrv01.domain.local:8001,prodsrv02.domain.
   local:8002,prodsrv03.domain.local:8003,prodsrv04.domain.local:8004
   </Location>
   ```

6. Type `:wq!` to save the file and exit.

7. Open and edit the Apache configuration `httpd.conf` file:

   ```
   [webadmin@web01]$ vi $APACHE_HOME/conf/httpd.conf
   ```

8. Locate the following lines at the end of file:

   ```
   # Supplemental configuration
   #
   # The configuration files in the conf/extra/ directory can be
   # included to add extra features or to modify the default
   configuration of
   # the server, or you may simply copy their contents here and
   change as
   # necessary.
   ```

9. Include the plug-in configuration file just after the previous lines:

   ```
   # Supplemental configuration
   #
   # The configuration files in the conf/extra/ directory can be
   # included to add extra features or to modify the default
   ```

```
configuration of
# the server, or you may simply copy their contents here and
change as
# necessary.

# WebLogic Plug-in Configuration
Include conf/extra/httpd-weblogic.conf
```

10. Type :wq! to save the file and exit.

11. Start the Apache HTTP Server.

    [webadmin@web01]$ $APACHE_HOME/bin/apachectl start

12. Repeat the previous steps and configure the web02 machine too with the appropriate web02 hostname.

How it works...

The plug-in distribution files were extracted and the files from the lib directory were copied to the $APACHE_HOME/lib directory of the Apache installation, including the mod_wl. so plug-in itself.

Also a new configuration file was created so the WebLogic plug-in configuration is kept apart from the Apache configuration. The syntax to include the new httpd-weblogic.conf file was added to the original configuration httpd.conf file. This procedure follows the default httpd.conf behavior of including extra configuration files.

The httpd-weblogic.conf file used as a sample in this recipe is configured so that all requests to Apache are distributed to the WebLogic cluster.

The configuration file is displayed with more information:

```
#Loads the WebLogic plug-in module

LoadModule weblogic_module lib/mod_wl.so


#All requests - from the root path (/) and below - will be handled by the
WebLogic plug-in.

<Location />

  SetHandler weblogic-handler

#Defines the initial Cluster Address the plug-in will try to connect and
distribute the requests

  WebLogicCluster prodsrv01.domain.local:8001,prodsrv02.domain.
local:8002,prodsrv03.domain.local:8003,prodsrv04.domain.local:8004

</Location>
```

Before, the test request was handled by the Apache:

```
[webadmin@web01]$ curl http://web01
<html><body><h1>It works!</h1></body></html>
```

Now the request is proxied to WebLogic. The following result is displayed when the Server instances of the cluster are down:

```
[webadmin@web01]$ curl http://web01
<HTML><HEAD><TITLE>Weblogic Bridge Message</TITLE></HEAD>
<BODY><H2>Failure of server APACHE bridge:</H2><P><hr>No backend server
available for connection: timed out after 10 seconds or idempotent set to
OFF or method not idempotent.<hr> </BODY></HTML>
```

After starting the WebLogic Managed Servers of the cluster, the same request now returns a HTTP 404 – NOT FOUND code, because no applications are deployed in the cluster yet:

```
[webadmin@web01]$ curl http://web01
<!DOCTYPE HTML PUBLIC "-//W3C//DTD HTML 4.0 Draft//EN">
<HTML>
<HEAD>
<TITLE>Error 404--Not Found</TITLE>
</HEAD>
_ code snipped _
```

There's more...

A single Web Tier with the WebLogic plug-in can be used to balance the requests to other WebLogic domains and clusters.

Proxying requests to other WebLogic clusters

It's possible to segregate the incoming HTTP requests with a specific context path to a different WebLogic cluster using the same Apache configuration.

The following is an example of the configuration in `httpd-weblogic.conf`:

```
LoadModule weblogic_module lib/mod_wl.so
<IfModule mod_weblogic.c>
    Debug ALL
    WLLogFile /tmp/wl-proxy.log
</IfModule>

<Location /app01>
    SetHandler weblogic-handler
```

```
    WebLogicCluster prodsrv01.domain.local:8001,prodsrv02.domain.
local:8002,prodsrv03.domain.local:8003,prodsrv04.domain.local:8004
</Location>

<Location /app02>
    SetHandler weblogic-handler
    WebLogicCluster prodsrv21:20001,prodsrv22:20002
</Location>
```

In the previous example, requests to `http://website.domain.local/app01` will be handled and proxied to the `PROD_Cluster` cluster. Requests to `http://website.domain.local/app02` will be proxied to another WebLogic domain with a cluster named `PROD2_Cluster`. Any other request, `http://website.domain.local/anyother`, for example, will be handled by the Apache HTTP Server.

Context Path	WLS Cluster	Cluster Address
`/app01`	`PROD_Cluster`	`prodsrv01.domain.local:8001,`
		`prodsrv02.domain.local:8002,`
		`prodsrv03.domain.local:8003,`
		`prodsrv04.domain.local:8004`
`/app02`	`PROD2_Cluster`	`prodsrv21:20001,prodsrv22:2002`
Other	None	None. Handled by Apache.

The configuration is very flexible and a lot of combinations are possible to fulfil the architectures requirements.

See also

▸ *Installing Apache HTTP Server for the Web tier*

Defining a network channel for cluster communications

When configuring the **Listen Address** value with a hostname as in the previous recipes, WebLogic Server instances use the specific **network interface card** (**NIC**) bound to the hostname's IP address for network traffic. The traffic includes all inbound and outbound requests and the Unicast cluster communications.

In a production environment with high network traffic, it is possible to improve network utilization by adding an additional NIC to be used by the Unicast cluster communications, segregating the application traffic, and the cluster communication traffic.

This recipe will create a new channel named `clusterChannel` and configure the `PROD_Cluster` cluster to use it.

Getting ready

This recipe assumes that all machines used by the cluster have two network interface cards. The first NIC is `eth0` used by the default WebLogic channel. The second NIC is `eth1` and will be used for the new WebLogic network channel.

All the Managed Server instances of the cluster must define a new channel with the same name `clusterChannel`. The `clusterChannel` points to the IP address or hostname of the NIC `eth1` of the machine that hosts the instance. The hostnames bound to the `eth1` for the `PROD_Server01`, `PROD_Server02`, `PROD_Server03`, and `PROD_Server04` Managed Servers are `channel01.domain.local`, `channel02.domain.local`, `channel03.domain.local`, and `channel04.domain.local` respectively.

How to do it...

Carry out the following steps to create a new channel:

1. Access the Administration Console with your web browser at `http://prod01.domain.local:7001/console`.

2. Click Expand the **Environment** tree on the left and click on **Servers**.

3. Click on the `PROD_Server01` link to navigate to **General | Configuration** of the first Managed Server of the cluster.

4. Click on the **Protocols** tab and then on the **Channels** tab to navigate to **Protocols | Channels** of the PROD_Server01 link. Click on the **New** button, as shown in the following screenshot:

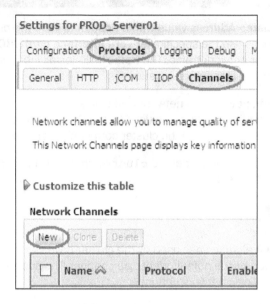

5. Type clusterChannel in the **Name** field. Change the **Protocol** drop-down menu to **cluster-broadcast** and click on the **Next** button.

6. Now, type channel01.domain.local in the **Listen Address** field, type 8001 in both the **Listen Port** and **External Listen Port** fields. Leave the **External Listen Address** empty. Click on the **Next** button, as shown in the following screenshot:.

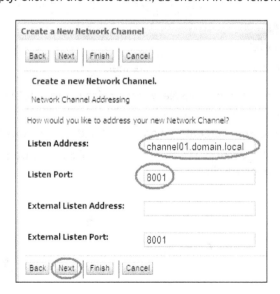

7. Select the checkboxes **Enabled**, **HTTP Enabled for This Protocol**, and **Outbound Enabled**. Leave the **Tunneling Enabled** checkbox in its default unchecked state. Click on the **Finish** button, as shown in the following screenshot:

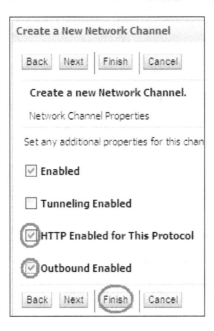

8. Add a new channel to each of the Managed Servers repeating the steps on the PROD_Server02, PROD_Server03, and PROD_Server04 instances. Use channel02.domain.local, channel03.domain.local, and channel04.domain.local as the **Listen Address** value and 8002, 8003, and 8004 as the **Listen Port** and **External Listen Port** values respectively.

9. Click on the **Clusters** link on the navigation tree on the left and click on PROD_Cluster to navigate to **General | Configuration** of the cluster.

10. Click on the **Messaging** tab and type `clusterChannel` on the **Unicast Broadcast Channel** text field (as shown in the following screenshot). Click on the **Save** button.

11. Click on the **Activate Changes** button to finish.

How it works...

The names `channel01.domain.local`, `channel02.domain.local`, `channel03.domain.local`, and `channel04.domain.local` are the hostnames bound to the `eth1` IP address of each machine.

The `PROD_Cluster` cluster is now using the `clusterChannel` network channel to communicate through a different NIC. The cluster data is being carried by `eth1` and the application traffic uses `eth0`.

There's more...

The WLST can also be used to create the network channel.

Defining the cluster channel using WLST

The change can be made using WLST:

1. Log in as a `wls` user to shell and start WLST:

   ```
   [wls@prod01]$ $WL_HOME/common/bin/wlst.sh
   ```

2. Connect to the Administration Server using `wlsadmin` as the user, `<pwd>` as the password and `t3://prod01.domain.local:7001` as the server URL:

```
wls:/offline> connect("wlsadmin","<pwd>","t3://prod01.domain.
local:7001")
```

3. Run the following WLST commands to create the cluster and the server instances:

```
edit()
startEdit()


cd('/Servers/PROD_Server01')
cmo.createNetworkAccessPoint('clusterChannel')
cd('/Servers/PROD_Server01/NetworkAccessPoints/clusterChannel')
cmo.setProtocol('cluster-broadcast')
cmo.setListenAddress('channel01.domain.local')
cmo.setEnabled(true)
cmo.setHttpEnabledForThisProtocol(true)
cmo.setTunnelingEnabled(false)
cmo.setOutboundEnabled(true)
cmo.setTwoWaySSLEnabled(false)
cmo.setClientCertificateEnforced(false)


cd('/Servers/PROD_Server02')
cmo.createNetworkAccessPoint('clusterChannel')
cd('/Servers/PROD_Server02/NetworkAccessPoints/clusterChannel')
cmo.setProtocol('cluster-broadcast')
cmo.setListenAddress('channel02.domain.local')
cmo.setEnabled(true)
cmo.setHttpEnabledForThisProtocol(true)
cmo.setTunnelingEnabled(false)
cmo.setOutboundEnabled(true)
cmo.setTwoWaySSLEnabled(false)
cmo.setClientCertificateEnforced(false)


cd('/Servers/PROD_Server03')
cmo.createNetworkAccessPoint('clusterChannel')
cd('/Servers/PROD_Server03/NetworkAccessPoints/clusterChannel')
cmo.setProtocol('cluster-broadcast')
```

```
cmo.setListenAddress('channel03.domain.local')
cmo.setEnabled(true)
cmo.setHttpEnabledForThisProtocol(true)
cmo.setTunnelingEnabled(false)
cmo.setOutboundEnabled(true)
cmo.setTwoWaySSLEnabled(false)
cmo.setClientCertificateEnforced(false)


cd('/Servers/PROD_Server04')
cmo.createNetworkAccessPoint('clusterChannel')
cd('/Servers/PROD_Server04/NetworkAccessPoints/clusterChannel')
cmo.setProtocol('cluster-broadcast')
cmo.setListenAddress('channel04.domain.local')
cmo.setEnabled(true)
cmo.setHttpEnabledForThisProtocol(true)
cmo.setTunnelingEnabled(false)
cmo.setOutboundEnabled(true)
cmo.setTwoWaySSLEnabled(false)
cmo.setClientCertificateEnforced(false)


cd('/Clusters/PROD_Cluster')
cmo.setClusterBroadcastChannel('clusterChannel')

activate()
exit()
```

See also

- *Using Unicast for cluster communications*
- *Using Multicast for cluster communications*
- *Defining a network channel for cluster communications*
- *Configuring high availability for Administration Server*

Configuring high availability for Administration Server

The Administration Server is a single WebLogic Server instance responsible for the configuration and management of the WebLogic domain. By default, the Administration Server runs on the machine that the domain was created.

Unlike WebLogic clustering, WebLogic Server does not provide out of the box high availability options for the Administration Server, if this machine fails.

> Thanks to the **Managed Servers Independence Mode** (**MSI**) Managed Servers will keep running even if the Administration Server is down.
>
> Managed Servers can also be started by using only Node Manager and WLST or by using the start-up shell scripts without the need of the Administration Server.

This recipe will provide the steps to prepare the environment in case the machine that hosts the Administration Server fails.

Getting ready

By default, the Administration Server binds to all IP addresses of the machine, but sets the `prod01` machine as its default hostname.

The first step is to set the **Listen Address** field to a unique hostname or alias decoupled from the original hostname of the machine. This recipe will use a new hostname `adminhost. domain.local`, which will initially point to the IP Address of `prod01` machine or to a VIP to `prod01` that can be migrated later.

Also a copy of the Administration Server directory must be provisioned on all machines in the domain so the Administration Server can be started on one of them when needed.

How to do it...

Change the Administration Server **Listen Address** value:

1. Access the Administration Console with your web browser at `http://prod01. domain.local:7001/console`.
2. Click on the **Lock & Edit** button to start a new edit session.
3. Expand the **Environment** tree on the left and click on **Servers**.

4. Click on the `PROD_AdminServer (admin)` link to navigate to **General | Configuration** of the Administration Server.

5. Type `adminhost` in the **Listen Address** field.

6. Click on the **Save** button and then on the **Activate Changes** button.

7. Shutdown all Server instances, including the Administration Server.

8. Start the Administration Server.

9. The Administration Console should now be accessible at `http://adminhost.domain.local:7001/console`.

Copy the Administration Server files to all machines:

1. Log in as a `wls` user to `prod01` shell and copy to the Administration Server directory to `prod02`:

   [wls@prod01] $ cd $DOMAIN_HOME/servers

   [wls@prod01] $ scp -rp PROD_AdminServer wls@prod02:$DOMAIN_HOME/servers/

> The Administration Server directory must always be updated on all machines. A recent backup can also be restored when needed. Remember to define a backup routine of your files.

2. Restart all instances and the configuration part is finished.

Starting the Administration Server on the `prod02` machine:

1. In a situation where `prod01` is unavailable, the `adminhost.domain.local` hostname must be changed to point to the IP address of `prod02` or the `adminhost.domain.local` VIP should move to `prod02`.

2. Log in as a `wls` user to the `prod02` shell and start the Administration Server. Make sure you use a recent copy of the Administration Server directory:

   [wls@prod02] $ cd $DOMAIN_HOME/bin

   [wls@prod02] $ nohup ./startWebLogic.sh &

3. The Administration Server is now running on `prod02` and the Administration Console is still accessible at the same address `http://adminhost.domain.local:7001/console`.

How it works...

All instances of the domain are now using the `adminhost.domain.local` hostname as the Administration Server hostname.

The Administration Server should be started normally on the `prod01` machine and listens for the IP address bound to `adminhost.domain.local`, which points to an IP address on the `prod01` machine as well.

If the `prod01` machine crashes, change the `adminhost.domain.local` IP address to the `prod02` machine or move the VIP to `prod02` and start the Administration Server on `prod02`.

 This change can be made by setting up the DNS Server or by making changes to the `/etc/hosts` file of the machines among a variety of other options. Please contact your network administrators to change the IP address of the `adminhost.domain.local` properly.

Follow the usual procedure to start the Administration Server, but now on `prod02` machine. As soon the Administration Server starts, all Managed Servers will reconnect automatically to it looking for the `adminhost.domain.local` new location and new IP address.

 In earlier versions, the DNS cache of the JDK didn't have a default time-to-live (TTL), so a WebLogic Server instance didn't recognize that a hostname had its IP address changed until restarting the instance. To avoid the need of a restart, a JVM argument had to be added to change the TTL.

In WebLogic 12c (using JDK > 1.6), the JVM argument is not needed anymore. Now the JDK sets a default DNS TTL to 30s.

There's more...

Update the start and stop scripts after changing the Administration Server's **Listen Address** value.

Changing the start/stop scripts

WebLogic Administrators who use the shell scripts provided in $DOMAIN_HOME/bin to start and stop WebLogic Managed Servers must change the scripts to use the new Administration Server hostname adminhost.domain.local:

1. Log in as a wls user to the prod01 shell and change to the $DOMAIN_HOME/bin directory:

   ```
   [wls@prod01]$ cd $DOMAIN_HOME/bin
   ```

2. Edit the startManagedWebLogic.sh, stopManagedWebLogic.sh, and stopManagedWebLogic.sh files and replace all occurrences of the prod01 word to adminhost.domain.local and save the files:

   ```
   [wls@prod01]$ sed -i 's/prod01/adminhost.domain.local/g'
   startManagedWebLogic.sh stopManagedWebLogic.sh stopWebLogic.sh
   ```

3. Copy the changed files to the other machines in the domain:

   ```
   [wls@prod01]$ scp startManagedWebLogic.sh stopManagedWebLogic.sh
   stopWebLogic.sh wls@prod02:$DOMAIN_HOME/bin
   ```

See also

▶ *Defining a Hostname/Alias for the Listen Address value*

3
Configuring JDBC Resources for High Availability

In this chapter, we will cover the following recipes:

- ▶ Creating a JDBC data source
- ▶ Creating a multi data source
- ▶ Defining the multi data source HA Strategy
- ▶ Creating a GridLink data source
- ▶ Managing JDBC data sources
- ▶ Tuning data sources for reliable connections
- ▶ Tuning multi data sources – surviving RAC node failures
- ▶ Updating the Oracle JDBC driver

Introduction

WebLogic Server 12c provides database connectivity through the use of the JDBC API.

JDBC API stands for Java database connectivity and allows Java applications to make calls to a database in the form of SQL statements. The connection to the database is encapsulated by the vendor's JDBC driver. WebLogic Server 12c provides JDBC drivers for the most commonly used databases, such as DB2, Informix, Microsoft SQL Server, MySQL, Oracle, PostgreSQL, Sybase, and others. A third-party JDBC driver can also be added, such as the Teradata JDBC drivers.

The JDBC data source contains the parameters, such as the database host address, database port, instance, and service name, needed to connect to the database. The data source also includes transaction options and a pool for reusing the database connections, optimizing the time spent opening these connections.

This chapter will go through some requirements of a hypothetic application named DBApp; it will show how to create and configure the JDBC resources required by it. With reliability and high availability in mind, the chapter will focus on connecting to an Oracle database and the additional steps needed when using Oracle RAC.

Deeper JDBC transaction tunings, such as Two Phase Commit, Logging Last Resource, and Global Transaction Support with no XA driver, among other options, are dependent on the application's development and will not be the focus of this chapter.

Creating a JDBC data source

Consider that the DBApp application is deployed on the PROD_Cluster cluster and requires a data source to connect to the database. The application looks for a non-XA data source with the **Java Naming and Directory Interface (JNDI)** as jdbc/ds-nonXA.

The database is an Oracle database that is running in the dbhost hostname and listening to the port 1521. The listener is accepting requests to the service name dbservice.

In this recipe, a new JDBC data source to connect to the Oracle database will be created and configured for the application DBApp.

Getting ready

The data source will be named ds-nonXA using the required JNDI jdbc/ds-nonXA. The target will be the cluster PROD_Cluster, the same target as that of the DBApp application. The database username is dbuser and the password is dbpwd.

How to do it...

Carry out the following steps to create a JDBC data source:

1. Access the Administration Console with your web browser at http://adminhost.domain.local:7001/console.

2. Click on the **Lock & Edit** button to start a new edit session.

3. Click on the plus sign to open the **Services** tree on the left, and then click on **Data Sources**.

4. Click on the **New** button and then click on **Generic Data Source**.

5. Type ds-nonXA in the **Name** field and jdbc/ds-nonXA in the **JNDI Name** field.

6. Select the **Oracle** option from the **Database Type** drop-down menu. Click on the **Next** button.

7. Choose *Oracle's Driver (Thin) for Service connections; Versions:9.0.1 and later from the **Database Driver** drop-down menu. Click on the **Next** button.

8. Leave the default values for the **Transaction options** and click on the **Next** button.

9. On the **Connection Properties** page, type dbservice in the **Database Name** field, dbhost in the **Host Name** field, and 1521 in the **Port** field. Complete the **Database User Name**, **Password**, and **Confirm Password** fields by typing dbuser and dbpwd as the username and password respectively. Click on the **Next** button.

10. Click on the **Next** button on the **Test Database Connection** page.

11. Select the **All servers in the cluster** radio button from the PROD_Cluster cluster. Click on the **Finish** button.

12. Then, click on the **Activate Changes** button.

How it works...

A new non-XA JDBC data source was created with the parameters required by the DBApp application. The non-XA Oracle JDBC driver is the **thin** version. All other parameters were left as their default values.

Name	Type	JNDI Name	Targets
ds-nonXA	Generic	jdbc/ds-nonXA	PROD_Cluster

The Oracle driver class name used for non-XA data sources is oracle.jdbc.OracleDriver.

There's more...

We will now see how to create the JDBC data source through WLST.

Creating the JDBC data source using WLST

1. Log in as a wls user to shell and start WLST:

   [wls@prod01]$ $WL_HOME/common/bin/wlst.sh

2. Connect to the Administration Server using wlsadmin as the user, <pwd> as the password, and t3://adminhost.domain.local:7001 as the server URL:

   wls:/offline> connect("wlsadmin","<pwd>","t3://adminhost.domain.local:7001")

3. Run the following WLST commands to create the data source:

```
edit()

startEdit()


cd('/')

cmo.createJDBCSystemResource('ds-nonXA')

cd('/JDBCSystemResources/ds-nonXA/JDBCResource/ds-nonXA')

cmo.setName('ds-nonXA')

cd('/JDBCSystemResources/ds-nonXA/JDBCResource/ds-nonXA/
JDBCDataSourceParams/ds-nonXA')

set('JNDINames',jarray.array([String('jdbc/ds-nonXA')], String))

cd('/JDBCSystemResources/ds-nonXA/JDBCResource/ds-nonXA/
JDBCDriverParams/ds-nonXA')

cmo.setUrl('jdbc:oracle:thin:@dbhost:1521/dbservice')

cmo.setDriverName('oracle.jdbc.OracleDriver')

cmo.setPassword('dbpwd')

cd('/JDBCSystemResources/ds-nonXA/JDBCResource/ds-nonXA/
JDBCConnectionPoolParams/ds-nonXA')

cmo.setTestTableName('SQL SELECT 1 FROM DUAL\r\n')

cd('/JDBCSystemResources/ds-nonXA/JDBCResource/ds-nonXA/
JDBCDriverParams/ds-nonXA/Properties/ds-nonXA')

cmo.createProperty('user')

cd('/JDBCSystemResources/ds-nonXA/JDBCResource/ds-nonXA/
JDBCDriverParams/ds-nonXA/Properties/ds-nonXA/Properties/user')

cmo.setValue('dbuser')

cd('/JDBCSystemResources/ds-nonXA/JDBCResource/ds-nonXA/
JDBCDataSourceParams/ds-nonXA')

cmo.setGlobalTransactionsProtocol('OnePhaseCommit')

cd('/JDBCSystemResources/ds-nonXA')

set('Targets',jarray.array([ObjectName('com.bea:Name=PROD_
Cluster,Type=Cluster')], ObjectName))


activate()

exit()
```

See also

▶ *Creating a multi data source*

Creating a multi data source

The multi data source should be used when connecting to an Oracle RAC database. The multi data source is a data source abstraction that groups all the individual data sources that connect to each node of the Oracle RAC database.

Consider that the DBApp application requires an XA connection with a JNDI name jdbc/ds-XA added to a database.

The database is an Oracle RAC database with two nodes. The first node has an instance name instance-rac01 and runs in the dbhost-rac01 hostname and listens to the port 1521. The listener accepts requests to the service name dbservice-rac01. The second node is the instance instance-rac02, and it runs in the dbhost-rac02 hostname, listens to the port 1521, and has a service name dbservice-rac02.

In this recipe, a new JDBC multi data source will be created and configured for the DBApp application.

Getting ready

Before creating the multi data source, the individual data sources pointing to each RAC node must be created. Two data sources will be created with the names ds-XA-rac01 and ds-XA-rac02 and with the JNDI names jdbc/ds-XA-rac01 and jdbc/ds-XA-rac02.

The multi data source will be named ds-XA and includes both data sources.

How to do it...

Carry out the following steps to create a multi data source:

1. Access the Administration Console with your web browser at http://adminhost.domain.local:7001/console.
2. Click on the **Lock & Edit** button to start a new edit session.
3. Click on the plus sign to open the **Services** tree on the left, and then click on **Data Sources**.
4. Click on the **New** button and then click on **Generic Data Source**.
5. Type ds-XA-rac01 in the **Name** field and jdbc/ds-XA-rac01 in the **JNDI Name** field. Leave the **Database Type** drop-down menu with the **Oracle** option selected. Click on the **Next** button.

6. Choose `*Oracle's Driver (Thin XA) for RAC Service-Instance connections; Versions:10 and later` from the **Database Driver** drop-down menu. Click on the **Next** button.

7. Then, click on the **Next** button in the **Transaction Options** page.

8. On the **Connection Properties** page, type `dbservice-rac01` in the **Service Name** field, `instance-rac01` in the **Database Name** field, `dbhost-rac01` in the **Host Name** field, and `1521` in the **Port** field. Complete the **Database User Name**, **Password**, and **Confirm Password** fields by typing `dbuser`, and `dbpwd` as the username and password respectively. Click on the **Next** button.

9. Click on the **Next** button in the **Test Database Connection** page.

10. Select the **All servers in the cluster** radio button from the `PROD_Cluster` cluster. Click on the **Finish** button.

11. Repeat the previous steps and create another data source. Add `ds-XA-rac02` as **Name**, `jdbc/ds-XA-rac02` as **JNDI Name**, `dbservice-rac02` as **Service Name**, `instance-rac02` as **Database Name**, and `dbhost-rac02` in the **Host Name** field.

	Name ⌃	Type	JNDI Name	Targets
☐	ds-XA-rac01	Generic	jdbc/ds-XA-rac01	PROD_Cluster
☐	ds-XA-rac02	Generic	jdbc/ds-XA-rac02	PROD_Cluster

12. Create the multi data source by clicking on the **New** button then on the **Multi Data Source** link.

13. Type `ds-XA` in the **Name** field and `jdbc/ds-XA` in the **JNDI Name** field. Leave the other options as their default values. Click on the **Next** button.

14. Select the **All servers in the cluster** radio button from the `PROD_Cluster` cluster. Click on the **Next** button.

15. Select the **XA Driver** option. Click on **Next**.

16. Select both data sources `ds-XA-rac01` and `ds-XA-rac02` from the left of the **Add Data Source** page. Click on the **>>** button in the center of both sides to move them to the right. Click on **Finish**.

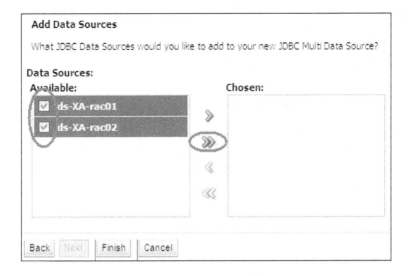

Add Data Sources

What JDBC Data Sources would you like to add to your new JDBC Multi Data Source?

Data Sources:

Available:
- ☑ ds-XA-rac01
- ☑ ds-XA-rac02

Chosen:

Back | Next | Finish | Cancel

17. Finally, click on the **Activate Changes** button.

How it works...

The multi data source `ds-XA` was created with the data sources `ds-XA-rac01` and `ds-XA-rac02` as members.

The multi data source manages the application requests for a database connection and uses **Algorithm Type** to define the strategy for high availability.

> If using the `Failover` algorithm, be sure to enable the **Failover Request if Busy** checkbox of the multi data source.

The multi data source is responsible for managing the load and failover; so if the Oracle database uses the **SCAN** address feature, it's recommended to set up a **GridLink** data source instead.

> It is still possible to use the SCAN address with the multi data source by defining the instance name in the data source URL. Also, data source members of a multi data source must always target to a unique Oracle RAC node, so using JDBC URL parameters such as `LOAD_BALANCE=ON` and `FAILOVER=ON` is not supported when using XA multi data sources.

The Oracle driver class name used for XA data sources is `oracle.jdbc.xa.client.OracleXADataSource`.

There's more...

Creating the multi data source using WLST

1. Log in as a `wls` user to shell and start WLST:

    ```
    [wls@prod01]$ $WL_HOME/common/bin/wlst.sh
    ```

2. Connect to the Administration Server using `wlsadmin` as the user, `<pwd>` as the password, and `t3://adminhost.domain.local:7001` as the server URL:

    ```
    wls:/offline> connect("wlsadmin","<pwd>","t3://adminhost.domain.
    local:7001")
    ```

3. Run the following WLST commands to create the first data source:

    ```
    edit()
    startEdit()


    #create the ds-XA-rac01 data source
    cmo.createJDBCSystemResource('ds-XA-rac01')
    cd('/JDBCSystemResources/ds-XA-rac01/JDBCResource/ds-XA-rac01')
    cmo.setName('ds-XA-rac01')
    cd('/JDBCSystemResources/ds-XA-rac01/JDBCResource/ds-XA-rac01/
    JDBCDataSourceParams/ds-XA-rac01')
    set('JNDINames',jarray.array([String('jdbc/ds-XA-rac01')],
    String))
    cd('/JDBCSystemResources/ds-XA-rac01/JDBCResource/ds-XA-rac01/
    JDBCDriverParams/ds-XA-rac01')
    cmo.setUrl('jdbc:oracle:thin:@(DESCRIPTION=(ADDRESS_
    LIST=(ADDRESS=(PROTOCOL=TCP)(HOST=dbhost-rac01)(PORT=1521)))
    (CONNECT_DATA=(SERVICE_NAME=dbservice-rac01)(INSTANCE_
    NAME=instance-rac01)))')
    cmo.setDriverName('oracle.jdbc.xa.client.OracleXADataSource')
    cmo.setPassword('dbpwd');
    cd('/JDBCSystemResources/ds-XA-rac01/JDBCResource/ds-XA-rac01/
    JDBCConnectionPoolParams/ds-XA-rac01')
    cmo.setTestTableName('SQL SELECT 1 FROM DUAL\r\n')
    cd('/JDBCSystemResources/ds-XA-rac01/JDBCResource/ds-XA-rac01/
    JDBCDriverParams/ds-XA-rac01/Properties/ds-XA-rac01')
    cmo.createProperty('user')
    cd('/JDBCSystemResources/ds-XA-rac01/JDBCResource/ds-XA-rac01/
    JDBCDriverParams/ds-XA-rac01/Properties/ds-XA-rac01/Properties/
    user')
    ```

```
cmo.setValue('dbuser')
```

```
cd('/JDBCSystemResources/ds-XA-rac01/JDBCResource/ds-XA-rac01/
JDBCDataSourceParams/ds-XA-rac01')
```

```
cmo.setGlobalTransactionsProtocol('TwoPhaseCommit')
```

```
cd('/JDBCSystemResources/ds-XA-rac01')
```

```
set('Targets',jarray.array([ObjectName('com.bea:Name=PROD_
Cluster,Type=Cluster')], ObjectName))
```

4. Run the following WLST commands to create the second data source:

```
#create the ds-XA-rac02 data source
```

```
cd('/')
```

```
cmo.createJDBCSystemResource('ds-XA-rac02')
```

```
cd('/JDBCSystemResources/ds-XA-rac02/JDBCResource/ds-XA-rac02')
```

```
cmo.setName('ds-XA-rac02')
```

```
cd('/JDBCSystemResources/ds-XA-rac02/JDBCResource/ds-XA-rac02/
JDBCDataSourceParams/ds-XA-rac02')
```

```
set('JNDINames',jarray.array([String('jdbc/ds-XA-rac02')],
String))
```

```
cd('/JDBCSystemResources/ds-XA-rac02/JDBCResource/ds-XA-rac02/
JDBCDriverParams/ds-XA-rac02')
```

```
cmo.setUrl('jdbc:oracle:thin:@(DESCRIPTION=(ADDRESS_
LIST=(ADDRESS=(PROTOCOL=TCP)(HOST=dbhost-rac02)(PORT=1521)))
(CONNECT_DATA=(SERVICE_NAME=dbservice-rac02)(INSTANCE_
NAME=instance-rac02)))')
```

```
cmo.setDriverName('oracle.jdbc.xa.client.OracleXADataSource')
```

```
cmo.setPassword('dbpwd');
```

```
cd('/JDBCSystemResources/ds-XA-rac02/JDBCResource/ds-XA-rac02/
JDBCConnectionPoolParams/ds-XA-rac02')
```

```
cmo.setTestTableName('SQL SELECT 1 FROM DUAL\r\n')
```

```
cd('/JDBCSystemResources/ds-XA-rac02/JDBCResource/ds-XA-rac02/
JDBCDriverParams/ds-XA-rac02/Properties/ds-XA-rac02')
```

```
cmo.createProperty('user')
```

```
cd('/JDBCSystemResources/ds-XA-rac02/JDBCResource/ds-XA-rac02/
JDBCDriverParams/ds-XA-rac02/Properties/ds-XA-rac02/Properties/
user')
```

```
cmo.setValue('dbuser')
```

```
cd('/JDBCSystemResources/ds-XA-rac02/JDBCResource/ds-XA-rac02/
JDBCDataSourceParams/ds-XA-rac02')
```

```
cmo.setGlobalTransactionsProtocol('TwoPhaseCommit')
```

```
cd('/JDBCSystemResources/ds-XA-rac02')
```

```
set('Targets',jarray.array([ObjectName('com.bea:Name=PROD_
Cluster,Type=Cluster')], ObjectName))
```

5. Run the following WLST commands to create the multi data source:

```
#create the multi data source ds-xa
cd('/')
cmo.createJDBCSystemResource('ds-XA')
cd('/JDBCSystemResources/ds-XA/JDBCResource/ds-XA')
cmo.setName('ds-XA')
cd('/JDBCSystemResources/ds-XA/JDBCResource/ds-XA/
JDBCDataSourceParams/ds-XA')
set('JNDINames',jarray.array([String('jdbc/ds-XA')], String))
cmo.setAlgorithmType('Failover')
cmo.setDataSourceList('ds-XA-rac01,ds-XA-rac02')
cd('/JDBCSystemResources/ds-XA')
set('Targets',jarray.array([ObjectName('com.bea:Name=PROD_
Cluster,Type=Cluster')], ObjectName))
activate()
exit()
```

See also

▸ *Creating a JDBC data source*

▸ *Defining the multi data source HA Strategy*

▸ *Creating a GridLink data source*

▸ *Tuning data sources for reliable connections*

▸ *Tuning multi data sources – surviving RAC node failures*

Defining the multi data source HA Strategy

The multi data source has two strategy options for highly available connections for an Oracle RAC database. The strategy is defined by the **Algorithm Type** parameter.

In this recipe, the multi data source ds-XA will be changed from the default Failover algorithm to the Load Balance strategy.

Getting ready

This recipe will change the parameters of the ds-XA data source, so make sure the multi data source and the individual data sources ds-XA-rac01 and ds-XA-rac02 have already been created from the previous recipe.

How to do it...

Carry out the following steps to configure the high availability strategy for the multi data source:

1. Access the Administration Console with your web browser at http://adminhost.domain.local:7001/console.

2. Click on the **Lock & Edit** button to start a new edit session.

3. Expand the **Services** tree on the left, and then click on **Data Sources**.

4. Click on the ds-XA multi data source.

5. Change **Algorithm Type** to Load Balance. Then click on the **Save** button.

6. Finally, click on the **Activate Changes** button.

How it works...

With the Load Balance algorithm, the multi data source is responsible for load balancing the application requests to reserve a database connection in a round-robin fashion. If one Oracle RAC node goes down, the multi data source continues to return good connections transparently to the applications from the other RAC node.

The Failover algorithm returns a connection from the first data source of the member list. If the connection fails or all connections of the pool are in use, the other data source members will be used.

 The multi data source does not provide failover for active and in-use connections.

There's more...

The multi data source algorithm can be changed using WLST.

Changing the multi data source algorithm type using WLST

1. Log in as a `wls` user to shell and start WLST:

   ```
   [wls@prod01]$ $WL_HOME/common/bin/wlst.sh
   ```

2. Connect to the Administration Server using `wlsadmin` as the user, `<pwd>` as the password, and `t3://adminhost.domain.local:7001` as the server URL:

   ```
   wls:/offline> connect("wlsadmin","<pwd>","t3://adminhost.domain.
   local:7001")
   ```

3. Run the following WLST commands to change the multi data source algorithm:

   ```
   edit()
   startEdit()

   cd('/JDBCSystemResources/ds-XA/JDBCResource/ds-XA/
   JDBCDataSourceParams/ds-XA')
   cmo.setAlgorithmType('Load-Balancing')

   activate()
   exit()
   ```

See also

- *Creating a JDBC data source*
- *Creating a multi data source*
- *Tuning data sources for reliable connections*
- *Tuning multi data sources – surviving RAC node failures*

Creating a GridLink data source

The GridLink data source is a new type of data source that has been available in WebLogic Server since Version 10.3.4. The GridLink is used to connect to Oracle RAC databases and is a recommended alternative to the multi data sources since it provides some useful features, such as fast connection failover, runtime connection load balancing, graceful handling of Oracle RAC outages, GridLink affinity, and SCAN addresses.

The same `DBApp` application requirement from the earlier recipe will be used, but in this recipe a GridLink data source will be used instead of a multi data source.

Consider that the DBApp application requires an XA connection with a JNDI name jdbc/ds-GridLinkXA to a database. The database is an Oracle RAC database with two nodes. The first node runs in the dbhost-rac01 hostname and listens to the port 1521. The second node runs in the dbhost-rac02 hostname and also listens to the port 1521. The database has a service name dbservice. The ONS service is running on the onshost hostname, port 6200.

Getting ready

Create the GridLink data source with the JNDI name jdbc/ds-GridLinkXA in the Administration Console. Make sure the Administration Server is running.

How to do it...

Carry out the following steps to create a new GridLink data source:

1. Access the Administration Console with your web browser at http://adminhost.domain.local:7001/console.

2. Click on the **Lock & Edit** button to start a new edit session.

3. Click on the plus sign to open the **Services** tree on the left, and then click on **Data Sources**.

4. Click on the **New** button and then click on **GridLink Data Source**.

5. Type ds-GridLinkXA in the **Name** field and jdbc/ds-GridLinkXA in the **JNDI Name** field. Choose *Oracle's Driver (Thin XA) for GridLink Connections Versions:11 and later from the **Database Driver** drop-down menu. Click on the **Next** button.

6. Click on the **Next** button on the **Transaction Options** page.

7. Leave the **Enter individual listener information** option selected on the **GridLink data source connection Properties Options** page and click on the **Next** button.

8. On the **Connection Properties** page, type dbservice in the **Service Name** field. Type dbhost-rac01:1521 in the **Host and Port** field and click on the **Add** button. Add the second host by typing dbhost-rac02:1521 in the **Host and Port** field and clicking on the **Add** button. Complete the database **User Name**, **Password**, and **Confirm Password** fields by typing dbuser and dbpwd as the username and password respectively. Leave the **Protocol** field with the TCP value. Click on the **Next** button.

9. Click on the **Next** button on the **Test GridLink Database Connection** page.

10. On the **ONS Client Configuration** page, type onshost:6200 in the **ONS host and port** field and click on the **Add** button. Then click on **Next**.

11. Click on the **Next** button on the **Test ONS client configuration** page.

12. Select the **All servers in the cluster** radio button from the PROD_Cluster cluster. Click on the **Finish** button.

13. Finally, click on the **Activate Changes** button.

How it works...

The GridLink data source has some advantages over the multi data source.

The multi data source uses the test connection feature to guarantee a reliable connection to the database. The GridLink data source on the other hand uses the call back mechanism of Oracle RAC **Fast Application Notification** (**FAN**). This means that the GridLink data source actively responds to events and notifications coming from the database, such as the fluctuation of RAC services.

Another improvement is the load balancing mechanism. The multi data source configured with the Load Balance algorithm distributes the application requests to borrow a connection from the data source members of the multi data source in a round-robin fashion. GridLink improves the distribution load by receiving load balancing events from the database. These events indicate the recommended connection distribution among the RAC nodes.

 If FAN is disabled, GridLink uses the round-robin Load Balance algorithm.

There's more...

The GridLink data source can also be created using WLST.

Creating a GridLink data source using WLST

1. Log in as a wls user to shell and start WLST:

   [wls@prod01] $ $WL_HOME/common/bin/wlst.sh

2. Connect to the Administration Server using wlsadmin as the user, <pwd> as the password, and t3://adminhost.domain.local:7001 as the server URL:

   wls:/offline> connect("wlsadmin","<pwd>","t3://adminhost.domain. local:7001")

3. Run the following WLST commands to create the GridLink data source:

   edit()
   startEdit()

   cmo.createJDBCSystemResource('ds-GridLinkXA')

```
cd('/JDBCSystemResources/ds-GridLinkXA/JDBCResource/ds-
GridLinkXA')
cmo.setName('ds-GridLinkXA')
cd('/JDBCSystemResources/ds-GridLinkXA/JDBCResource/ds-GridLinkXA/
JDBCDataSourceParams/ds-GridLinkXA')
set('JNDINames',jarray.array([String('jdbc/ds-GridLinkXA')],
String))
cd('/JDBCSystemResources/ds-GridLinkXA/JDBCResource/ds-GridLinkXA/
JDBCDriverParams/ds-GridLinkXA')
cmo.setUrl('jdbc:oracle:thin:@(DESCRIPTION=(ADDRESS_
LIST=(ADDRESS=(PROTOCOL=TCP)(HOST=dbhost-rac01)(PORT=1521))
(ADDRESS=(PROTOCOL=TCP)(HOST=dbhost-rac02)(PORT=1521)))(CONNECT_
DATA=(SERVICE_NAME=dbservice)))\r\n')
cmo.setDriverName('oracle.jdbc.xa.client.OracleXADataSource')
cmo.setPassword('dbpwd')
cd('/JDBCSystemResources/ds-GridLinkXA/JDBCResource/ds-GridLinkXA/
JDBCConnectionPoolParams/ds-GridLinkXA')
cmo.setTestTableName('SQL SELECT 1 FROM DUAL\r\n')

cd('/JDBCSystemResources/ds-GridLinkXA/JDBCResource/ds-GridLinkXA/
JDBCDriverParams/ds-GridLinkXA/Properties/ds-GridLinkXA')
cmo.createProperty('user')
cd('/JDBCSystemResources/ds-GridLinkXA/JDBCResource/ds-GridLinkXA/
JDBCDriverParams/ds-GridLinkXA/Properties/ds-GridLinkXA/
Properties/user')
cmo.setValue('dbuser')
cd('/JDBCSystemResources/ds-GridLinkXA/JDBCResource/ds-GridLinkXA/
JDBCDataSourceParams/ds-GridLinkXA')
cmo.setGlobalTransactionsProtocol('TwoPhaseCommit')
cd('/JDBCSystemResources/ds-GridLinkXA/JDBCResource/ds-GridLinkXA/
JDBCOracleParams/ds-GridLinkXA')
cmo.setFanEnabled(true)
cmo.setOnsWalletFile('')
cmo.unSet('OnsWalletPasswordEncrypted')
cmo.setOnsNodeList('onshost:6200 \r\n')
cmo.setFanEnabled(true)
cmo.setOnsWalletFile('')
cmo.unSet('OnsWalletPasswordEncrypted')
cmo.setOnsNodeList('onshost:6200 \r\n')
cd('/JDBCSystemResources/ds-GridLinkXA')
set('Targets',jarray.array([ObjectName('com.bea:Name=PROD_
Cluster,Type=Cluster')], ObjectName))

activate()
exit()
```

See also

▸ *Creating a multi data source*

Managing JDBC data sources

The WebLogic JDBC subsystem can be controlled when needed. A WebLogic Administrator can start, stop, shrink, pause, suspend, and reset the data source on demand. The statement cache can also be cleared if needed.

In this recipe, the `ds-nonXA` data source will be used as an example.

Getting ready

The JDBC operations use the Administration Console, so make sure the Administration Server is running.

How to do it...

To control the data source operations, carry out the following steps:

1. Access the Administration Console with your web browser at `http://adminhost.domain.local:7001/console`.

2. Click on the plus sign to open the **Services** tree on the left, and then click on **Data Sources**.

3. Click on the `ds-nonXA` link to open the data source and then click on the **Control** tab.

4. Select the checkbox from `ds-nonXA` and click on the button of the desired operation: **Shrink**, **Reset**, **Clear Statement Cache**, **Suspend**, **Resume**, **Shutdown**, or **Start**.

How it works...

The data source control operations are useful in situations such as when an Oracle RAC node is down or during a database maintenance window.

The **Shrink** operation closes the idle connections of the pool, freeing the database connections and resources in use. It reduces the opened connections until the greater value is between the **minimum capacity** parameter and the in-use connection.

The **Reset** operation resets the pool, closing and reopening all the database connections.

The **Clear Statement Cache** operation clears the callable and prepared statement caches.

 The **Clear Statement Cache** operation is useful when there are changes in DBMS objects such as stored procedures. Some exceptions and errors can be caused by deprecated cached statements.

The **Suspend** operation disables the data source. Although it leaves the connection state unchanged in the pool, the applications cannot borrow connections. The **Suspend** operation can also be forced. In this case, all connections are closed.

The **Resume** operation resumes a suspended data source.

The **Shutdown** operation shuts down the data source. If there are connections in use by the application, the application operation, in the course of time, will fail and return an error. The **Shutdown** operation can be forced. In this case, if the connections are in use, WebLogic will forcibly close all of them and will shut down the data source.

The **Start** operation starts a stopped data source.

See also

▸   *Creating a JDBC data source*
▸   *Creating a multi data source*
▸   *Creating a GridLink data source*

Tuning data sources for reliable connections

In the previous recipes, some data sources required by the DBApp application were created.

Some default parameter values are not the best option to use out of the box, so in this recipe the parameters of the GridLink ds-GridLinkXA data source will be tuned to avoid unreliable connections being delivered to the applications.

The changes are generic to the GridLink and Generic data source types and can be applied to all previously created data sources.

Getting ready

Access the Administration Console to tune the ds-GridLinkXA data source parameter. Make sure the ds-GridLinkXA GridLink was created in the previous recipe and that the Administration Server is running.

How to do it...

To set the data source tunings, proceed with the following steps:

1. Access the Administration Console with your web browser at `http://adminhost.domain.local:7001/console`.

2. Click on the **Lock & Edit** button to start a new edit session.

3. Click on the plus sign to open the **Services** tree on the left, and then click on **Data Sources**.

4. Click on the `ds-GridLinkXA` link to open the data source, and then click on the **Connection Pool** tab under the main **Configuration** tab.

5. Type 0 in the **Initial Capacity** field and 15 in the **Maximum Capacity** and **Minimum Capacity** fields. Click on the **Save** button and then click on the **Advanced** link to open the advanced options.

6. Check the **Test Connection on Reserve** checkbox. Type 900 in the **Test Frequency** field and type 0 in the **Seconds to Trust an Idle Connection** field. Leave the other options as their default values (as shown in the following screenshot) and click on the **Save** button.

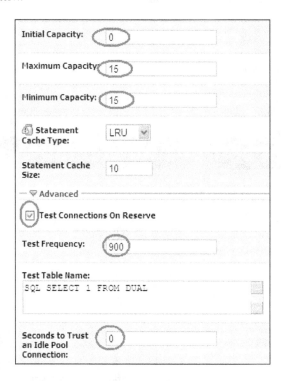

7. Finally, click on the **Activate Changes** button.

How it works...

This recipe changes a GridLink data source but this can work for Generic data source types as well.

During the WebLogic Server startup process, the data sources are deployed and the connections to the databases are opened according to the **Initial Capacity** parameter.

If a data source connection cannot be established with the database during startup for some reason, the Managed Server starts in the ADMIN state instead of in the RUNNING state. The commonly used procedure in this situation is to click on the **Resume** button; the server instance resumes to the RUNNING state and starts accepting and processing the application requests. However, the data source remains undeployed and uninitialized, and errors will occur with the applications that use this data source. Even if the database goes back online, the data source will not start automatically.

 To avoid the ADMIN state on startup, set the data source **Initial Capacity** to 0 so it won't open any connection to the database during the server startup process. The Managed Server instance will start in the RUNNING state, and as soon as the database goes back online, the data source will reconnect to it without intervention.

The drawback is that since WebLogic will start in the RUNNING state, even with the database out, the application requests that use the data source will return errors. Therefore, it is a good idea to use the option that best suits the application's requirements.

It's also a common recommendation to set **Initial Capacity** and **Maximum Capacity** to the same value so all connections would already be open when needed. The value of 15 for **Maximum Capacity** was used as an example.

 In WebLogic Server 12c, a better recommendation for production environments would be to set **Initial Capacity** to 0 and **Minimum Capacity** and **Maximum Capacity** to the same value. The **Minimum Capacity** parameter was added in WebLogic Server 10.3.6.

With the **Test Connection on Reserve** option enabled, WebLogic tests the connection with the database using the query specified in the **Test Table Name** field, just before lending the connection to the application. The value of 0 seconds in the **Seconds to Trust an Idle Connection** field forces the test to be made in every request. The **Test Frequency** field was also increased to 900 seconds instead of the default value of 120 seconds.

Although this set of configurations increases the database overhead, it usually compensates by avoiding unreliable connections being delivered to the application. WebLogic Administrators should be aware that every unexpected error in a production environment can cause financial losses and loss of credibility with the final user. So tuning WebLogic for stability should be a priority.

The values used in this recipe are based on an online application that receives requests during a 24 x 7 period. A batch application that runs once a day for a few hours should use some different settings, such as a **Minimum Capacity** of 0, so the connections to the database are closed when the application is idle. Tune the parameters according to your application requirements.

There's more...

The data source configuration changes can be made with WLST.

Tuning the data sources using WLST

1. Log in as a wls user to shell and start WLST:

   [wls@prod01] $ $WL_HOME/common/bin/wlst.sh

2. Connect to the Administration Server using wlsadmin as the user, <pwd> as the password, and t3://adminhost.domain.local:7001 as the server URL:

   wls:/offline> connect("wlsadmin","<pwd>","t3://adminhost.domain.local:7001")

3. Run the following WLST commands to tune the data source:

   ```
   edit()
   startEdit()

   cd('/JDBCSystemResources/ds-GridLinkXA/JDBCResource/ds-GridLinkXA/
   JDBCConnectionPoolParams/ds-GridLinkXA')
   cmo.setInitialCapacity(0)
   cmo.setMinCapacity(15)
   cmo.setMaxCapacity(15)
   cmo.setTestConnectionsOnReserve(true)
   cmo.setTestFrequencySeconds(900)
   cmo.setSecondsToTrustAnIdlePoolConnection(0)

   activate()
   exit()
   ```

See also

- ▸ *Creating a JDBC data source*
- ▸ *Creating a Multi data source*
- ▸ *Creating a GridLink data source*
- ▸ *Tuning multi data sources - surviving RAC node failures*

Tuning multi data sources – surviving RAC node failures

The multi data source default configuration doesn't provide the best settings for surviving an Oracle RAC node failure properly.

This recipe tunes the `ds-XA-rac01` and `ds-XA-rac02` data sources and the `ds-XA` multi data source.

Getting ready

Access the Administration Console to tune the data sources parameters. Make sure the `ds-XA-rac01` and `ds-XA-rac02` data sources and the `ds-XA` multi data source were created in the previous recipe and that the Administration Server is running.

How to do it...

To set the multi data source configurations, complete the following steps:

1. Access the Administration Console with your web browser at `http://adminhost.domain.local:7001/console`.

2. Click on the **Lock & Edit** button to start a new edit session.

3. Click on the plus sign to open the **Services** tree on the left, and then click on **Data Sources**.

4. Click on the `ds-XA` link to open the multi data source configuration page.

5. Check the **Failover Request if Busy** checkbox and type 5 in the **Test Frequency Seconds** field. Click on the **Save** button, as shown in the following screenshot:

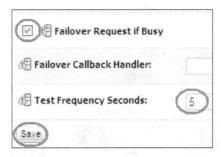

6. Click on the **Data Sources** link on the left navigation tree again. Click on the ds-XA-rac01 data source link and then on the **Connection Pool** tab.

7. In the **URL** field, add the following parameters to the text value: (ENABLE=BROKEN) (LOAD_BALANCE=OFF) (FAILOVER=OFF). The final **URL** should be jdbc:oracle:thin:@(DESCRIPTION=(ENABLE=BROKEN)(LOAD_ BALANCE=OFF)(FAILOVER=OFF)(ADDRESS_LIST=(ADDRESS=(PROTOCOL=TCP) (HOST=dbhost-rac01)(PORT=1521)))(CONNECT_DATA=(SERVICE_ NAME=dbservice-rac01)(INSTANCE_NAME=instance-rac01))).

8. Add the line oracle.net.CONNECT_TIMEOUT=10000 to the **Properties** field.

9. If not already tuned from the previous recipe, type 0 in the **Initial Capacity** field and 15 in the **Maximum Capacity** and **Minimum Capacity** fields. Click on the **Advanced** link to open the advanced options.

10. Check the **Test Connection on Reserve** checkbox. Type 900 in the **Test Frequency** field and type 0 in the **Seconds to Trust an Idle Connection** field.

11. Leave the other options as their default values and click on the **Save** button.

12. Repeat steps 6 to 10 with the ds-XA-rac02 data source.

13. Finally, click on the **Activate Changes** button.

How it works...

This recipe performs some additional tuning on the data sources and multi data sources.

The **Failover Request if Busy** option is not enabled by default and is recommended to be enabled when using multi data sources with the Failover algorithm. It works by providing a connection from the next data source member on the list when all the connections from the primary data source member are in use (overloaded).

WebLogic Server closes all the connections of a data source and disables it if the connection to the database fails to be created two consecutive times. By default, the multi data source rechecks the database every 120 seconds based on the multi data source **Test Frequency Seconds** parameter. Changing the **Test Frequency Seconds** parameter to 5 seconds is recommended.

The (ENABLE=BROKEN)(LOAD_BALANCE=OFF)(FAILOVER=OFF) parameters added to the URL field are recommended settings for the data source members of multi data sources.

The ENABLE=BROKEN parameter adds an internal TCP keepalive on the JDBC client side, improving the network connection reliability with the database.

The JDBC client load balance and JDBC connect time failover must be disabled with the LOAD_BALANCE=OFF and FAILOVER=OFF parameters since these features must be provided by the multi data source.

The oracle.net.CONNECT_TIMEOUT=10000 parameter adds a connect timeout of 10 seconds.

All other tunings, such as **Initial Capacity,** are described in the previous recipe.

There's more...

The data source configuration changes can be made with WLST.

Tuning the multi data sources using WLST

1. Log in as a wls user to shell and start WLST:

    [wls@prod01]$ $WL_HOME/common/bin/wlst.sh

2. Connect to the Administration Server using wlsadmin as the user, <pwd> as the password, and t3://adminhost.domain.local:7001 as the server URL:

    wls:/offline> connect("wlsadmin","<pwd>","t3://adminhost.domain.local:7001")

3. Run the following WLST commands to tune the multi data source:

    ```
    edit()
    startEdit()

    cd('/JDBCSystemResources/ds-XA/JDBCResource/ds-XA/JDBCDataSourceParams/ds-XA')
    cmo.setFailoverRequestIfBusy(true)

    cd('/JDBCSystemResources/ds-XA/JDBCResource/ds-XA/JDBCConnectionPoolParams/ds-XA')
    cmo.setTestFrequencySeconds(5)
    ```

4. Run the following WLST commands to tune the first data source:

```
# tune ds-XA-rac01

cd('/JDBCSystemResources/ds-XA-rac01/JDBCResource/ds-XA-rac01/
JDBCDriverParams/ds-XA-rac01')

cmo.setUrl('jdbc:oracle:thin:@(DESCRIPTION=(ENABLE=BROKEN)(LOAD_
BALANCE=OFF)(FAILOVER=OFF)(ADDRESS_LIST=(ADDRESS=(PROTOCOL=TCP)
(HOST=dbhost-rac01)(PORT=1521)))(CONNECT_DATA=(SERVICE_
NAME=dbservice-rac01)(INSTANCE_NAME=instance-rac01)))')

cd('/JDBCSystemResources/ds-XA-rac01/JDBCResource/ds-XA-rac01/
JDBCDriverParams/ds-XA-rac01/Properties/ds-XA-rac01')

cmo.destroyProperty(getMBean('/JDBCSystemResources/ds-XA-rac01/
JDBCResource/ds-XA-rac01/JDBCDriverParams/ds-XA-rac01/Properties/
ds-XA-rac01/Properties/user'))

cmo.createProperty('user')

cd('/JDBCSystemResources/ds-XA-rac01/JDBCResource/ds-XA-rac01/
JDBCDriverParams/ds-XA-rac01/Properties/ds-XA-rac01/Properties/
user')

cmo.setValue('dbuser')

cd('/JDBCSystemResources/ds-XA-rac01/JDBCResource/ds-XA-rac01/
JDBCDriverParams/ds-XA-rac01/Properties/ds-XA-rac01')

cmo.createProperty('oracle.net.CONNECT_TIMEOUT')

cd('/JDBCSystemResources/ds-XA-rac01/JDBCResource/ds-XA-rac01/
JDBCDriverParams/ds-XA-rac01/Properties/ds-XA-rac01/Properties/
oracle.net.CONNECT_TIMEOUT')

cmo.setValue('10000')

cd('/JDBCSystemResources/ds-XA-rac01/JDBCResource/ds-XA-rac01/
JDBCConnectionPoolParams/ds-XA-rac01')

cmo.setMaxCapacity(15)

cmo.setMinCapacity(15)

cmo.setSecondsToTrustAnIdlePoolConnection(0)

cmo.setTestConnectionsOnReserve(true)

cmo.setTestFrequencySeconds(900)

cmo.setInitialCapacity(0)
```

5. Run the following WLST commands to tune the second data source:

```
# tune ds-XA-rac02

cd('/JDBCSystemResources/ds-XA-rac02/JDBCResource/ds-XA-rac02/
JDBCDriverParams/ds-XA-rac02')
```

```
cmo.setUrl('jdbc:oracle:thin:@(DESCRIPTION=(ENABLE=BROKEN)(LOAD_
BALANCE=OFF)(FAILOVER=OFF)(ADDRESS_LIST=(ADDRESS=(PROTOCOL=TCP)
(HOST=dbhost-rac02)(PORT=1521)))(CONNECT_DATA=(SERVICE_
NAME=dbservice-rac02)(INSTANCE_NAME=instance-rac02)))')

cd('/JDBCSystemResources/ds-XA-rac02/JDBCResource/ds-XA-rac02/
JDBCDriverParams/ds-XA-rac02/Properties/ds-XA-rac02')

cmo.destroyProperty(getMBean('/JDBCSystemResources/ds-XA-rac02/
JDBCResource/ds-XA-rac02/JDBCDriverParams/ds-XA-rac02/Properties/
ds-XA-rac02/Properties/user'))

cmo.createProperty('user')

cd('/JDBCSystemResources/ds-XA-rac02/JDBCResource/ds-XA-rac02/
JDBCDriverParams/ds-XA-rac02/Properties/ds-XA-rac02/Properties/
user')

cmo.setValue('dbuser')

cd('/JDBCSystemResources/ds-XA-rac02/JDBCResource/ds-XA-rac02/
JDBCDriverParams/ds-XA-rac02/Properties/ds-XA-rac02')

cmo.createProperty('oracle.net.CONNECT_TIMEOUT')

cd('/JDBCSystemResources/ds-XA-rac02/JDBCResource/ds-XA-rac02/
JDBCDriverParams/ds-XA-rac02/Properties/ds-XA-rac02/Properties/
oracle.net.CONNECT_TIMEOUT')

cmo.setValue('10000')

cd('/JDBCSystemResources/ds-XA-rac02/JDBCResource/ds-XA-rac02/
JDBCConnectionPoolParams/ds-XA-rac02')

cmo.setMaxCapacity(15)

cmo.setMinCapacity(15)

cmo.setSecondsToTrustAnIdlePoolConnection(0)

cmo.setTestConnectionsOnReserve(true)

cmo.setTestFrequencySeconds(900)

cmo.setInitialCapacity(0)

activate()
exit()
```

See also

▶ *Creating a JDBC data source*
▶ *Creating a multi data source*
▶ *Creating a GridLink data source*
▶ *Tuning data sources for reliable connections*

Updating the Oracle JDBC driver

Oracle WebLogic Server 12c (Version 12.1.1.0 at the time of writing this book) contains the Oracle Database 11g Release 2 (Version 11.2.0.3) JDBC drivers.

This recipe shows the steps to update the JDBC drivers to a different version.

Getting ready

Download the updated JDBC drivers from the Oracle website.

The Oracle JDBC driver filename is `ojdbc6.jar`. Create a temporary folder, such as `~/jdbctemp`, and download the file to it.

The procedure is done manually, so make sure that none of the WebLogic Server instances are running, including the Administration Server.

How to do it...

Back up the original JDBC driver and copy the updated file to the WebLogic installation folder:

1. Log in as a `wls` user to the `prod01` shell and run the following commands:

   [wls@prod01]$ cd $WL_HOME/server/lib

   [wls@prod01]$ mv ojdbc6.jar ojdbc6.original

   [wls@prod01]$ cp ~/jdbctemp/ojdbc6.jar .

2. Repeat the step in `prod02` and all machines of the cluster.
3. Start the Administration Server and all the Managed Servers.

How it works...

Updating the Oracle JDBC drivers is a straightforward process.

Just make a backup copy of the JDBC driver file `ojdbc6.jar`, replace it with the new file version, and start the WebLogic Server instances.

There's more...

The Oracle JDBC driver itself can be invoked to display its version.

Verify the driver version

1. Log in as a `wls` user to shell and navigate to the folder of the downloaded file:

    ```
    [wls@prod01]$ cd ~/jdbctemp
    ```

2. Run the following Java command to display the driver version:

    ```
    [wls@prod01]$ /oracle/jvm/bin/java -jar ojdbc6.jar
    ```

3. The JDBC driver Version will be displayed on the screen:

    ```
    Oracle 11.2.0.3.0 JDBC 4.0 compiled with JDK6 on Fri_
    Nov_04_08:05:20_PDT_2011

    #Default Connection Properties Resource

    #Sun Apr 07 04:08:20 BRT 2013
    ```

See also

-   *Creating a JDBC data source*
-   *Creating a multi data source*
-   *Creating a GridLink data source*

4
Configuring JMS Resources for Clustering and High Availability

In this chapter we will cover the following recipes:

- ▸ Creating the file stores
- ▸ Creating the JDBC stores
- ▸ Creating the JMS servers
- ▸ Creating the JMS module
- ▸ Configuring the subdeployment target
- ▸ Creating the distributed queue destination and the connection factory
- ▸ Starting/stopping consumers for a JMS destination
- ▸ Using the Server affinity to tune the distributed destinations' load balance
- ▸ Creating a pinned queue with clustering and HA with service migration
- ▸ Configuring the messaging bridge with source and target distributed destinations
- ▸ Relying on SAF to transfer JMS messages to another WebLogic domain

Introduction

The **Java Message Service** (**JMS**) is a standard Java API that enables an enterprise application to communicate asynchronously with other applications by sending and receiving messages. The Oracle WebLogic Server 12*c* messaging subsystem is fully compatible with the JMS 1.1 specification.

The JMS API defines two models of communication: point-to-point and publisher/subscriber. Point-to-point communication uses a JMS queue and publisher/subscriber communication uses a JMS topic. Although similar in configuration, JMS queues and JMS topics are destinations that work in very different ways.

In the point-to-point model, a sender first publishes and enqueues a message to the queue. The message is then dequeued and processed by the single consumer that is listening to this queue. The enqueue and dequeue processes are independent, loosely coupled, and asynchronous. The message can be held by the queue until a consumer starts listening for incoming messages. In the point-to-point model, the message is delivered to only one recipient.

In the publisher/subscriber model, a publisher sends a message to a topic and this message is consumed by every subscriber of the topic. In the publisher/subscriber model, the message can be delivered to multiple recipients.

A hypothetical scenario with an `JMSApp` enterprise application deployed in `PROD_Cluster` will be used as an example in this chapter. The application requires performance and high availability and uses a JMS queue under the JNDI name `jms.appqueue`, and a connection factory with the JNDI name `jms.appcf`. A clustered JMS offers a more reliable solution than a JMS in a single Managed Server. The platform can be scaled when needed and the load is distributed across multiple Managed Servers.

The following recipes contain the steps needed by a WebLogic Administrator to properly configure the `JMSApp` application to use the WebLogic JMS subsystem with clustering and high availability. A specific JMS module will be created to isolate the configuration, which includes the JMS servers and the JMS queue destination.

Creating the file stores

Oracle WebLogic Server 12*c* makes use of its own storage solution, known as the **Persistent Store**. The persistent store can be used by the JMS subsystem to persist the JMS messages of a JMS destination. It can also be used by the **transaction log** (**TLOG**) for keeping information of committed transactions on course or to store WLDF diagnostic information, among other functionalities.

The persistent store can be file-based or JDBC-based. All WebLogic Server instances include a default file-based persistent store. The default persistent store is located at `$DOMAIN_HOME/servers/<instance_name>/data/store/default`.

In this recipe a new custom file store will be created in all Managed Servers of the PROD_ Cluster cluster.

Getting ready

For the cluster PROD_Cluster, we will consider the file stores FileStore01, FileStore02, FileStore03, and FileStore04 for the instances PROD_Server01, PROD_Server02, PROD_Server03, and PROD_Server04 respectively.

Managed Server	Persistent store
PROD_Server01	FileStore01
PROD_Server02	FileStore02
PROD_Server03	FileStore03
PROD_Server04	FileStore04

The file stores will be saved in the $DOMAIN_HOME/filestores directory, so make sure the directory is created before creating the file stores.

How to do it...

Create the $DOMAIN_HOME/filestores directory in all machines, as follows:

1. Log in as a wls user to the prod01 shell and create the directory.

   [wls@prod01]$ cd $DOMAIN_HOME

   [wls@prod01]$ mkdir filestores

2. Repeat this step for prod02.

Create the file stores using the Administration Console, as follows:

1. Access the Administration Console with your web browser at http://adminhost. domain.local:7001/console.

2. Click on the **Lock & Edit** button to start a new edit session.

3. Expand the **Services** tree on the left and click on **Persistent Stores**.

4. Click on the **New** button and click on the **Create File Store** link to start creating a new persistent store.

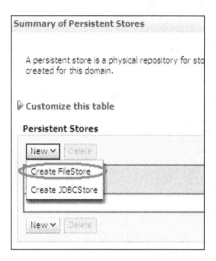

5. Type `FileStore01` in the **Name** field. Click on the **Target** drop-down menu and select the `PROD_Server01` option.

6. Type `/oracle/Middleware/user_projects/domains/PROD_DOMAIN/ filestores` in the **Directory** field to point to the newly created directory and Click on the **OK** button.

7. Repeat the previous steps and create the remaining file stores, FileStore02, FileStore03, and FileStore04 targeting the corresponding Managed Servers, PROD_Server02, PROD_Server03, and PROD_Server04.

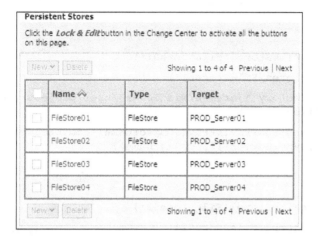

8. Click on the **Activate Changes** button to finish.

How it works...

The file stores were created in all Managed Servers of the cluster and will be used as persistent stores for the JMS servers.

> Although it is possible to use the default file store for the JMS servers, creating a separate file store is recommended to decouple and isolate the configuration for the JMSApp application. Using the default store also eliminates the possibility of using a migratable target.

There's more...

In the following section, the file store will be created using WLST.

Creating the file store using WLST

1. Log in as a wls user to the shell and start WLST.

   [wls@prod01]$ $WL_HOME/common/bin/wlst.sh

2. Connect to the Administration Server using wlsadmin as user, <pwd> as the password, and t3://adminhost.domain.local:7001 as the server URL.

   wls:/offline>connect("wlsadmin","<pwd>","t3://adminhost.domain.local:7001")

3. Run the following WLST commands to create the file stores:

```
edit()
startEdit()

cd('/')
cmo.createFileStore('FileStore01')
cd('/FileStores/FileStore01')
cmo.setDirectory('/oracle/Middleware/user_projects/domains/PROD_
DOMAIN/filestores')
set('Targets',jarray.array([ObjectName('com.bea:Name=PROD_
Server01,Type=Server')], ObjectName))

cd('/')
cmo.createFileStore('FileStore02')
cd('/FileStores/FileStore02')
cmo.setDirectory('/oracle/Middleware/user_projects/domains/PROD_
DOMAIN/filestores')
set('Targets',jarray.array([ObjectName('com.bea:Name=PROD_
Server02,Type=Server')], ObjectName))

cd('/')
cmo.createFileStore('FileStore03')
cd('/FileStores/FileStore03')
cmo.setDirectory('/oracle/Middleware/user_projects/domains/PROD_
DOMAIN/filestores')
set('Targets',jarray.array([ObjectName('com.bea:Name=PROD_
Server03,Type=Server')], ObjectName))

cd('/')
cmo.createFileStore('FileStore04')
cd('/FileStores/FileStore04')
cmo.setDirectory('/oracle/Middleware/user_projects/domains/PROD_
DOMAIN/filestores')
set('Targets',jarray.array([ObjectName('com.bea:Name=PROD_
Server04,Type=Server')], ObjectName))

activate()
exit()
```

▶ *Creating the JMS servers*

Creating the JDBC stores

The persistent store can also persist the data in the database by using the JDBC store. In this recipe a new JDBC store will be created in all Managed Servers of the `PROD_Cluster` cluster.

The database that will host the stores is an Oracle RAC database with two nodes. The first node has an instance name `instance-rac01`, runs in the `dbhost-rac01` hostname, and listens to the port `1521`. The listener accepts requests to the service name `dbservice-rac01`. The second node is the instance `instance-rac02`, runs in the `dbhost-rac02` hostname, listens to the port `1521`, and has a service name `dbservice-rac02`.

Getting ready

A multi data source will be created with the name `ds-store` and JNDI name `jdbc/ds-store`. The data source members will be called `ds-store-rac01` and `ds-store-rac02` with the JNDI names `jdbc/ds-store-rac01` and `jdbc/ds-store-rac02`.

For the cluster `PROD_Cluster`, we will consider the JDBC stores `JDBCStore01`, `JDBCStore02`, `JDBCStore03`, and `JDBCStore04` for the instances `PROD_Server01`, `PROD_Server02`, `PROD_Server03`, and `PROD_Server04` respectively.

Managed Server	Persistent store
PROD_Server01	JDBCStore01
PROD_Server02	JDBCStore02
PROD_Server03	JDBCStore03
PROD_Server04	JDBCStore04

How to do it...

Create the data sources and the multi data source:

1. Access the Administration Console with your web browser at `http://adminhost.domain.local:7001/console`.
2. Click on the **Lock & Edit** button to start a new edit session.
3. Click on the **Services** tree on the left and then click on **Data Sources**.
4. Click on the **New** button and click on **Generic Data Source**.

5. Type `ds-store-rac01` in the **Name** field and `jdbc/ds-store-rac01` in the **JNDI Name**. Leave the **Database Type** drop-down menu with the **Oracle** option selected. Click on the **Next** button.

6. Choose `*Oracle's Driver (Thin) for RAC Service-Instance connections; Versions:10 and later` from the **Database** driver drop-down menu. Click on the **Next** button.

7. Disable the **Supports Global Transactions** checkbox and click on the **Next** button.

8. In the **Connection Properties** page, type `dbservice-rac01` in the **Service Name** field, `instance-rac01` in the **Database Name** field, `dbhost-rac01` in the **Host Name** field, and `1521` in the **Port** field. Fill in the **Database User Name**, **Password**, and **Confirm Password** fields with `dbuser` and `dbpwd`. Leave the **Protocol** field with the default `TCP` value. Click on the **Next** button.

9. Click on the **Next** button in the **Test Database Connection** page.

10. Click on the **All servers in the cluster** radio button from the `PROD_Cluster` cluster. Click on the **Finish** button.

11. Repeat the previous steps and create another data source. Use `ds-store-rac02` as **Name**, `jdbc/ds-store-rac02` as **JNDI Name**, `dbservice-rac02` as **Service Name**, `instance-rac02` as **Database Name,** and `dbhost-rac02` as **Host Name**.

12. Create the multi data source by clicking on the **New** button and then the **Multi Data Source** link.

13. Type `ds-store` in the **Name** field and `jdbc/ds-store` in the **JNDI Name** field. Leave the **Algorithm Type** option in the default **Failover** option. Click on the **Next** Button.

14. Click on the **All servers in the cluster** radio button from the `PROD_Cluster` cluster. Click on the **Next** button.

15. Click on the **Non-XA Driver** option in the **Select Data Source Type** page. Click on **Next**.

16. Select both data sources `ds-store-rac01` and `ds-store-rac02` from the left of the **Add Data Source** page. Click on the **>**button in the center of both sides to move them to the right. Click on **Finish**.

17. Click on the **Activate Changes** button.

Create the JDBC stores using the Administration Console:

1. Access the Administration Console again with your web browser at `http://adminhost.domain.local:7001/console`.

2. Click on the **Lock & Edit** button to start a new edit session.

3. Click on the plus sign to open the **Services** tree on the left and click on **Persistent Stores**.

4. Click on the **New** button and click the **Create JDBCStore** link to start creating a new persistent store.

5. Type JDBCStore01 in the **Name** field. Click on the **Target** drop-down menu and select the PROD_Server01 option. Select the ds-store value in the **Data Source** field. Type JDBCStore01 again in the **Prefix Name** field and click on the **OK** button.

6. Repeat the previous steps and create the remaining JDBC stores, JDBCStore02, JDBCStore03, and JDBCStore04 targeting the corresponding Managed Servers, PROD_Server02, PROD_Server03, and PROD_Server04. Use the same ds-store data source for all JDBC stores.

7. Click on the **Activate Changes** button to finish.

How it works...

The JDBC stores were created in all Managed Servers of the cluster and can be used as persistent stores for the JMS servers.

The JDBC store uses a multi data source pointing to an Oracle RAC database with two RAC nodes.

 It's mandatory to use non-XA data sources and a multi data source with the Failover algorithm with the JDBC store. Make sure to tune all JDBC parameters according to how they were tuned in the previous chapter.

There's more...

The JDBC store can be created using WLST.

Creating the JDBC store using WLST

1. Log in as a wls user to the shell and start WLST.

   ```
   [wls@prod01]$ $WL_HOME/common/bin/wlst.sh
   ```

2. Connect to the Administration Server using wlsadmin as user, <pwd> as the password, and t3://adminhost.domain.local:7001 as the server URL.

   ```
   wls:/offline>connect("wlsadmin","<pwd>","t3://adminhost.domain.local:7001")
   ```

3. Run the following WLST commands to create the first data source:

   ```
   edit()
   startEdit()

   # create the ds-store-rac01 data source
   cd('/')
   ```

```
cmo.createJDBCSystemResource('ds-store-rac01')

cd('/JDBCSystemResources/ds-store-rac01/JDBCResource/ds-store-
rac01')

cmo.setName('ds-store-rac01')

cd('/JDBCSystemResources/ds-store-rac01/JDBCResource/ds-store-
rac01/JDBCDataSourceParams/ds-store-rac01')

set('JNDINames',jarray.array([String('jdbc/ds-store-rac01')],
String))

cd('/JDBCSystemResources/ds-store-rac01/JDBCResource/ds-store-
rac01/JDBCDriverParams/ds-store-rac01')

cmo.setUrl('jdbc:oracle:thin:@(DESCRIPTION=(ADDRESS_
LIST=(ADDRESS=(PROTOCOL=TCP)(HOST=dbhost-rac01)(PORT=1521)))
(CONNECT_DATA=(SERVICE_NAME=dbservice-rac01)(INSTANCE_
NAME=instance-rac01)))')

cmo.setDriverName('oracle.jdbc.OracleDriver')

cmo.setPassword('dbpwd');

cd('/JDBCSystemResources/ds-store-rac01/JDBCResource/ds-store-
rac01/JDBCConnectionPoolParams/ds-store-rac01')

cmo.setTestTableName('SQL SELECT 1 FROM DUAL\r\n')


cd('/JDBCSystemResources/ds-store-rac01/JDBCResource/ds-store-
rac01/JDBCDriverParams/ds-store-rac01/Properties/ds-store-rac01')

cmo.createProperty('user')

cd('/JDBCSystemResources/ds-store-rac01/JDBCResource/ds-store-
rac01/JDBCDriverParams/ds-store-rac01/Properties/ds-store-rac01/
Properties/user')

cmo.setValue('dbuser')

cd('/JDBCSystemResources/ds-store-rac01/JDBCResource/ds-store-
rac01/JDBCDataSourceParams/ds-store-rac01')

cmo.setGlobalTransactionsProtocol('None')

cd('/JDBCSystemResources/ds-store-rac01')

set('Targets',jarray.array([ObjectName('com.bea:Name=PROD_
Cluster,Type=Cluster')], ObjectName))
```

4. Run the following WLST commands to create the second data source:

```
# create the ds-store-rac02 data source
cd('/')
cmo.createJDBCSystemResource('ds-store-rac02')
cd('/JDBCSystemResources/ds-store-rac02/JDBCResource/ds-store-
rac02')
```

```
cmo.setName('ds-store-rac02')

cd('/JDBCSystemResources/ds-store-rac02/JDBCResource/ds-store-
rac02/JDBCDataSourceParams/ds-store-rac02')

set('JNDINames',jarray.array([String('jdbc/ds-store-rac02')],
String))

cd('/JDBCSystemResources/ds-store-rac02/JDBCResource/ds-store-
rac02/JDBCDriverParams/ds-store-rac02')

cmo.setUrl('jdbc:oracle:thin:@(DESCRIPTION=(ADDRESS_
LIST=(ADDRESS=(PROTOCOL=TCP)(HOST=dbhost-rac02)(PORT=1521)))
(CONNECT_DATA=(SERVICE_NAME=dbservice-rac02)(INSTANCE_
NAME=instance-rac02)))')

cmo.setDriverName('oracle.jdbc.OracleDriver')

cmo.setPassword('dbpwd');

cd('/JDBCSystemResources/ds-store-rac02/JDBCResource/ds-store-
rac02/JDBCConnectionPoolParams/ds-store-rac02')

cmo.setTestTableName('SQL SELECT 1 FROM DUAL\r\n')

cd('/JDBCSystemResources/ds-store-rac02/JDBCResource/ds-store-
rac02/JDBCDriverParams/ds-store-rac02/Properties/ds-store-rac02')

cmo.createProperty('user')

cd('/JDBCSystemResources/ds-store-rac02/JDBCResource/ds-store-
rac02/JDBCDriverParams/ds-store-rac02/Properties/ds-store-rac02/
Properties/user')

cmo.setValue('dbuser')

cd('/JDBCSystemResources/ds-store-rac02/JDBCResource/ds-store-
rac02/JDBCDataSourceParams/ds-store-rac02')

cmo.setGlobalTransactionsProtocol('None')

cd('/JDBCSystemResources/ds-store-rac02')

set('Targets',jarray.array([ObjectName('com.bea:Name=PROD_
Cluster,Type=Cluster')], ObjectName))
```

5. Run the following WLST commands to create the multi data source:

```
# create the multi data source
cd('/')

cmo.createJDBCSystemResource('ds-store')


cd('/JDBCSystemResources/ds-store/JDBCResource/ds-store')

cmo.setName('ds-store')

cd('/JDBCSystemResources/ds-store/JDBCResource/ds-store/
JDBCDataSourceParams/ds-store')

set('JNDINames',jarray.array([String('jdbc/ds-store')], String))
```

```
cmo.setAlgorithmType('Failover')

cmo.setDataSourceList('ds-store-rac01,ds-store-rac02')

cd('/JDBCSystemResources/ds-store')

set('Targets',jarray.array([ObjectName('com.bea:Name=PROD_
Cluster,Type=Cluster')], ObjectName))


activate()
```

6. Run the following WLST commands to create the JDBC stores:

```
edit()

startEdit()


# create the JDBC stores


cd('/')

cmo.createJDBCStore('JDBCStore01')

cd('/JDBCStores/JDBCStore01')

cmo.setDataSource(getMBean('/JDBCSystemResources/ds-store'))

cmo.setPrefixName('JDBCStore01')

set('Targets',jarray.array([ObjectName('com.bea:Name=PROD_
Server01,Type=Server')], ObjectName))


cd('/')

cmo.createJDBCStore('JDBCStore02')

cd('/JDBCStores/JDBCStore02')

cmo.setDataSource(getMBean('/JDBCSystemResources/ds-store'))

cmo.setPrefixName('JDBCStore02')

set('Targets',jarray.array([ObjectName('com.bea:Name=PROD_
Server02,Type=Server')], ObjectName))


cd('/')

cmo.createJDBCStore('JDBCStore03')

cd('/JDBCStores/JDBCStore03')

cmo.setDataSource(getMBean('/JDBCSystemResources/ds-store'))

cmo.setPrefixName('JDBCStore03')

set('Targets',jarray.array([ObjectName('com.bea:Name=PROD_
Server03,Type=Server')], ObjectName))
```

```
cd('/')

cmo.createJDBCStore('JDBCStore04')

cd('/JDBCStores/JDBCStore04')

cmo.setDataSource(getMBean('/JDBCSystemResources/ds-store'))

cmo.setPrefixName('JDBCStore04')

set('Targets',jarray.array([ObjectName('com.bea:Name=PROD_
Server04,Type=Server')], ObjectName))


activate()

exit()
```

See also

▶ *Creating the JMS servers*

Creating the JMS servers

The JMS server is a WebLogic resource that provides a container for the JMS queues and JMS topics' destinations. A JMS server can manage several destinations at a time and it uses the specified persistent store to persist the messages. The persistent store of the JMS server can be the default persistent store of the WebLogic Server instance, a custom file store or a JDBC store.

Following the roadmap configuration for the JMSApp application, a JMS server will be created for each of the Managed Servers of the cluster PROD_Cluster, and each one will be configured to use the file stores created before.

Getting ready

For the cluster PROD_Cluster, we will consider JMSServer01, JMSServer02, JMSServer03, and JMSServer04 as the JMS Servers for instances PROD_Server01, PROD_Server02, PROD_Server03, and PROD_Server04 respectively.

Each JMS server will use the custom file store created in the previous recipe. The JDBC stores can also be used instead of the file stores.

Managed Server	JMS server	Persistent store
PROD_Server01	JMSServer01	FileStore01
PROD_Server02	JMSServer02	FileStore02
PROD_Server03	JMSServer03	FileStore03
PROD_Server04	JMSServer04	FileStore04

How to do it...

To create the JMS servers, carry out the following steps:

1. Access the Administration Console with your web browser at `http://adminhost.`
   `domain.local:7001/console`.

2. Click on the **Lock & Edit** button to start a new edit session.

3. Click on the plus sign to open the **Services** tree on the left; click on **Messaging** and
   then on **JMS Servers**.

4. Click on the **New** button to open the **Create a New JMS Server** page.

5. Type `JMSServer01` in the **Name** field and choose `FileStore01` from the
   Persistent Store drop-down menu. Click on the **Next** button.

6. Choose `PROD_Server01` from the **Target** drop-down menu. Click on the
   Finish button.

7. Repeat the previous steps and create `JMSServer02, JMSServer03, JMSServer04`
   using the file stores `FileStore01, FileStore02, FileStore03,` and
   `FileStore04`.

	Name ⌃	Persistent Store	Target
☐	JMSServer01	FileStore01	PROD_Server01
☐	JMSServer02	FileStore02	PROD_Server02
☐	JMSServer03	FileStore03	PROD_Server03
☐	JMSServer04	FileStore04	PROD_Server04

8. Click on the **Activate Changes** button to finish.

How it works...

The JMS servers were created pointing to their specific file stores. The JMS servers are still
working as independent units and the configuration for clustering will be achieved with the
creation of the JMS module and the JMS destinations and resources.

The JDBC stores created in the previous recipe can also be used as persistent stores to the
JMS servers.

There's more...

The JMS servers can be created with WLST.

Creating the JMS servers using WLST

1. Log in as a `wls` user to the shell and start WLST.

   [wls@prod01]$ $WL_HOME/common/bin/wlst.sh

2. Connect to the Administration Server using `wlsadmin` as user, `<pwd>` as the password, and `t3://adminhost.domain.local:7001` as the server URL.

   wls:/offline>connect("wlsadmin","<pwd>","t3://adminhost.domain. local:7001")

3. Run the following WLST commands to create the JMS servers:

   ```
   edit()
   startEdit()

   cd('/')
   cmo.createJMSServer('JMSServer01')
   cd('/JMSServers/JMSServer01')
   cmo.setPersistentStore(getMBean('/FileStores/FileStore01'))
   set('Targets',jarray.array([ObjectName('com.bea:Name=PROD_
   Server01,Type=Server')], ObjectName))

   cd('/')
   cmo.createJMSServer('JMSServer02')
   cd('/JMSServers/JMSServer02')
   cmo.setPersistentStore(getMBean('/FileStores/FileStore02'))
   set('Targets',jarray.array([ObjectName('com.bea:Name=PROD_
   Server02,Type=Server')], ObjectName))

   cd('/')
   cmo.createJMSServer('JMSServer03')
   cd('/JMSServers/JMSServer03')
   cmo.setPersistentStore(getMBean('/FileStores/FileStore03'))
   set('Targets',jarray.array([ObjectName('com.bea:Name=PROD_
   Server03,Type=Server')], ObjectName))

   cd('/')
   ```

```
cmo.createJMSServer('JMSServer04')

cd('/JMSServers/JMSServer04')

cmo.setPersistentStore(getMBean('/FileStores/FileStore04'))

set('Targets',jarray.array([ObjectName('com.bea:Name=PROD_
Server04,Type=Server')], ObjectName))


activate()

exit()
```

Creating the JMS servers with JDBC stores using WLST

1. Log in as a `wls` user to the shell and start WLST.

   ```
   [wls@prod01]$ $WL_HOME/common/bin/wlst.sh
   ```

2. Connect to the Administration Server using `wlsadmin` as user, `<pwd>` as the password, and `t3://adminhost.domain.local:7001` as the server URL.

   ```
   wls:/offline>connect("wlsadmin","<pwd>","t3://adminhost.domain.
   local:7001")
   ```

3. Run the following WLST commands to create the JMS servers:

   ```
   edit()

   startEdit()


   cd('/')

   cmo.createJMSServer('JMSServer01')

   cd('/JMSServers/JMSServer01')

   cmo.setPersistentStore(getMBean('/JDBCStores/JDBCStore01'))

   set('Targets',jarray.array([ObjectName('com.bea:Name=PROD_
   Server01,Type=Server')], ObjectName))


   cd('/')

   cmo.createJMSServer('JMSServer02')

   cd('/JMSServers/JMSServer02')

   cmo.setPersistentStore(getMBean('/JDBCStores/JDBCStore02'))

   set('Targets',jarray.array([ObjectName('com.bea:Name=PROD_
   Server02,Type=Server')], ObjectName))


   cd('/')

   cmo.createJMSServer('JMSServer03')

   cd('/JMSServers/JMSServer03')
   ```

```
cmo.setPersistentStore(getMBean('/JDBCStores/JDBCStore03'))
set('Targets',jarray.array([ObjectName('com.bea:Name=PROD_
Server03,Type=Server')], ObjectName))


cd('/')
cmo.createJMSServer('JMSServer04')
cd('/JMSServers/JMSServer04')
cmo.setPersistentStore(getMBean('/JDBCStores/JDBCStore04'))
set('Targets',jarray.array([ObjectName('com.bea:Name=PROD_
Server04,Type=Server')], ObjectName))


activate()
exit()
```

See also

- ▸ *Creating the file stores*
- ▸ *Creating the JDBC stores*
- ▸ *Creating the JMS module*

Creating the JMS module

The JMS module is a WebLogic global system resource that aggregates and stores JMS resources and JMS-related configurations such as queues, topics, connection factories, quotas, distributed queues, and distributed topics.

There are two types of JMS modules: the JMS application module and the JMS system module. In this recipe, the JMS system module will be covered since it is the module WebLogic administrators use for creation and configuration. Although it has the same functions as those of a system module, the JMS application module should be handled by the developer and has to be included and packaged inside the application's EAR file.

The system module is also preferred over the application module because the application module can be handled only by manually editing the XML. The system module, on the other hand, can be managed through the Administration Console, WLST, or JMX.

Continuing the setup process for the JMS resources needed by the JMSApp application, create a new JMS module called JMSAppModule in PROD_DOMAIN.

Getting ready

The JMS module will be created using the Administration Console, so make sure the Administration Server is running.

How to do it...

Carry out the following steps to create the JMS module:

1. Access the Administration Console with your web browser at `http://adminhost.domain.local:7001/console`.

2. Click on the **Lock & Edit** button to start a new edit session.

3. Click on the plus sign to open the **Services** tree on the left; click on **Messaging** and then on **JMS Modules**.

4. Click on the **New** button to open the **Create JMS System Module** page.

5. Type `JMSAppModule` in the **Name** field. Leave the **Descriptor File Name** and **Location in Domain** text fields blank. Click on the **Next** button.

6. Check the **All Servers in the cluster** radio button to target the `JMSAppModule` to the cluster `PROD_Cluster`. Click on the **Next** button.

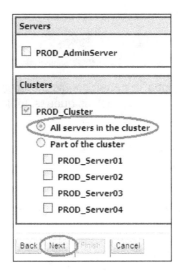

7. Click on the **Finish** button, leaving the checkbox **Would you like to add resources to this JMS system module?** unchecked.

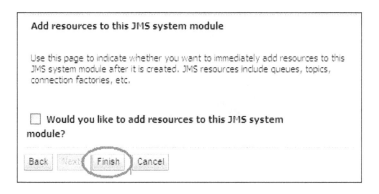

8. Click on the **Activate Changes** button to finish.

How it works...

The JMS module JMSAppModule was created in the PROD_DOMAIN domain and is ready to be configured and used by the JMSApp application.

The module configuration is saved at the $DOMAIN_HOME/config/jms directory and uses the filename convention <module-name>-jms.xml. In this case, the filename created is jmsappmodule-jms.xml.

There's more...

The JMS module can be created with WLST.

Creating the JMS module using WLST

1. Log in as a wls user to the shell and start WLST.

   ```
   [wls@prod01]$ $WL_HOME/common/bin/wlst.sh
   ```

2. Connect to the Administration Server using wlsadmin as user, <pwd> as the password, and t3://adminhost.domain.local:7001 as the server URL.

   ```
   wls:/offline>connect("wlsadmin","<pwd>","t3://adminhost.domain.local:7001")
   ```

3. Run the following WLST commands to create the JMS module:

   ```
   edit()
   startEdit()
   ```

```
cd('/')
cmo.createJMSSystemResource('JMSAppModule')

cd('/JMSSystemResources/JMSAppModule')
set('Targets',jarray.array([ObjectName('com.bea:Name=PROD_
Cluster,Type=Cluster')], ObjectName))

activate()
exit()
```

See also

- ▶ *Creating the JMS servers*
- ▶ *Configuring the subdeployment targeting*

Configuring the subdeployment target

The JMS module JMSAppModule is targeted to the cluster PROD_Cluster, meaning the JMS resources added to the module will use the PROD_Cluster cluster as the default target. Because of the JMS resource, such as a distributed queue, the default target is not the best option for production.

WebLogic Server has a feature called subdeployment targeting to handle this special targeting. The subdeployment allows a JMS resource to use a different target from the default JMS module target, using a single or multiple WebLogic Server instances, WebLogic clusters, or JMS servers as target.

 Subdeployment is a not a precise term and confuses WebLogic administrators. Subdeployment is better referred to as advanced targeting.

In this recipe a new subdeployment called JMSAppSub will be created targeting only the JMS servers created for the JMSApp application.

Getting ready

The subdeployment JMSAppSub will be created using the Administration Console. Make sure the Administration Server is running and the JMSAppModule module is created.

How to do it...

Carry out the following steps to configure the JMS subdeployment:

1. Access the Administration Console with your web browser at `http://adminhost.domain.local:7001/console`.

2. Click on the **Lock & Edit** button to start a new edit session.

3. Click on the plus sign to open the **Services** tree on the left; click on **Messaging** and then on **JMS Modules**.

4. Click on the `JMSAppModule` link and then the **Subdeployments** tab. Now click on the **New** button.

5. Type `JMSAppSub` in the **Name** text field under **Subdeployments** and click on the **Next** button.

6. Click and enable only the checkboxes JMSServer01, JMSServer02, JMSServer03, and JMSServer04 and click on the **Finish** button.

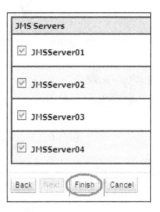

7. Click on the **Activate Changes** button to finish.

How it works...

The subdeployment JMSAppSub was created for the JMS module JMSAppModule, pointing to the JMS servers JMSServer01, JMSServer02, JMSServer03, and JMSServer04, meaning that any JMS resource targeting to the subdeployment will be restricted for use by the selected JMS servers only.

In the next recipe, the JMS resources required by the JMSApp application will be configured to target the subdeployment JMSAppModule.

There's more...

The subdeployment can also be created with WLST.

Configuring the subdeployment using WLST

1. Log in as a wls user to the shell and start WLST:

   [wls@prod01]$ $WL_HOME/common/bin/wlst.sh

2. Connect to the Administration Server using wlsadmin as user, <pwd> as the password, and t3://adminhost.domain.local:7001 as the server URL.

   wls:/offline>connect("wlsadmin","<pwd>","t3://adminhost.domain.local:7001")

3. Run the following WLST commands:

```
edit()
startEdit()

cmo.createSubDeployment('JMSAppSub')

cd('/JMSSystemResources/JMSAppModule/SubDeployments/JMSAppSub')
set('Targets',jarray.array([ObjectName('com.bea:Name=JMSServer
01,Type=JMSServer'), ObjectName('com.bea:Name=JMSServer02,Type
=JMSServer'), ObjectName('com.bea:Name=JMSServer03,Type=JMSSer
ver'), ObjectName('com.bea:Name=JMSServer04,Type=JMSServer')],
ObjectName))

activate()
exit()
```

See also

► *Creating the JMS servers*
► *Creating the distributed queue destination and the connection factory*

Creating the distributed queue destination and the connection factory

Oracle WebLogic Server 12c has two types of queues: the **queue** and the **distributed queue**. The queue is a JMS resource targeted to a single Managed Server.

A distributed queue must be used when working with WebLogic clustering. The distributed queue is a logical entity that groups single queues distributed across the JMS servers and Managed Servers of the cluster but is accessible as a single and transparent JNDI name. JMS applications require that all resource and JNDI names be unique across the entire application environment, including the WebLogic domains involved, the clusters, Managed Servers, and JMS resources.

The members (queues) of the distributed queue can use weighted or uniform distribution.

 Use the uniformly distributed queue for JMS clustering. The weighted distribution is more complicated to create and manage and it is deprecated in WebLogic Server 12c.

A JMS queue must be created to handle the JMSApp application's messages. In this recipe, the uniformly distributed queue called JMSAppQueue and the connection factory called JMSAppConnectionFactory will be created and added to the JMSAppModule module.

Getting ready

The queue will be added using the Administration Console. The persistent stores, JMS servers, JMS module, and subdeployment of the previous recipes must already be created.

How to do it...

Carry out the following steps to create a new distributed queue:

1. Access the Administration Console with your web browser at http://adminhost. domain.local:7001/console.

2. Click on the **Lock & Edit** button to start a new edit session.

3. Click on the plus sign to open the **Services** tree on the left; click on **Messaging** and then on **JMS Modules**.

4. Click on the JMSAppModule link to open the **Configuration** page. Click on the **New** button.

5. Select the **Distributed Queue** option from the **Create a New JMS System Module Resource** page and click on the **Next** button.

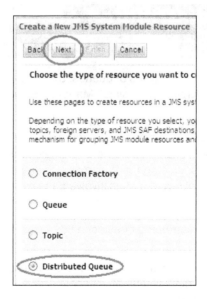

6. Type `JMSAppQueue` in the **Name** field and `jms.appqueue` in the **JNDI Name field**. Leave the default values **Uniform** in the **Destination Type** field and **None** in the **Template** drop-down menus. Click on the **Next** button.

7. Click on the **Advanced Targeting** button.

8. From the **Subdeployments** drop-down menu, select the **JMSAppSub** option and click on the **Finish** button.

9. Click on the **New** button again and choose the **Connection Factory** radio button. Click on the **Next** button.

10. Type `JMSAppConnectionFactory` in the **Name** field and `jms.appcf` in the **JNDI Name** field. Leave all other fields at their default values and click the **Next** button.

11. Click on the **Finish** button to confirm the `PROD_Cluster` cluster as target.

12. Click on the **Activate Changes** button to finish.

How it works...

The distributed queue JMSAppQueue and the connection factory JMSAppConnectionFactory were created and added to the JMS module.

Name ⌃	Type	JNDI Name	Subdeployment	Targets
☐ JMSAppConnectionFactory	Connection Factory	jms.appcf	Default Targetting	PROD_Cluster
☐ JmsAppQueue	Uniform Distributed Queue	jms.appqueue	JMSAppSub	JMSServer01, JMSServer02, JMSServer03, JMSServer04

The uniformly distributed queue is targeted to the JMSAppSub subdeployment. The uniform distribution means that WebLogic create a queue member of the distributed queue in each of the JMS servers of the subdeployment automatically.

Avoid targeting a uniformly distributed queue to a cluster, otherwise WebLogic will create a queue member in every JMS server found in the cluster. Use the subdeployment targeting with specific JMS servers for a more controlled configuration.

WebLogic has two connection factories enabled by default that can be used by the application—weblogic.jms.ConnectionFactory and weblogic.jms.XAConnectionFactory.

It's recommended that an application use a custom connection factory since the two default connection factories cannot be tuned.

The custom connection factory JMSAPPConnectionFactory was created with the JNDI name jms.appcf and is ready to be used by the JMSApp.

There's more...

The JMS resources can be created using WLST.

Creating the distributed queue and connection factory using WLST

1. Log in as a wls user to the shell and start WLST.

    ```
    [wls@prod01] $ $WL_HOME/common/bin/wlst.sh
    ```

2. Connect to the Administration Server using `wlsadmin` as user, `<pwd>` as the password, and `t3://adminhost.domain.local:7001` as the server URL.

```
wls:/offline>connect("wlsadmin","<pwd>","t3://adminhost.domain.
local:7001")
```

3. Run the following WLST commands:

```
edit()
startEdit()


cmo.createUniformDistributedQueue('JmsAppQueue')

cd('/JMSSystemResources/JMSAppModule/JMSResource/JMSAppModule/
UniformDistributedQueues/JmsAppQueue')

cmo.setJNDIName('jms.appqueue')

cd('/JMSSystemResources/JMSAppModule/SubDeployments/JMSAppSub')

set('Targets',jarray.array([ObjectName('com.bea:Name=JMSServer01,T
ype=JMSServer'), ObjectName('com.bea:Name=JMSServer02,Type=JMSServ
er'), ObjectName('com.bea:Name=JMSServer03,Ty

pe=JMSServer'), ObjectName('com.bea:Name=JMSServer04,Type=JMSServ
er')], ObjectName))

cd('/JMSSystemResources/JMSAppModule/JMSResource/JMSAppModule/
UniformDistributedQueues/JmsAppQueue')

cmo.setSubDeploymentName('JMSAppSub')


cd('/JMSSystemResources/JMSAppModule/JMSResource/JMSAppModule')

cmo.createConnectionFactory('JMSAppConnectionFactory')

cd('/JMSSystemResources/JMSAppModule/JMSResource/JMSAppModule/
ConnectionFactories/JMSAppConnectionFactory')

cmo.setJNDIName('jms.appcf')

cd('/JMSSystemResources/JMSAppModule/JMSResource/JMSAppModule/
ConnectionFactories/JMSAppConnectionFactory/SecurityParams/
JMSAppConnectionFactory')

cmo.setAttachJMSXUserId(false)

cd('/JMSSystemResources/JMSAppModule/JMSResource/JMSAppModule/
ConnectionFactories/JMSAppConnectionFactory/ClientParams/
JMSAppConnectionFactory')

cmo.setClientIdPolicy('Restricted')

cmo.setSubscriptionSharingPolicy('Exclusive')

cmo.setMessagesMaximum(10)

cd('/JMSSystemResources/JMSAppModule/JMSResource/JMSAppModule/
ConnectionFactories/JMSAppConnectionFactory/TransactionParams/
```

```
JMSAppConnectionFactory')
cmo.setXAConnectionFactoryEnabled(true)

activate()
exit()
```

See also

▶ *Configuring the subdeployment targeting*

Starting/stopping consumers for a JMS destination

The WebLogic JMS subsystem allows a JMS destination queue to have its message operations controlled when needed. A queue destination can have its consumers paused and resumed on demand.

Getting ready

In this recipe, the JMSAppQueue queue will be used as an example. The message operations will use the Administration Console, so make sure the Administration Server is up and running.

How to do it...

To pause the consumers operations for the JMSAppQueue queue, do the following:

1. Access the Administration Console with your web browser at `http://adminhost.domain.local:7001/console`.

2. Click on the **Lock & Edit** button to start a new edit session.

3. Click on the plus sign to open the **Services** tree on the left; click on **Messaging** and then **JMS Servers**.

4. Click on the JMSServer01 link to open the **Configuration** page. Click on the **Monitoring** tab and then on the **Active Destinations** tab.

5. Click on the checkbox from the JMSAppModule!JMSServer01@JmsAppQueue queue and click on the **Consumption** button. Then click on the **Pause** link.

6. Click the **Yes** button to confirm.

7. Repeat these steps for the JMSServer02, JMSServer03, and JMSServer04 JMS servers.

To resume the consumers operations of the JMSAppQueue queue, do the following:

1. Access the Administration Console with your web browser at http://adminhost. domain.local:7001/console.

2. Click on the **Lock & Edit** button to start a new edit session.

3. Expand the **Services** tree on the left; click on **Messaging** and then on **JMS Servers**.

4. Click on the JMSServer01 link to open the **Configuration** page. Click on the **Monitoring** tab and then on the **Active Destinations** tab.

5. Click on the checkbox from the JMSAppModule!JMSServer01@JmsAppQueue queue and click on the **Consumption** button. Then click on the **Resume** link.

6. Click on the **Yes** button to confirm.

7. Repeat these steps for the JMSServer02, JMSServer03, and JMSServer04 JMS servers.

How it works...

The consumer operations can be temporarily paused through the Administration Console when the JMS messages dequeue must stop in a situation of a maintenance window or a troubleshooting process.

There's more...

JMS destinations can be controlled through WLST as well. This is discussed in the following sections.

Pausing the consumers using WLST

This operation can be made by using WLST:

1. Log in as a `wls` user to the shell and start WLST.

   [wls@prod01] $ $WL_HOME/common/bin/wlst.sh

2. Connect to the Administration Server using `wlsadmin` as user, `<pwd>` as the password, and `t3://adminhost.domain.local:7001` as the server URL.

   wls:/offline>connect("wlsadmin","<pwd>","t3://adminhost.domain. local:7001")

3. Run the following WLST commands:

   domainRuntime()

   cd('/ServerRuntimes/PROD_Server01/JMSRuntime/PROD_Server01.jms/ JMSServers/JMSServer01/Destinations/JMSAppModule!JMSServer01@ JmsAppQueue')

   cmo.pauseConsumption()

   cd('/ServerRuntimes/PROD_Server02/JMSRuntime/PROD_Server02.jms/ JMSServers/JMSServer02/Destinations/JMSAppModule!JMSServer02@ JmsAppQueue')

   cmo.pauseConsumption()

   cd('/ServerRuntimes/PROD_Server03/JMSRuntime/PROD_Server03.jms/ JMSServers/JMSServer03/Destinations/JMSAppModule!JMSServer03@ JmsAppQueue')

   cmo.pauseConsumption()

   cd('/ServerRuntimes/PROD_Server04/JMSRuntime/PROD_Server04.jms/ JMSServers/JMSServer04/Destinations/JMSAppModule!JMSServer04@ JmsAppQueue')

   cmo.pauseConsumption()

   exit()

Resuming the consumers using WLST

This operation can be made by using WLST:

1. Log in as a `wls` user to the shell and start WLST.

   [wls@prod01]$ $WL_HOME/common/bin/wlst.sh

2. Connect to the Administration Server using `wlsadmin` as user, `<pwd>` as the password, and `t3://adminhost.domain.local:7001` as the server URL.

   wls:/offline>connect("wlsadmin","<pwd>","t3://adminhost.domain.local:7001")

3. Run the following WLST commands:

   domainRuntime()

   cd('/ServerRuntimes/PROD_Server01/JMSRuntime/PROD_Server01.jms/JMSServers/JMSServer01/Destinations/JMSAppModule!JMSServer01@JmsAppQueue')

   cmo.resumeConsumption()

   cd('/ServerRuntimes/PROD_Server02/JMSRuntime/PROD_Server02.jms/JMSServers/JMSServer02/Destinations/JMSAppModule!JMSServer02@JmsAppQueue')

   cmo.resumeConsumption()

   cd('/ServerRuntimes/PROD_Server03/JMSRuntime/PROD_Server03.jms/JMSServers/JMSServer03/Destinations/JMSAppModule!JMSServer03@JmsAppQueue')

   cmo.resumeConsumption()

   cd('/ServerRuntimes/PROD_Server04/JMSRuntime/PROD_Server04.jms/JMSServers/JMSServer04/Destinations/JMSAppModule!JMSServer04@JmsAppQueue')

   cmo.resumeConsumption()

   exit()

See also

▶ *Creating the JMS servers*

Using the Server affinity to tune the distributed destinations' load balance

The connection factory is the JMS resource used by the client application to control the behavior of the load balance algorithm used when publishing JMS messages to the distributed destination and its queue or topic members.

An application deployed in a production environment should preferably use a custom connection factory that can be tuned to fit the application requirements so as to avoid using the default WebLogic connection factories. The JMS message-publishing and load-balancing behavior can be tuned by changing the server affinity configuration of the connection factory. By default, the load-balancing and server-affinity options of the connection factory are enabled.

The JMSApp application uses the connection factory JMSAppCF created in the previous recipe to connect and publish JMS messages to the distributed queue JMSAppQueue.

Disabling the server affinity of the connection factory will force the load balance when publishing the JMS messages to the distributed queue. There is the drawback of the overhead of an additional TCP connection from the source Managed Server where the application request is running to the target Managed Server where the queue member of the distributed queue is hosted.

This recipe shows the steps to configure the server affinity.

Getting ready

To change the server affinity configuration, access the Administration Console.

How to do it...

To set the server affinity, follow these steps:

1. Access the Administration Console with your web browser at `http://adminhost.domain.local:7001/console`.
2. Click on the **Lock & Edit** button to start a new edit session.
3. Expand the **Services** tree on the left; click on **Messaging** and then on **JMS Modules**.
4. Click on the JMSAppModule link to open its **Configuration** page.
5. Click on the JMSAppConnectionFactory link and then click on the **Load Balance** tab to open the load-balancing options.

6. Disable the **Server Affinity Enabled** checkbox and click on the **Save** button.

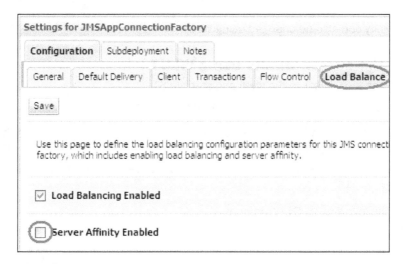

7. Click on the **Activate Changes** button to finish.

How it works...

To illustrate the flow of the process, suppose an application request is being processed in the first Managed Server, PROD_Server01. The application will use the connection factory JMSAppCF to publish a JMS message to the JMSAppQueue distributed queue. Thanks to the server affinity option being enabled, the JMS message will be published to the local queue member of the JMSAppQueue distributed queue that is running in the same Managed Server, PROD_Server01.

In order to prioritize the delivery of a JMS message to a queue member of the distributed queue, the balancing algorithm verifies some characteristics such as if the queue member is local to the Managed Server, if it has a consumer, or if it has a persistent store. The disabled server affinity removes the influence of being a local queue. So, with the server affinity disabled, the same request running in PROD_Server01 will balance the load and publish the JMS messages to all queue members of the distributed queue, JMSAppQueue, running in all Managed Servers, PROD_Server01, PROD_Server02, PROD_Server03, and PROD_Server04.

Disabling the server affinity is useful for distributing the JMS messages to the members of the distributed queue when the application requests are not yet balanced across the Managed Servers. An example is when the application requests are not load-balanced at the web tier or when a single request publishes a large amount of messages.

Analyze each application case and use the option that better suits an even distribution of the load in production.

There's more...

The server affinity can also be changed using WLST.

Changing the server affinity using WLST

1. Log in as a `wls` user to the shell and start WLST.

    ```
    [wls@prod01]$ $WL_HOME/common/bin/wlst.sh
    ```

2. Connect to the Administration Server using `wlsadmin` as user, `<pwd>` as the password, and `t3://adminhost.domain.local:7001` as the server URL.

    ```
    wls:/offline>connect("wlsadmin","<pwd>","t3://adminhost.domain.
    local:7001")
    ```

3. Run the following WLST commands:

    ```
    edit()
    startEdit()

    cd('/JMSSystemResources/JMSAppModule/JMSResource/JMSAppModule/
    ConnectionFactories/JMSAppConnectionFactory/LoadBalancingParams/
    JMSAppConnectionFactory')
    cmo.setServerAffinityEnabled(false)
    activate()
    exit()
    ```

See also

 ▸ *Creating the distributed queue destination and the connection factory*
 ▸ *Configuring messaging bridge with source and target distributed destinations*

Creating a pinned queue with clustering and HA with service migration

WebLogic clustering is used for scalability, high availability, and parallel processing of the user and server requests. The cluster distributes the load across the cluster's Managed Server instances, and for the JMS queues each Server instance has its own queue member of a distributed queue.

An application requirement may need a single JMS queue, pinned to a Managed Server and not configured as a distributed queue, even though the WebLogic cluster is being used.

The requirement is valid but using a queue pinned to a single Managed Server brings a single point of failure to a production environment. If the Managed Server hosting the pinned queue crashes, the queue will be unavailable.

To handle this situation, WebLogic has a feature called Service Migration where the pinned queue can be moved from one Managed Server to another automatically when needed, bringing high availability to a pinned service.

In this recipe, we are assuming that the application `JMSApp` requires a `JMSAppPinnedQueue` queue to be configured as a pinned queue. WebLogic will be configured to handle the Service migration for it.

Getting ready

A new persistent store and a new JMS server targeting a migratable target will be created. The persistent store will be created as a file store. A JDBC store can also be used.

 The directory hosting the file stores must be shared with all machines of the `PROD_Cluster` cluster. Use a shared storage solution (**NAS, SAS, and SAN**).

The shared storage `/shared/filestores` directory will be used as a reference in this recipe.

How to do it...

Follow the ensuing steps to configure the service migration:

 Access the Administration Console with your web browser at `http://adminhost.domain.local:7001/console`.

1. Click on the **Lock & Edit** button to start a new edit session.
2. Expand the **Environment** tree on the left and then click on the **Clusters** link.
3. Click on the `PROD_Cluster` link and then on the **Migration** tab. Select the **Consensus** option from the **Migration Basis** drop-down menu. Click on the **Save** button.
4. Click on the **Migratable Targets** link from the navigation tree on the left.

5. Click on the `PROD_Server01 (migratable)` link and then on the **Migration** tab. Select **Auto-Migrate Exactly-Once Services** from the **Service Migration Policy** drop-down menu. Click on the **Save** button.

6. Click on the **Activate Changes** button to finish.

Create one migratable file store and one migratable JMS server using the Administration Console:

1. Access the Administration Console with your web browser at `http://adminhost. domain.local:7001/console`.

2. Expand the **Services** tree on the left and then click on **Persistent Stores**.

3. Click on the **New** button and click on the **Create File Store** link to start creating a new persistent store.

4. Type `FileStoreMigratable` in the **Name** field. Click on the **Target** drop-down menu and select the `PROD_Server01 (migratable)` option. Type `/shared/filestores` in the **Directory** field to point to the shared directory and click on the **OK** button.

5. Expand the **Services** tree on the left; click on **Messaging** and then on **JMS Servers**.

6. Click on the **New** button to open the **Create a New JMS Server** page.

7. Type `JMSServerMigratable` in the **Name** field and choose **FileStoreMigratable** from the **Persistent Store** drop-down menu. Click on the **Next** button.

8. Choose `PROD_Server01 (migratable)` from the **Target** drop-down menu. Click on the **Finish** button.

9. Click on the **Activate Changes** button to finish.

Create a new JMS module named `JMSAppModulePinned`, configure the subdeployment `JMSAppSubPinned`, and add a new JMS queue named `JMSAppPinnedQueue`:

1. Access the Administration Console with your web browser at `http://adminhost.domain.local:7001/console`.

2. Click on the **Lock & Edit** button to start a new edit session.

3. Click on the plus sign to open the **Services** tree on the left; click on **Messaging** and then on **JMS Modules**.

4. Click on the **New** button to open the **Create JMS System Module** page.

5. Type `JMSAppModulePinned` in the **Name** field. Leave the **Descriptor File Name** and **Location in Domain** text fields blank. Click on the **Next** button.

6. Check the **All Servers in the cluster** radio button to target the `JMSAppModulePinned` value to the `PROD_Cluster` cluster. Click on the **Next** button.

7. Click on the **Finish** button, leaving the checkbox **Would you like to add resources to this JMS system module?** unchecked.

8. Expand the **Services** tree on the left; click on **Messaging** and then on **JMS Modules**.

9. Click on the JMSAppModulePinned link to open the **Configuration** page. Then click on the **Subdeployments** tab and click on the **New** button.

10. Type JMSAppSubPinned in the **subdeployment's Name** text field and click on the **Next** button.

11. Enable the checkbox **JMSServerMigratable** and click on the **Finish** button.

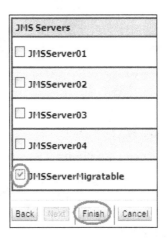

12. Click the **Configuration** tab to open the **JMS Module configuration** page and click on the **New** button.

13. Select the **Queue** radio button from the **Create a New JMS System Module Resource** page and click on the **Next** button.

14. Type JMSAppQueuePinned in the **Name** field and jms.appqueuepinned in the **JNDI Name** text field. Leave the **Template** option as **None**. Click on the **Next** button.

15. Select JMSAppSubPinned in the **subdeployment's Name** field and click on the **Finish** button, leaving the JMSServerMigratable radio button selected.

16. Click on the **Activate Changes** button to finish.

How it works...

The `Consensus` option is the migration basis configured for the `PROD_Cluster` cluster. It requires the Node Manager to be running, to keep the leasing information updated in the memory.

The new persistent store, `FileStoreMigratable`, and the new JMS server, `JMSServerMigratable`, were created and targeted to the migratable target, `PROD_Server01 (migratable)`, which was configured to use `Auto-Migrate Exactly-Once Services` as the migration policy. One migratable target from a Managed Server must be elected to be the primary host of the service.

A JMS module, `JMSAppModulePinned`, was created with a new subdeployment, `JMSAppSubPinned`, targeting `JMSServerMigratable`. The queue `JMSAppPinnedQueue` was created and uses the `JMSAppSubPinned` subdeployment.

This configuration guarantees `JMSAppPinnedQueue` is always running in at least one Managed Server of the cluster, giving preference to run at the `PROD_Server01` server. If `PROD_Server01` goes down or crashes, the queue is automatically migrated to another running instance with no intervention.

 Remember that the file store must reside in a shared storage so that all machines of the cluster can access it.

See also

▶ *Creating the distributed queue destination and the connection factory*

Configuring messaging bridge with source and target distributed destinations

The messaging bridge is used to forward JMS messages from one source queue to another target queue.

In this recipe, a bridge will be created to forward the JMS messages from the `JMSAppQueue` distributed queue to a hypothetic distributed queue with a JNDI name `jms.remotequeue`, hosted by a separate WebLogic domain named `REMOTE_DOMAIN`. The `REMOTE_DOMAIN` domain is configured with a cluster with two Managed Servers instances running at the addresses `t3://remote01.domain.local:9001` and `t3://remote02.domain.local:9002`. A remote connection factory is available under the JNDI name `jms.remoteappcf`. Both local and remote queues are distributed destinations.

Getting ready

The Administrative Console is used to configure the messaging bridge, so make sure the Administration Server is up and running.

The bridge destinations use the `jms-xa-adp` (XA) or `jms-notran-adp` (non-XA) resource adapters to connect to the destinations. They are not deployed by default so you have to deploy them. In this recipe, since the bridge is non-XA, the resource adapter `jms-notran-adp` should be deployed. WebLogic can automatically deploy the resource adapter when you create the bridge, but it's recommended you deploy it manually.

How to do it...

Create the directory to host the deployment plan to all machines, as follows:

1. Login as a `wls` user to the `prod01` shell and create the directory.

   ```
   [wls@prod01]$ cd $DOMAIN_HOME
   [wls@prod01]$ mkdir plans
   ```

2. Repeat this step for `prod02`.

Deploy the `jms-notran-adp` resource adapter, as follows:

1. Access the Administration Console with your web browser at `http://adminhost.domain.local:7001/console`.

2. Click on the **Lock & Edit** button to start a new edit session.

3. Click on the **Deployments** link on the navigation tree to the left.

4. Click on the **Install** button.

5. Type `/oracle/Middleware/wlserver_12.1/server/lib` in the **Path** field and click on **Next**.

6. Select the `jms-notran-adp.rar` resource adapter and click on the **Next** button.

7. Select the **Install this deployment as an application** radio button and click on **Next**.

8. Select the **All servers in the cluster** radio button from the `PROD_Cluster` target and click on the **Next** button.

9. Select the **I will make the deployment accessible from the following location** radio button; leave the other options in their default values and click on **Next**.

10. Click on the **Finish** button to open the **Deployment's Configuration** screen.

11. Click on the **Configuration** and then the **Outbound Connection Pools** tabs.

12. Click on the **+** button from the `weblogic.jms.bridge.AdapterConnectionFactory` link and click on the `eis/jms/WLSConnectionFactoryJNDINoTX` link.

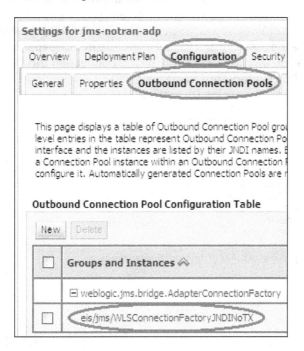

13. Click on the **Connection Pool** tab and change the **Max Capacity** field to the desired value (use 2x the number of bridges). Click on the **Save** button.

14. Type the full path, `/oracle/Middleware/user_projects/domains/PROD_DOMAIN/plans/jms-notran-adp-Plan.xml`, in the **Path** field. Click on the **OK** button.

15. Replicate the file `/oracle/Middleware/user_projects/domains/PROD_DOMAIN/plans/jms-notran-adp-Plan.xml` to all the machines of the cluster.

16. Click on the **Activate Changes** button to finish.

17. Go to the **Deployments** page again, select the checkbox to the left of the `jms-notran-adp` deployment, and click on the **Start** button and then the **Servicing all request** link.

Create the JMS bridge destinations as follows:

1. Access the Administration Console with your web browser at `http://adminhost.domain.local:7001/console`.

2. Click on the **Lock & Edit** button to start a new edit session.

3. Expand the **Services** tree on the left and then click on **+Messaging, +Bridges**, and **JMS Bridge Destinations**.

4. Click on the **New** button to open the **Create a New JMS Bridge Destination** page. Type `BridgeSource_01` in the **Name** field and select the `eis.jms.WLSConnectionFactoryJNDINoTX` value from the **Adapter JNDI Name** drop-down menu. Leave the default blank value for the **Adapter Classpath** field and type `t3://prodsrv01.domain.local:8001` on the **Connection URL** field, `jms.appcf` on the **Connection Factory JNDI Name** field, and `jms.appqueue` on the **Destination JNDI Name** field. Click on the **OK** button.

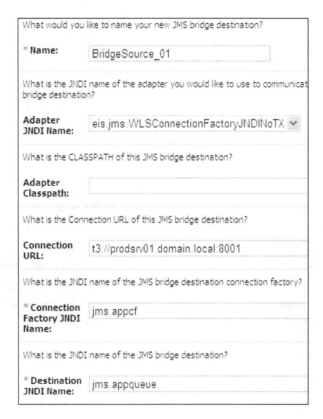

5. Repeat the previous steps for creating the `BridgeSource_02`, `BridgeSource_03`, and `BridgeSource_04` bridge destinations, using `t3://prodsrv02.domain.local:8002`, `t3://prodsrv03.domain.local:8003`, and `t3://prodsrv04.domain.local:8004` as the values to the **Connection URL** field.

6. Click on the **New** button again to create the remote destination target.

7. Type `BridgeTarget` in the **Name** field, select the `eis.jms.`
   `WLSConnectionFactoryJNDINoTX` from the **Adapter JNDI Name field**, and
   type `t3://remote01.domain.local:9001,remote02.domain.local:9002`
   in the **Connection URL** field. Type `jms.remoteappcf` on the **Connection Factory
   JNDI Name** field and `jms.remotequeue` on the **Destination JNDI Name** field. Click
   on the **OK** button.

8. Click on the **Activate Changes** button to finish.

Create the messaging bridges as follows:

1. Access the Administration Console with your web browser at `http://adminhost.`
   `domain.local:7001/console`.

2. Click on the **Lock & Edit** button to start a new edit session.

3. Expand the **Services** tree on the left; click on **Messaging** and then
   on **Bridges**.

4. Click on the **New** button to open the **Create a New Bridge** page.

5. Type `Bridge_01` in the **Name** field, leave the **Selector** field blank and select the
   Quality of Service field as the **Atmost-once** option. Enable the checkbox **Started**
   and click on the **Next** button.

6. In the **Select an Existing Source Destination** drop-down menu, choose
   `BridgeSource_01` and click on the **Next** button.

7. Leave the **Messaging Provider** option in the default `WebLogic Server 7.0 or
   higher` and click on **Next**.

8. Select the **BridgeTarget** option from the **Select an Existing Target Destination**
   drop-down menu. Click on **Next**.

9. Again, leave the **Messaging Provider** option in the default `WebLogic Server 7.0
   or higher` and click on **Next**.

10. On the target screen, enable only the `PROD_Server01` checkbox and click on **Next**.

11. Click on the **Finish** button.

12. Repeat the previous steps to create the remaining bridges according to the
    following table:

Bridge	Source Destination	Target Destination	Target
Bridge_01	BridgeSource_01	BridgeTarget	PROD_Server01
Bridge_02	BridgeSource_02	BridgeTarget	PROD_Server02
Bridge_03	BridgeSource_03	BridgeTarget	PROD_Server03
Bridge_04	BridgeSource_04	BridgeTarget	PROD_Server04

13. Click on the **Activate Changes** button to finish.

How it works...

One message bridge per queue member must be created when using a distributed destination like the `JMSAppQueue` queue to guarantee every message from every member is forwarded.

The target destination, `BridgeTarget`, uses a remote connection factory, `jms.remoteappcf`, to connect to the remote queue. Since the remote queue `jms.remotequeue` is also distributed, disable the server affinity option of the remote connection factory `jms.remoteappcf` so the messages are load-balanced to all members of the distributed queue `jms.remotequeue`.

Depending on the number of bridges created in the WebLogic domain, you should tune the max connections settings of the resource adapter. The recommendation is to set the max connections value as 2 times the number of bridges. If you have 20 bridges, change the max connections to at least 40.

 If the resource adapter deployment plan is changed, copy the updated file to every machine of the cluster. In this case, copy the `/oracle/Middleware/user_projects/domains/PROD_DOMAIN/plans/jms-notran-adp-Plan.xml` file to every machine in the same path. Using a shared folder to host the file is also a valid option.

There's more...

The message bridge can be configured using WLST.

Configuring the message bridge using WLST:

This change can be made using WLST.

1. Log in as a `wls` user to the shell and start WLST.

   [wls@prod01]$ $WL_HOME/common/bin/wlst.sh

2. Connect to the Administration Server using `wlsadmin` as user, `<pwd>` as the password, and `t3://adminhost.domain.local:7001` as the server URL:

   wls:/offline>connect("wlsadmin","<pwd>","t3://adminhost.domain.local:7001")

3. Run the following WLST commands to create the bridge sources:

   edit()

   startEdit()

   cd('/')

   cmo.createJMSBridgeDestination('BridgeSource_01')

```
cd('/JMSBridgeDestinations/BridgeSource_01')
cmo.setClasspath('')
cmo.setConnectionURL('t3://prodsrv01.domain.local:8001')
cmo.setAdapterJNDIName('eis.jms.WLSConnectionFactoryJNDIXA')
cmo.setConnectionFactoryJNDIName('jms.appcf')
cmo.setDestinationJNDIName('jms.appqueue')


cd('/')
cmo.createJMSBridgeDestination('BridgeSource_02')
cd('/JMSBridgeDestinations/BridgeSource_02')
cmo.setClasspath('')
cmo.setConnectionURL('t3://prodsrv02.domain.local:8002')
cmo.setAdapterJNDIName('eis.jms.WLSConnectionFactoryJNDIXA')
cmo.setConnectionFactoryJNDIName('jms.appcf')
cmo.setDestinationJNDIName('jms.appqueue')


cd('/')
cmo.createJMSBridgeDestination('BridgeSource_03')
cd('/JMSBridgeDestinations/BridgeSource_03')
cmo.setClasspath('')
cmo.setConnectionURL('t3://prodsrv03.domain.local:8003')
cmo.setAdapterJNDIName('eis.jms.WLSConnectionFactoryJNDIXA')
cmo.setConnectionFactoryJNDIName('jms.appcf')
cmo.setDestinationJNDIName('jms.appqueue')


cd('/')
cmo.createJMSBridgeDestination('BridgeSource_04')
cd('/JMSBridgeDestinations/BridgeSource_04')
cmo.setClasspath('')
cmo.setConnectionURL('t3://prodsrv04.domain.local:8004')
cmo.setAdapterJNDIName('eis.jms.WLSConnectionFactoryJNDIXA')
cmo.setConnectionFactoryJNDIName('jms.appcf')
cmo.setDestinationJNDIName('jms.appqueue')
```

4. Run the following WLST commands to create the bridge target:

```
cd('/')
cmo.createJMSBridgeDestination('BridgeTarget')
cd('/JMSBridgeDestinations/BridgeTarget')
cmo.setClasspath('')
cmo.setConnectionURL('t3://remote01.domain.local:9001,remote02.
domain.local:9002')
cmo.setAdapterJNDIName('eis.jms.WLSConnectionFactoryJNDIXA')
cmo.setConnectionFactoryJNDIName('jms.remoteappcf')
cmo.setDestinationJNDIName('jms.remotequeue')
```

5. Run the following WLST commands to create the bridges and associate the sources and the target:

```
cd('/')
cmo.createMessagingBridge('Bridge_01')
cd('/MessagingBridges/Bridge_01')
set('Targets',jarray.array([ObjectName('com.bea:Name=PROD_
Server01,Type=Server')], ObjectName))
cmo.setSourceDestination(getMBean('/JMSBridgeDestinations/
BridgeSource_01'))
cmo.setTargetDestination(getMBean('/JMSBridgeDestinations/
BridgeTarget'))
cmo.setStarted(true)
cmo.setSelector('')
cmo.setQualityOfService('Atmost-once')


cd('/')
cmo.createMessagingBridge('Bridge_02')
cd('/MessagingBridges/Bridge_02')
set('Targets',jarray.array([ObjectName('com.bea:Name=PROD_
Server02,Type=Server')], ObjectName))
cmo.setSourceDestination(getMBean('/JMSBridgeDestinations/
BridgeSource_02'))
cmo.setTargetDestination(getMBean('/JMSBridgeDestinations/
BridgeTarget'))
cmo.setStarted(true)
cmo.setSelector('')
cmo.setQualityOfService('Atmost-once')
```

```
cd('/')
cmo.createMessagingBridge('Bridge_03')
cd('/MessagingBridges/Bridge_03')
set('Targets',jarray.array([ObjectName('com.bea:Name=PROD_
Server03,Type=Server')], ObjectName))
cmo.setSourceDestination(getMBean('/JMSBridgeDestinations/
BridgeSource_03'))
cmo.setTargetDestination(getMBean('/JMSBridgeDestinations/
BridgeTarget'))
cmo.setStarted(true)
cmo.setSelector('')
cmo.setQualityOfService('Atmost-once')


cd('/')
cmo.createMessagingBridge('Bridge_04')
cd('/MessagingBridges/Bridge_04')
set('Targets',jarray.array([ObjectName('com.bea:Name=PROD_
Server04,Type=Server')], ObjectName))
cmo.setSourceDestination(getMBean('/JMSBridgeDestinations/
BridgeSource_04'))
cmo.setTargetDestination(getMBean('/JMSBridgeDestinations/
BridgeTarget'))
cmo.setStarted(true)
cmo.setSelector('')
cmo.setQualityOfService('Atmost-once')


activate()
exit()
```

See also

▶ *Creating the distributed queue destination and the connection factory*

▶ *Using the Server affinity to tune the distributed destinations load balance*

▶ *Relying on SAF to transfer JMS messages to another WebLogic domain*

Relying on SAF to transfer JMS messages to another WebLogic domain

Store-and-Forward (**SAF**) is another mechanism WebLogic provides to transfer messages from one source to a target destination.

The WebLogic messaging bridge and the SAF work in a similar way although the SAF is recommended over the messaging bridge when used to transfer messages between domains with WebLogic Version 9.0 or later. JMS SAF also simplifies the configuration since there is no need to configure a local JMS queue destination as the SAF creates a local representation of the remote queue.

In this recipe, a SAF agent will be created to forward the JMS messages to a hypothetic distributed queue with a JNDI name `jms.remotequeue`, hosted by a separate WebLogic domain `REMOTE_DOMAIN`. The `REMOTE_DOMAIN` domain is configured with a cluster with the two Managed Servers instances running at the `t3://remote01.domain.local:9001` and `t3://remote02.domain.local:9002` addresses. The local representation of the remote queue in the `PROD_DOMAIN` domain will be configured under the JNDI name `jms.remotequeue-saf`.

Getting ready

This recipe assumes the `REMOTE_DOMAIN` domain is up and running and the SAF agent can connect to the remote destinations. The configuration is changed by accessing the Administration Console, so make sure the Administration Server is running.

How to do it...

Create the SAF agents as follows:

1. Access the Administration Console with your web browser at `http://adminhost.domain.local:7001/console`.

2. Click on the **Lock & Edit** button to start a new edit session.

3. Click on the plus sign to open the **Services** tree on the left; click on **+ Messaging** and then on **Store-and-Forward Agents**.

4. Click on the **New** button to open the **Create a New Store-and-Forward Agent** page. Type `SAFAgent_01` in the **Name** field and select the `FileStore01` option in the **Persistent Store** drop-down menu. Change the **Agent Type** option to **Sending-only** and click on the **Next** button.

5. Select the `PROD_Server01` server as **Target**. Click on the **Finish** button.

6. Repeat the previous steps and create the SAFAgent_02, SAFAgent_03, and SAFAgent_04 agents. Use FileStore02, FileStore03, and FileStore04 as the values for the **Persistent Store** drop-down menu and PROD_Server02, PROD_Server03, and PROD_Server04 as the values for the **Target** drop-down menu.

7. Click on the **Activate Changes** button to finish.

Create the SAF resources as follows:

1. Access the Administration Console with your web browser at http://adminhost.domain.local:7001/console.

2. Click on the **Lock & Edit** button to start a new edit session.

3. Expand the **Services** tree on the left; click on **Messaging** and then on **JMS Modules**.

4. Click on the JMSAppModule link to open the **Configuration** page. Click on the **New** button and select the **Remote SAF Context** radio button and then click on the **Next** button.

5. Type RemoteSAFContextApp in the **Name** field and t3://remote01.domain.local:9001,remote02.domain.local:9002 in the **URL** field. Type in the username and password of an already registered user of REMOTE_DOMAIN in the fields **User Name**, **Password**, and **Confirm Password**. Click on the **OK** button.

6. Click on the **New** button again and select the **SAF Imported Destinations** radio button and click on **Next**.

7. Type SAFImportedDestinationsApp in the **Name** field, choose the RemoteSAFContextApp value from the **Remote SAF Context** drop-down menu, and click on the **Next** button.

8. Click on the **Next** button to confirm the target to **All servers in the cluster** of PROD_Cluster.

9. Click on the SAFImportedDestinationsApp value from the JMS resource list of the JMSAppModule module; then click on the **Queues** tab.

10. Click on the **New** button and type SAFRemoteQueue in the **Name** field. Type jms.remotequeue in the **Remote JNDI Name** field and click on the **OK** button.

11. Click on the created SAF queue, SAFRemoteQueue, and type jms.remotequeue-saf in the **Local JNDI Name** field. Click on the **Save** button.

12. Click on the **Activate Changes** button to finish.

How it works...

The SAF agent and SAF resources were configured in PROD_DOMAIN to forward messages to the jms.remotequeue queue hosted by the REMOTE_DOMAIN domain. The JNDI representation of the jms.remotequeue queue in the PROD_DOMAIN domain is jms.remotequeue-saf.

The SAF agent was configured to use the persistent stores FileStore01, FileStore02, FileStore03, and FileStore04 to persist the messages.

With this configuration, every message posted to the jms.remotequeue-saf agent from the PROD_DOMAIN domain is forwarded to the jms.remotequeue queue of the REMOTE_DOMAIN domain.

There's more...

The SAF agent and resources can be configured using WLST.

Configuring the SAF agents and SAF resources using WLST

This change can be made using WLST:

1. Log in as a wls user to the shell and start WLST.

    [wls@prod01] $ $WL_HOME/common/bin/wlst.sh

2. Connect to the Administration Server using wlsadmin as user, <pwd> as the password, and t3://adminhost.domain.local:7001 as the server URL.

    wls:/offline>connect("wlsadmin","<pwd>","t3://adminhost.domain.local:7001")

3. Create the SAF agents by running the following WLST commands:

    edit()

    startEdit()

    cd('/')

    cmo.createSAFAgent('SAFAgent_01')

    cd('/SAFAgents/SAFAgent_01')

    cmo.setStore(getMBean('/FileStores/FileStore01'))

    set('Targets',jarray.array([ObjectName('com.bea:Name=PROD_Server01,Type=Server')], ObjectName))

    cmo.setServiceType('Sending-only')

    cd('/')

```
cmo.createSAFAgent('SAFAgent_02')

cd('/SAFAgents/SAFAgent_02')

cmo.setStore(getMBean('/FileStores/FileStore02'))

set('Targets',jarray.array([ObjectName('com.bea:Name=PROD_
Server02,Type=Server')], ObjectName))

cmo.setServiceType('Sending-only')


cd('/')

cmo.createSAFAgent('SAFAgent_03')

cd('/SAFAgents/SAFAgent_03')

cmo.setStore(getMBean('/FileStores/FileStore03'))

set('Targets',jarray.array([ObjectName('com.bea:Name=PROD_
Server03,Type=Server')], ObjectName))

cmo.setServiceType('Sending-only')


cd('/')

cmo.createSAFAgent('SAFAgent_04')

cd('/SAFAgents/SAFAgent_04')

cmo.setStore(getMBean('/FileStores/FileStore04'))

set('Targets',jarray.array([ObjectName('com.bea:Name=PROD_
Server04,Type=Server')], ObjectName))

cmo.setServiceType('Sending-only')


activate()
```

4. Connect to the Administration Server using `wlsadmin` as user, `<pwd>` as the password, and `t3://adminhost.domain.local:7001` as the server URL.

```
edit()

startEdit()


cd('/JMSSystemResources/JMSAppModule/JMSResource/JMSAppModule')

cmo.createSAFRemoteContext('RemoteSAFContextApp')

cd('/JMSSystemResources/JMSAppModule/JMSResource/JMSAppModule/
SAFRemoteContexts/RemoteSAFContextApp/SAFLoginContext/
RemoteSAFContextApp')

cmo.setLoginURL('t3://remote01.domain.local:9001,remote02.domain.
local:9002')

cmo.setUsername('<remote username>')
```

```
cmo.setPassword('<remote password>')


cd('/JMSSystemResources/JMSAppModule/JMSResource/JMSAppModule')
cmo.createSAFImportedDestinations('SAFImportedDestinationsApp')


cd('/JMSSystemResources/JMSAppModule/JMSResource/JMSAppModule/
SAFImportedDestinations/SAFImportedDestinationsApp')
cmo.setJNDIPrefix(None)
cmo.setSAFRemoteContext(getMBean('/JMSSystemResources/
JMSAppModule/JMSResource/JMSAppModule/SAFRemoteContexts/
RemoteSAFContextApp'))
cmo.setSAFErrorHandling(None)
cmo.setTimeToLiveDefault(0)
cmo.setUseSAFTimeToLiveDefault(false)
cmo.setDefaultTargetingEnabled(true)


cmo.createSAFQueue('SAFRemoteQueue')
cd('/JMSSystemResources/JMSAppModule/JMSResource/JMSAppModule/
SAFImportedDestinations/SAFImportedDestinationsApp/SAFQueues/
SAFRemoteQueue')
cmo.setRemoteJNDIName('jms.remotequeue')


activate()
exit()
```

See also

▸ *Configuring messaging bridge with source and target distributed destinations*

5
Monitoring WebLogic Server 12c

In this chapter, we will cover the following recipes:

- ▶ Customizing the Administration Console tables
- ▶ Using the JRockit Mission Control Management Console
- ▶ Monitoring Linux with SAR
- ▶ Sending e-mail notifications with WLDF
- ▶ Generating an SMNP trap
- ▶ Creating a Monitoring Dashboard custom view
- ▶ Viewing historical data in the monitoring dashboard using a database

Introduction

Oracle WebLogic Server 12c provides some out of the box monitoring tools that will help maintain and support WebLogic production environments.

Although there are several other vendors offering WebLogic Server monitoring applications, it's important for a WebLogic Administrator to learn how to use the embedded tools provided, such as the Administration Console, the Monitoring Dashboard, and other common tools such as SAR, WLDF, and SNMP.

This chapter focuses on showing the system administrators how to use the tools and features to monitor WebLogic. It does not intend to provide the metrics and thresholds that should be used.

Customizing the Administration Console tables

The Administration Console is the central tool for managing, configuring, and monitoring WebLogic.

This recipe shows how to customize the Administration Console tables to display more columns and more information and data that are hidden by default. This is a simple but essential feature to help monitor the WebLogic Server.

Getting ready

Access the Administration Console. The following procedure customizes the threads' monitoring table of the Managed Server Self-Tuning's thread pool.

How to do it...

Carry out the following steps to customize the Administration Console tables:

1. Access the Administration Console with your web browser at `http://adminhost.domain.local:7001/console`.

2. Click on the plus sign to open the **Environment** tree on the left and then click on the **Servers** link.

3. Click on any server, such as the `PROD_Server01` link. Click on the **Monitoring** tab and then on the **Threads** tab to open the **Threads** page.

4. Click on the second **Customize this table** link of the `Self-Tuning Thread Pool Threads` table.

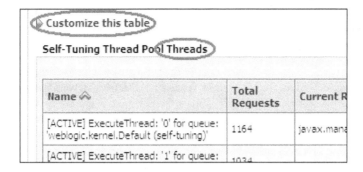

5. Click on the **>>** button to add the columns **Application**, **Module**, and **Work Manager**. Change the **Number of rows displayed per page** value to **1000**. Click on the **Apply** button.

How it works...

The Administration Console allows the user to customize and add more columns to the monitoring tables. In this recipe, the **Application**, **Module**, and **Work Manager** columns are added to the Self-Tuning Thread Pool Threads table.

The added columns are very useful to monitor the application requests being processed. The following table displays thread 0 processing a request of the testWeb application and thread 1 processing a request of the myApp application.

Name ⌃	...by	Application	Module	Work Manager
[ACTIVE] ExecuteThread: '0' for queue: 'weblogic.kernel.Default (self-tuning)'		testWeb	testWeb.war	default
[ACTIVE] ExecuteThread: '1' for queue: 'weblogic.kernel.Default (self-tuning)'		myApp	myApp.war	default
[ACTIVE] ExecuteThread: '3' for queue: 'weblogic.kernel.Default (self-tuning)'		testWeb	testWeb.war	default

Customizing the Administration Console monitoring tables is a common task and can be applied in a variety of tables, such as the data sources, the JMS queues, and transactions.

Using the JRockit Mission Control Management Console

Mission Control is a monitoring and troubleshooting application provided with Oracle JRockit.

From a monitoring point of view, Mission Control provides a Management Console to monitor the garbage-collection behavior, processor utilization by the JVM, memory allocation, thread utilization, and some other useful monitoring metrics.

Mission Control is a standalone application, so it must be started either locally from the same machine that WebLogic is running on or from a remote workstation.

 If you run Mission Control locally on the Linux server prod01, an **X** window must be available.

This recipe will run Mission Control in a Microsoft Windows desktop and will remotely connect and monitor the PROD_Server01 Managed Server.

Getting ready

Oracle JRockit must be downloaded and installed in the Windows desktop. Download Oracle JRockit 6 for Microsoft Windows at `http://www.oracle.com/technetwork/middleware/jrockit/downloads`. The filename is `jrockit-jdk1.6.0_XXX-windows-iaYY.exe`, where `XXX` stands for the JRockit release and JDK version and `YY` stands for 32 bits or 64 bits. Choose the version that matches your desktop and accept the license agreement to download it.

How to do it...

Enable the `PROD_Server01` Managed Server to accept JMX connections from Mission Control:

1. Access the Administration Console with your web browser at `http://adminhost.domain.local:7001/console`.

2. Click on the **Lock & Edit** button to start a new edit session.

3. Click on the plus sign to open the **Environment** tree on the left and then click **Servers**.

4. Click on the `PROD_Server01` link and then click the **Server Start** tab.

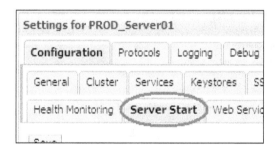

5. Add the following to the **Arguments** field and click on the **Save** button:

   ```
   -Xmanagement:autodiscovery=false,authenticate=false,ssl=fa
   lse,interface=prodsrv01.domain.local,port=8081 -Djava.rmi.
   server.hostname=prodsrv01.domain.local -Djavax.management.
   builder.initial=weblogic.management.jmx.mbeanserver.
   WLSMBeanServerBuilder
   ```

6. Click on the **Activate Changes** button.

7. Restart `PROD_Server01`.

Start Mission Control on the desktop, as follows:

1. Start Mission Control by double-clicking on the **Oracle JRockit Mission Control** icon.

2. On the **JVM Browser** panel to the left, right-click on the `Connectors` folder and click on the **New Connection** option.

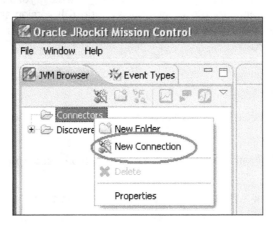

3. Type `prodsrv01.domain.local` in the **Host** field and `8081` in the **Port** field and click on the **Finish** button.

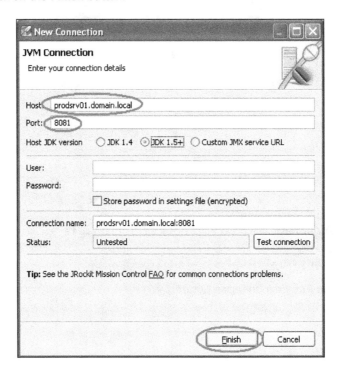

4. Right-click on the newly created connection, `prodsrv01.domain.local:8081`, and click on the **Start Console** menu option.

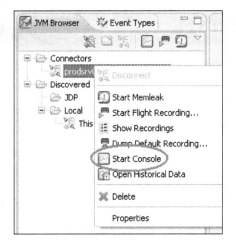

How it works...

Mission Control connects to the specified host and port defined in the `Xmanagement` start-up argument and starts monitoring the `PROD_Server01` JVM.

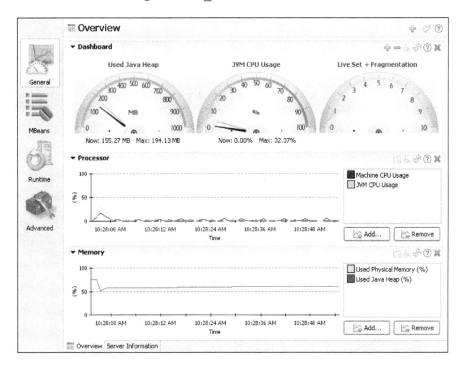

Add the start-up arguments to monitor the other WebLogic instances. Mission Control can connect to any running JRockit JVM.

Monitoring Linux with SAR

A Linux host with Red Hat Enterprise Linux or Oracle Linux can be monitored using the SAR command-line utility. The SAR is included in the SYSSTAT package bundle and is usually included with these Linux distributions.

SAR retrieves activity counters of the operational system, such as CPU, memory, disk, and network I/O usage. By default, it keeps a history of seven days, so it is a very useful tool to retrieve past reports and quickly search for behavioral patterns.

This recipe will retrieve some statistics from the `prod01` machine using the SAR command-line utility.

Getting ready

SAR should already be installed in a Red Hat or Oracle Linux distribution. If it is not installed, you can use the `yum` package management utility to install the SYSSTAT package, which includes SAR.

As root user, execute the `yum` command and follow the onscreen instructions to install SYSSTAT:

```
[root@prod01]$ yum install sysstat
```

 All SAR commands are executed from the Linux shell. Log in to the host first. The root user is used only to install the SYSSTAT package.

How to do it...

To retrieve the queue length and load averages from the current day, as a `wls` user execute the following command:

```
[wls@prod01]$ sar -q
```

This will display the following result:

```
08:20:01 AM   runq-sz   plist-sz   ldavg-1   ldavg-5   ldavg-15
08:30:01 AM         4       1896      0.31      0.93       0.91
08:40:01 AM         3       1903      0.10      0.35       0.61
08:50:01 AM         5       1908      0.70      1.02       0.91
09:00:01 AM         9       1920      0.14      0.32       0.60
09:10:01 AM         4       1900      0.89      0.58       0.61
09:20:01 AM         4       1902      0.49      0.95       0.97
09:30:01 AM        10       1931      0.18      0.47       0.74
09:40:01 AM         4       1900      1.66      1.51       1.13
09:50:01 AM         5       1907      0.82      0.79       0.91
10:00:01 AM        10       1914      1.25      1.02       0.97
10:10:01 AM         5       1901      1.00      1.84       1.59
```

To retrieve a past CPU usage from the 21st day of the month, as a `wls` user execute the following command:

```
[wls@prod01]$ sar -u -f /var/log/sa/sa21
```

This will display the following result:

```
08:20:01 AM   CPU   %user   %nice   %system   %iowait   %steal   %idle
08:30:01 AM   all    1.77    1.37      0.26      0.31     0.00   96.29
08:40:01 AM   all    2.39    1.37      0.29      0.37     0.00   95.58
08:50:01 AM   all    1.78    1.36      0.27      0.29     0.00   96.30
09:00:01 AM   all    1.88    1.36      0.26      0.28     0.00   96.21
09:10:01 AM   all    2.87    1.37      0.31      1.01     0.00   94.44
09:20:01 AM   all    2.42    1.37      0.29      0.30     0.00   95.63
09:30:01 AM   all    2.17    1.36      0.27      0.50     0.00   95.70
09:40:01 AM   all    2.38    1.36      0.30      0.37     0.00   95.59
09:50:01 AM   all    2.53    1.37      0.32      0.35     0.00   95.44
10:00:01 AM   all    2.83    1.37      0.31      0.43     0.00   95.06
10:10:01 AM   all    2.71    1.37      0.34      0.60     0.00   94.98
```

 The default SAR configuration keeps historical data for a week.

How it works...

The SAR utility is very flexible and provides a quick way to watch the host behavior for the current day and for the past seven days. SAR runs every 10 minutes and saves a summary at the end of the day.

These are the default values in the crontab and can be adjusted.

There's more...

Apart from the options discussed earlier, we can view more fine-grained data as well.

Collecting SAR data every minute

SAR can store statistical data in a more fine-grained time interval.

Log in as a `root` user to the shell and execute the following command:

```
[root@prod01]$ vi /etc/cron.d/sysstat
```

Locate the following lines:

```
# run system activity accounting tool every 10 minutes
*/10 * * * * root /usr/lib64/sa/sa1 1 1
```

Change these lines to the following:

```
# run system activity accounting tool every 1 minute
*/1 * * * * root /usr/lib64/sa/sa1 1 1
```

Type `:wq!` to save and close the file.

Sending e-mail notifications with WLDF

The **WebLogic Diagnostic Framework** (**WLDF**) is a set of functionalities to monitor, collect, and analyze runtime counters, metrics, and statistical and diagnostic data from various WebLogic Server components. The metrics can be gathered from the JRockit JVM, the WebLogic domain, the WebLogic clusters, Managed Servers, applications, and every component that exposes data through MBeans.

WebLogic Administrators can include active monitoring in production environments with WLDF. It is possible to configure WebLogic to send e-mail alerts when certain conditions and metrics are reached.

In this recipe, the WebLogic domain will be configured to send e-mail alerts when the WebLogic thread pool from a Managed Server has queued requests waiting to be processed.

Getting ready

A mail session called `EmailAlertMailSession` and a diagnostic module named `EmailAlertModule` will be created using the Administration Console, so make sure the Administration Server is running.

How to do it...

Follow these steps to create the `EmailAlertMailSession` mail session:

1. Access the Administration Console with your web browser at `http://adminhost.domain.local:7001/console`.

2. Click on the **Lock & Edit** button to start a new edit session.

3. Click on the plus sign to open the **Services** tree on the left and then click on **Mail Sessions**.

4. Click on the **New** button and type `EmailAlertMailSession` in the **Name** field. Type `mail/emailAlertMailSession` in the **JNDI Name** field.

5. Add to **JavaMail** the properties needed according to the SMTP Server used:

   `mail.smtp.host=<smtp-host>`

   `mail.smtp.port=<smtp-port>`

6. Click on the **Next** button and select the **All servers in the cluster** target. Click on the **Finish** button.

7. Click on the **Activate Changes** button to finish.

Follow these steps to create the `EmailAlertModule` WLDF module:

1. Access the Administration Console with your web browser at `http://adminhost.domain.local:7001/console`.

2. Click on the **Lock & Edit** button to start a new edit session.

3. Click on the plus sign to open the **Diagnostics** tree on the left and then click on **Diagnostic Modules**.

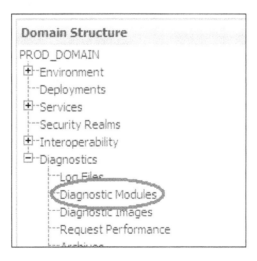

4. In the **Summary of Diagnostic Modules** page, click on the **New** button.

5. Type EmailAlertModule in the **Name** field and click on the **OK** button.

6. Click on the newly created EmailAlertModule WLDF module and then on the **Targets** tab. Select the **All servers in the cluster** radio button and click on the **Save** button.

7. Click on the **Configuration** tab and then the **Collected Metrics** tab. Change the **Sampling Period** value to 60000 and click on the **Save** Button.

8. Click on the **New** button in the **Collected Metrics in this Module** table to create a new Harvester.

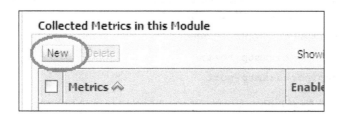

9. Choose ServerRuntime from the **MBean Server location** drop-down menu and click on the **Next** button.

10. Select weblogic.management.runtime.ThreadPoolRuntimeMBean from the **MBean Type** drop-down menu and click on the **Next** button.

11. Select the **QueueLength** item from the Collected Attributes table on the left and click on the **>** icon to move it to the **Chosen** table on the right. Click on the **Next** button.

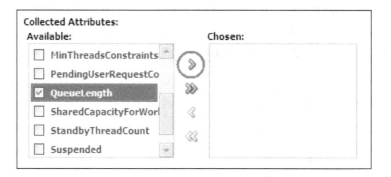

12. In the **Select Instances** page, leave the **Chosen Collected Instances** and **Instance Expressions** textboxes empty and then click on the **Finish** button.

Follow these steps to create the watches and notifications for the WLDF module:

1. Click on the **Watches and Notifications** tab and then on the **Notifications** tab below. Click on the **New** button to create a new notification.

2. Select the **SMTP (E-Mail)** option in the **Type** drop-down menu and click on the **Next** button.

3. Type `EmailAlertNotification` in the **Notification Name** field and click on the **Next** button.

4. Select the `EmailAlertMailSession` option from the **Mail Session Name** drop-down menu. Type an e-mail address in the **E-Mail Recipients** textbox and click on the **Finish** button. This e-mail address will receive the alerts.

5. Now click on the **Watches** tab and click on the **New** button to create a new watch.

6. Type `EmailAlertWatch` in the **Watch Name** field. Leave the **Collected Metrics** option selected in the **Watch Type** field and click on the **Next** button.

7. Click on the **Add Expressions** button to add a new expression rule.

8. Select the `ServerRuntime` option from the **MBean Server location** drop-down menu and then click on the **Next** button.

9. Select `weblogic.management.runtime.ThreadPoolRuntimeMBean` from the **MBean Type** drop-down menu and click on the **Next** button.

10. Select the **Enter a custom instance** radio button and type `com.bea:Name=Thread PoolRuntime,ServerRuntime=PROD_Server*Type=ThreadPoolRuntime` in the **Custom Instance** field. Click on the **Next** button.

11. Select the `QueueLength` option from the **Message Attribute** drop-down menu and select the **>** option from the **Operator** drop-down menu and type `100` in the **Value** field. Click on the **Finish** button.

12. On the following screen, click on the **Finish** button again.

13. Click on the **EmailAlertWatch** to assign the notification. Click the **Notifications** tab.

14. Select **EmailAlertNotification** from the **Available** table to the left and click on the **>** icon to move it to the **Chosen** table to the right. Click on the **Save** button.

15. Click on the **Activate Changes** button to finish.

How it works...

WLDF is a very powerful framework and helps WebLogic Administrators to properly monitor a WebLogic domain.

The diagnostic module was created with a WLDF Harvester for the `QueueLength` attribute of the `ThreadPoolRuntimeBean` MBean and a sampling period of `60000`. The sampling period is the interval between metric-collection cycles, in milliseconds. The data collected by the harvester is stored in a WLDF archive.

The default archive is stored in a file-based format at `$DOMAIN_HOME/servers/<serverName>/data/store/diagnostics`.

The WLDF archive can use a JDBC-based store to persist the collected data.

The scenario of 100 queued requests waiting to be processed can indicate a potential problem because all threads of the WebLogic Server thread pool could be busy and the requests will not be processed fast enough, causing the incoming requests to pile up. The `EmailAlertWatch` watch was created for such situations to observe when the `QueueLength` value is greater than `100`. When this condition is reached, the watch triggers an event to the `EmailAlertNotification` notification and an e-mail is sent to the specified recipients.

The notification can also be configured as an SNMP trap, a JMS message, a JMX operation, or a Diagnostic Image.

The WLDF is very flexible and can be configured with any attribute of the exposed MBean. Set up a watch expression that meets the condition and the monitoring requirements of your environment.

See also

▸ *Generating a SNMP trap*
▸ *Viewing historical data in the monitoring dashboard using a database*

Generating an SNMP trap

WebLogic provides **Simple Network Management Protocol** (**SNMP**) standards to monitor the domain, Managed Servers, and applications the same way the exposed MBean's attributes were monitored in the last recipe using WLDF.

In this recipe, an SNMP agent will be added to monitor all Managed Servers of the `PROD_Domain`, watching for the same `QueueLength` attribute of the `ThreadPoolRuntime` MBean.

An SNMP trap will be triggered by adding a gauge monitor to verify if the `QueueLength` value is above `100`.

Getting ready

The Server SNMP agent called `PROD_SNMPAgent` will be created using the Administration Console, so make sure the Administration Server is running.

This recipe assumes there is an SNMP Manager listening for an SNMP trap at the hostname `snmphost` on port 162.

How to do it...

Follow these steps to create the Server SNMP Agent:

1. Access the Administration Console with your web browser at `http://adminhost.domain.local:7001/console`.

2. Click on the **Lock & Edit** button to start a new edit session.

3. Click on the plus sign to open the **Diagnostics** tree on the left and then click on **SNMP**.

4. Click on the **New** button from the Server SNMP Agent. Type `PROD_SNMPAgent` in the **Name** field and click on the **OK** button.

5. Click on the newly created SNMP Agent, `PROD_SNMPAgent`.

6. Click on the **Enabled** checkbox to enable it. Type `1610` in the **SNMP UDP Port** field and `7050` in the **Master AgentX Port** field. Click on the **Save** button.

7. Click on the **Targets** tab and select the **All servers in the cluster** option from the `PROD_Cluster` target. Click on the **Save** button.

Follow these steps to create the gauge monitor and the SNMP trap:

1. Click on the **Configuration** tab and then on the **Gauge Monitors** tab. Click on the **New** button to create a new SNMP Gauge Monitor.

2. Type `QueueLengthGauge` in the **Name** field. Select the **ThreadPoolRuntime** option from the **Monitored MBean Type** drop-down menu. Click on the **Next** button.

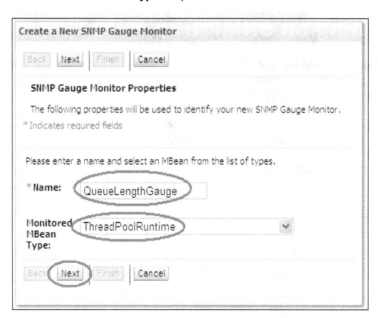

3. Select the **QueueLength** option from the **Monitored Attribute Name** drop-down menu and click on the **Finish** button.

4. Click on the newly created `QueueLengthGauge` gauge and type `100` in the **Threshold High** field. Click on the **Save** button.

5. Click on the **Servers** tab and enable the `PROD_Server01`, `PROD_Server02`, `PROD_Server03`, and `PROD_Server04` checkboxes. Click on the **Save** button.

6. Go to **Diagnostics | SNMP** on the left tree again and click on the `PROD_SNMPAgent` link.

7. Click on the **Trap Destinations** tab and click on the **New** button.

8. Type `QueueLengthTrap` in the **Name** field. Type `snmphost` in the **Host** field and `162` in the **Port** field. Click on the **OK** button.

9. Click on the **Activate Changes** button to finish.

How it works...

The same notification from the previous recipe was created, but in this recipe instead of sending an e-mail alert using WLDF, a SNMP trap is generated to a hypothetical SNMP Manager running at `snmphost` on port `162`.

The threshold condition is the same. The SNMP trap is sent when the `QueueLength` attribute from the WebLogic thread pool from a Managed Server of the `PROD_Cluster` value is above `100`.

The trap generated has the following format:

```
--- Snmp Trap Received ---
    Version         : v1
    Source          : UdpEntity:<source_ip>:1610
    Community       : public
    Enterprise      : enterprises.140.625
    AgentAddr       : <source_ip>
    TrapOID         : enterprises.140.625.0.75
    RawTrapOID      : 1.3.6.1.4.1.140.625.0.75
    Trap Objects    : {
    { enterprises.140.625.100.5=Sun Nov 11 15:50:55 BRST 2012 }
    { enterprises.140.625.100.10=PROD_Server02 }
    { enterprises.140.625.100.55=jmx.monitor.gauge.high }
    { enterprises.140.625.100.60=100 }
    { enterprises.140.625.100.65=435 }
    { enterprises.140.625.100.70=com.bea:Name=ThreadPoolRuntime,Server
Runtime=PROD_Server02,Type=ThreadPoolRuntime }
    { enterprises.140.625.100.75=ThreadPoolRuntime }
    { enterprises.140.625.100.80=QueueLength }
}
```

The previous SNMP trap example was triggered from `PROD_Server02` and the `QueueLength` attribute was `435` at the time.

There's more...

Now we will see how to create an SNMP agent through WLST.

Creating the SNMP Agent by using WLST

1. Log in as a `wls` user to the shell and start WLST.

   [wls@prod01]$ $WL_HOME/common/bin/wlst.sh

2. Connect to the Administration Server using `wlsadmin` as user, `<pwd>` as the password, and `t3://adminhost.domain.local:7001` as the server URL.

   wls:/offline> connect("wlsadmin","<pwd>","t3://adminhost.domain. local:7001")

3. Run the following WLST commands:

   ```
   edit()
   startEdit()
   cmo.createSNMPAgentDeployment('PROD_SNMPAgent')
   cd('/SNMPAgentDeployments/PROD_SNMPAgent')
   cmo.setMasterAgentXPort(7050)
   cmo.setEnabled(true)
   cmo.setSNMPPort(1610)
   cmo.setPrivacyProtocol('NoPriv')
   cmo.createSNMPGaugeMonitor('QueueLengthGauge')
   cd('/SNMPAgentDeployments/PROD_SNMPAgent/SNMPGaugeMonitors/
   QueueLengthGauge')
   cmo.setMonitoredMBeanType('ThreadPoolRuntime')
   cmo.setMonitoredAttributeName('QueueLength')
   set('EnabledServers',jarray.array([ObjectName('com.bea:Name=PROD_
   Server01,Type=Server'), ObjectName('com.bea:Name=PROD_
   Server02,Type=Server'), ObjectName('com.bea:Name=PROD_
   Server03,Type=Server'), ObjectName('com.bea:Name=PROD_
   Server04,Type=Server')], ObjectName))
   cmo.setThresholdHigh(100)
   cmo.setMonitoredMBeanName('(None)')
   cmo.setMonitoredMBeanName('')
   ```

```
cd('/SNMPAgentDeployments/PROD_SNMPAgent')

set('Targets',jarray.array([ObjectName('com.bea:Name=PROD_
Cluster,Type=Cluster')], ObjectName))

cmo.createSNMPTrapDestination('QueueLengthTrap')

cd('/SNMPAgentDeployments/PROD_SNMPAgent/SNMPTrapDestinations/
QueueLengthTrap')

cmo.setPort(16200)

cmo.setSecurityLevel('noAuthNoPriv')

activate()

exit()
```

See also

> ▸ *Sending e-mail notifications with WLDF*

Creating a Monitoring Dashboard custom view

The Monitoring Dashboard is embedded with the Oracle WebLogic Server 12c. The dashboard is an application deployed in the Administration Server and is accessible at the URL `http://adminhost.domain.local:7001/console/dashboard`.

The Monitoring Dashboard can graphically display the metrics collected from the WLDF and exposed by the MBeans.

In this recipe, a Dashboard custom view will be created to display the `Queue Length` attribute from the `ThreadPoolRuntime` MBean of the `PROD_Server01` Managed Server. This is the same attribute monitored in the previous recipes.

Getting ready

The Monitoring Dashboard is a functionality of the Administration Console. Make sure the Administration Server is running.

How to do it...

Carry out the following steps to create a custom view:

1. Access the Monitoring Dashboard with your web browser at `http://adminhost.domain.local:7001/console/dashboard`.

2. From the **View List** tab, click on **My Views** and then on the down arrow to display the drop-down menu. Click on the **New View** menu option.

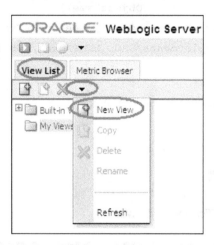

3. Type QueueLengthView to set the **View** name.

4. Click on the arrow down on the chart of the display pane to the right. Click on **New Chart**.

5. Click on the **Metric Browser** tab, select the PROD_Server01 option from the **Servers** drop-down menu, and click on the **GO** button.

6. Click on the ThreadPool item from the **Types** selection list and then on the ThreadPoolRuntime from the **Instances** selection list. Click on the QueueLength (int) option and drag it to the QueueLengthView chart on the right display panel.

7. Click on the green start button on the left to start collecting.

How it works...

A custom view was created with a new chart to display the `QueueLength` counter metrics. The `QueueLength` attribute is collected directly from the exposed `ThreadPoolRuntime` MBean.

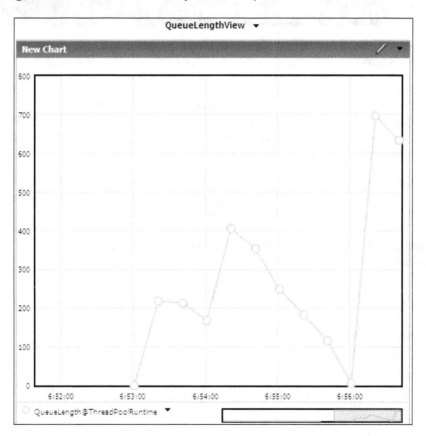

Other charts can be created and any other exposed runtime MBean attribute can be added. The QueueLength attribute from the other Managed Servers of the PROD_Cluster cluster can also be added to the same chart.

 The chart polls for the online and real-time statistics, keeping by default 100 samples of 20 second intervals each, giving about 30 minutes of time range.

See also

▸ *View Historical Data in the Monitoring Dashboard using a Database*

Viewing historical data in the monitoring dashboard using a database

In the previous recipe, a Dashboard custom view was created to display the QueueLength attribute of the ThreadPoolRuntime MBean of the Managed Servers of the PROD_Cluster cluster.

The Dashboard can collect the data from two sources. One is from the exposed MBeans, displaying polled runtime statistics like the previous recipe. The other form is from the WLDF archive data collected from a WLDF harverster. This stored data is called **collected metrics** by the Monitoring Dashboard.

In this recipe, the PROD_Server01, PROD_Server02, PROD_Server03, and PROD_Server04 WLDF archives will be configured to use a database instead of the default file-based archive to hold the data collected from a WLDF Harvester. A new custom view will be created to display this data and it will be able to display all the collected historical data instead of the default 30 minutes collected from the polled collector. The QueueLength attribute will be used.

The database is an Oracle database, running in the dbhost hostname and listening to the port 1521. The listener is accepting requests to the service named dbservice.

Getting ready

The recipe will use the database dbhost, so create a new JDBC data source named ds-wldf-archive, with a JNDI name jdbc/ds-wldf-archive targeted to the PROD_Cluster cluster.

The database tables WLS_EVENTS and WLS_HVST have to be created. WebLogic uses these tables to store the WLDF archive data.

The Monitoring Dashboard is a functionality of the Administration Console. Make sure the Administration Server is running.

How to do it...

Follow these steps to create tables in the Oracle `dbhost` database:

1. Connect to the database at `dbhost`, port `1521`, and service name `dbservice`.

2. Run the following SQL script:

```
DROP TABLE WLS_EVENTS;
CREATE TABLE WLS_EVENTS (
    RECORDID number NOT NULL,
    TIMESTAMP number default NULL,
    CONTEXTID varchar2(128) default NULL,
    TXID varchar2(32) default NULL,
    USERID varchar2(32) default NULL,
    TYPE varchar2(64) default NULL,
    DOMAIN varchar2(64) default NULL,
    SERVER varchar2(64) default NULL,
    SCOPE varchar2(64) default NULL,
    MODULE varchar2(64) default NULL,
    MONITOR varchar2(64) default NULL,
    FILENAME varchar2(64) default NULL,
    LINENUM number default NULL,
    CLASSNAME varchar2(250) default NULL,
    METHODNAME varchar2(64) default NULL,
    METHODDSC varchar2(4000) default NULL,
    ARGUMENTS clob default NULL,
    RETVAL varchar2(4000) default NULL,
    PAYLOAD blob default NULL,
    CTXPAYLOAD varchar2(4000),
    DYES timestamp default NULL,
    THREADNAME varchar2(128) default NULL
);
DROP TABLE WLS_HVST;
CREATE TABLE WLS_HVST (
    RECORDID number NOT NULL,
    TIMESTAMP number default NULL,
    DOMAIN varchar2(64) default NULL,
    SERVER varchar2(64) default NULL,
    TYPE varchar2(64) default NULL,
    NAME varchar2(250) default NULL,
    ATTRNAME varchar2(64) default NULL,
```

```
    ATTRTYPE number default NULL,
    ATTRVALUE varchar2(4000)
);

DROP SEQUENCE MON_EVENTS;
CREATE SEQUENCE MON_EVENTS
    START WITH 1
    INCREMENT BY 1
    NOMAXVALUE;

DROP TRIGGER TRIG_EVENTS;
CREATE TRIGGER TRIG_EVENTS
    BEFORE INSERT ON WLS_EVENTS
    FOR EACH ROW
    BEGIN
    SELECT MON_EVENTS.NEXTVAL INTO :NEW.RECORDID FROM DUAL;
    END;
/

DROP SEQUENCE MON_HVST;
CREATE SEQUENCE MON_HVST
    START WITH 1
    INCREMENT BY 1
    NOMAXVALUE;

DROP TRIGGER TRIG_HVST;
CREATE TRIGGER TRIG_HVST
    BEFORE INSERT ON WLS_HVST
    FOR EACH ROW
    BEGIN
    SELECT MON_HVST.NEXTVAL INTO :NEW.RECORDID FROM DUAL;
    END;
/
```

Follow these steps to create the JDBC data source:

1. Access the Administration Console with your web browser at `http://adminhost.domain.local:7001/console`.

2. Click on the **Lock & Edit** button to start a new edit session.

3. Click on the plus sign to open the **Services** tree on the left and then click **Data Sources**.

4. Click on the **New** button and click on **Generic Data Source**.

5. Type `ds-wldf-archive` in the **Name** field and `jdbc/ds-wldf-archive` in the **JNDI Name**. Leave the **Database Type** drop-down menu with the `Oracle` option selected. Click on the **Next** button.

6. Choose `*Oracle's Driver (Thin) for Service connections; Versions:9.0.1 and later` from the **Database Driver** drop-down menu. Click on the **Next** button.

7. Leave the **Transaction** options with the default values and click on the **Next** button.

8. In the **Connection Properties** page, type `dbservice` in the **Database Name** field, `dbhost` in the **Host Name** field, and `1521` in the **Port** field. Complete the **Database User Name, Password**, and **Confirm Password** fields with `dbuser` and `dbpwd`. Click on the **Next** button.

9. Click on the **Next** button in the **Test Database Connection** page.

10. Click on each Managed Server checkbox of the `PROD_Cluster` cluster. Don't click on the **All servers in the cluster** radio button. Click on the **Finish** button.

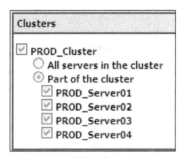

11. Click on the **Activate Changes** button to finish.

Follow these steps to configure the WLDF archive to store the data to a JDBC based store:

1. Access the Administration Console with your web browser at `http://adminhost.domain.local:7001/console`.

2. Click on the **Lock & Edit** button to start a new edit session.

3. Click on the plus sign to open the **Diagnostics** tree on the left and then click on **Archive**.

4. Click on the `PROD_Server01` Managed Server.

5. Select the `JDBC` option from the **Type** drop-down menu. Select the `ds-wldf-archive` option from the **Data Source** drop-down menu. Click on the **Save** button.

6. Repeat the previous steps for the `PROD_Server02`, `PROD_Server03`, and `PROD_Server04` Managed Servers.

7. Click on the **Activate Changes** button.

Follow these steps to create a new WLDF module and a new WLDF Harvester:

1. Access the Administration Console with your web browser at `http://adminhost.domain.local:7001/console`.

2. Click on the **Lock & Edit** button to start a new edit session.

3. Click on the plus sign to open the **Diagnostics** tree on the left and then click on **Diagnostic Modules**.

4. In the **Summary of Diagnostic Modules** page, click on the **New** button.

5. Type `QueueLengthModule` in the **Name** field and click on the **OK** button.

6. Click on the newly created `QueueLengthModule` module and click on the **Targets** tab. Select the **All servers in the cluster** radio button and click on the **Save** button.

7. Click on the **Configuration** tab and then the **Collected Metrics** tab. Change the **Sampling Period** to `60000` and click on the **Save** Button.

8. Click on the **New** button in the `Collected Metrics in this Module` table to create a new WLDF harvester.

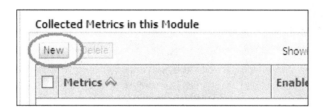

9. Choose `ServerRuntime` from the **MBean Server location** drop-down menu and click on the **Next** button.

10. Select `weblogic.management.runtime.ThreadPoolRuntimeMBean` from the **MBean Type** drop-down menu and click on the **Next** button.

11. Select the `QueueLength` item from the `Collected Attributes` table on the left and click the **>** icon to move it to the **Chosen** table on the right. Click on the **Finish** button.

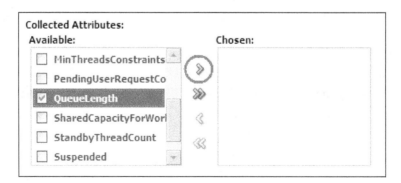

12. Click on the **Activate Changes** button and restart all Managed Servers.

Follow these steps to create a new custom view in the Monitoring Dashboard:

1. Access the Monitoring Dashboard with your web browser at `http://adminhost.domain.local:7001/console/dashboard`.

2. From the **View List** tab, click on **My Views** and then click on the down arrow to display the drop-down menu. Click on the **New View** menu option.

3. Type in `QueueLengthCollectedView` to set the **View** name.

4. Click on the down arrow on the chart of the display pane to the right. Click on **New Chart**.

5. Click on the **Metric Browser** tab and then enable the **Collected Metrics Only** checkbox. Select the `PROD_Server01` option from the **Servers** drop-down menu and click on the **OK** button.

6. Click on the **ThreadPool** item from the **Types** selection list and then click on **ThreadPoolRuntime** from the **Instances** selection list. Click on the `QueueLength (int)` option and drag it to the `QueueLengthCollectView` chart on to the display panel to the right.

7. Repeat steps 5 and 6 and add the metrics from the `PROD_Server02`, `PROD_Server03`, and `PROD_Server04` Managed Servers.

How it works...

A custom view was created with a new chart to display the `QueueLength` counter metrics of the WLDF archive stored in the database.

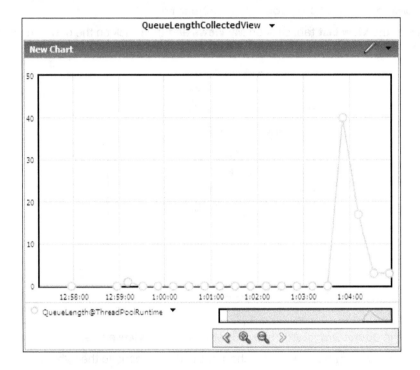

This chart can be used to display historical data and uses the time range stored in the database's WLDF archive. This is an important tool to understand the Managed Servers' behavioral data and past events in production environments.

See also

- ▸ *Sending e-mail notifications with WLDF*
- ▸ *Creating a Monitoring Dashboard custom view*

6
Troubleshooting WebLogic Server 12c

In this chapter, we will cover the following recipes:

- ▶ Changing log levels to debug
- ▶ Including the time taken field in access.log
- ▶ Enabling verbose garbage collection logging
- ▶ Taking thread dumps
- ▶ Enabling the JRockit Mission Control Flight Recorder
- ▶ Analyzing a heap dump
- ▶ Recovering the WebLogic admin password
- ▶ Recovering the data source password

Introduction

Problems in the WebLogic environment can be exemplified as application errors, a JVM crash, when the application hangs and stops responding or when the client starts to feel the application is responding slower than usual.

All these examples are common problems in a production environment and they are usually solved by simply bouncing/restarting the affected Managed Server.

If the same problem becomes more and more frequent, a troubleshooting process must be started. Troubleshooting is the analysis process to solve a specific problem.

The purpose of all troubleshooting processes is to find the source and root cause of the problem. The source of a problem can reside either in the application code or on the host machine, or the issue may only occur because of a bad WebLogic configuration or a network issue. The problem can also occur because of a WebLogic bug. A product bug must always be considered in software of this size and complexity.

A correct WebLogic analysis and diagnosis of the troubleshooting process is not an easy task. It is complex, complicated, and involves a deep knowledge of WebLogic core mechanisms and Java architecture. Incorrect diagnoses can lead to an imprecise root cause that in turn will generate wasted efforts in both development and infrastructure.

 What is the problem? is the question to be answered. If not answered properly, it will lead to an endless loop of workarounds, tunings, and fixes that will probably make things worse.

This chapter provides some recipes and steps to help the WebLogic troubleshooting process in production environments.

Changing log levels to debug

The level of logged information is essential during a troubleshooting analysis. Any additional log can give a hint that will help reveal the root cause of the problem in a production environment.

This recipe shows a hypothetical scenario to diagnose transaction problems. The log level setting of the `PROD_Server01` Managed Server will be changed to add more debugging information.

Getting ready

The log levels will be changed using the Administration Console, so make sure the Administration Server is running.

How to do it...

Carry out the following steps to change the log level for debugging:

1. Access the Administration Console by pointing your web browser to `http://adminhost.domain.local:7001/console`.

2. Click on the **Lock & Edit** button to start a new edit session.

3. Expand the **Environment** tree on the left, and then click on the **Servers** link.

4. Click on the `PROD_Server01` Managed Server link and then click on the **Logging** tab.

5. Click on the **Advanced** link to open the advanced options.

6. Change the **Minimum severity to log** drop-down menu to **Trace**.

7. Change the **Severity Level** value for the **Log file** value to **Trace**.

8. Change the **Severity Level** for the **Standard out** value to **Debug**.

9. Type -1 in the **stdout Stack Trace Depth** field.

10. Click on the **Save** button.

11. Click on the **Debug** tab.

12. Click on the **[+]** sign in the **weblogic** scope.

13. Check the **transaction** checkbox and click on the **Enable** button:

14. Finally, click on the **Activate Changes** button.

How it works...

Changing the log levels to display more information is the first common and useful task WebLogic administrators should set in production environments.

The `PROD_Server01` logfiles are located by default at `$DOMAIN_HOME/servers/PROD_Server01/logs/PROD_Server01.log` and `$DOMAIN_HOME/servers/PROD_Server01/logs/PROD_Server01.out`.

This recipe raises the level of logging and enables only the transaction debug. WebLogic has several other debug options that can be enabled, such as security, protocol, JMS, and deploy among others. Enable the option that best suits your troubleshooting needs.

 Debug and trace logging will write a lot of information to the output log, so do not forget to disable it at the analysis end.

There's more...

The log levels can also be changed using WLST.

Changing the log levels using WLST

1. Log in as a `wls` user to shell and start WLST:

   [wls@prod01]$ $WL_HOME/common/bin/wlst.sh

2. Connect to the Administration Server using `wlsadmin` as the user, `<pwd>` as the password and `t3://adminhost.domain.local:7001` as the server URL:

   wls:/offline> connect("wlsadmin","<pwd>","t3://adminhost.domain.local:7001")

3. Run the following WLST commands to create the file stores:

   edit()

   startEdit()

   cd('/Servers/PROD_Server01/Log/PROD_Server01')

   cmo.setStacktraceDepth(-1)

   cmo.setLoggerSeverity('Trace')

   cmo.setStdoutSeverity('Debug')

   cmo.setMemoryBufferSeverity('Debug')

   cd('/Servers/PROD_Server01/ServerDebug/PROD_Server01')

```
cmo.createDebugScope('weblogic.transaction')

cd('/Servers/PROD_Server01/ServerDebug/PROD_Server01/DebugScopes/
weblogic.transaction')
cmo.setEnabled(true)

activate()
exit()
```

See also

▶ *Including the time taken field in access.log*

▶ *Enabling verbose garbage collection logging*

Including the time taken field in access.log

The `access.log` file registers every HTTP request received by the WebLogic Server. It contains valuable information for the analysis in the production environments.

In this recipe, all Managed Servers of the `PROD_Cluster` cluster will be configured to add the `time taken` field to the `access.log` logfile. The default configuration does not include the time taken to process an HTTP request in the `access.log` file.

Getting ready

The `access.log` file has been configured using the Administration Console, so make sure the Administration Server is running.

How to do it...

Carry out the following steps to add the `time taken` field:

1. Access the Administration Console by pointing your web browser to `http://adminhost.domain.local:7001/console`.

2. Click on the **Lock & Edit** button to start a new edit session.

3. Expand the **Environment** tree on the left and then click on **Servers**.

4. Click on the **PROD_Server01** link. Click on the **Logging** tab and then on the **HTTP** tab.

5. Click on the **Advanced** link to open the advanced options.

6. Select the **Extended** option from the **Format** drop-down menu.

7. Type c-ip date time cs-method cs-uri sc-status bytes time-taken in **Extended Logging Format Fields** and click on the **Save** button.

8. Click on the **Activate Changes** button to finish.

9. Repeat the preceding steps for the PROD_Server02, PROD_Server03, and PROD_Server04 Managed Servers. Restart all the Managed Servers.

How it works...

The access.log file of the PROD_Server01 Managed Server is located at $DOMAIN_HOME/servers/PROD_Server01/logs/access.log.

The extended logging format adds the last field with the time taken for an HTTP request in seconds. The field is very helpful to watch how much time the HTTP requests are taking to execute.

```
10.2.8.2 2012-11-14 11:04:02 GET  /myApp/get.jsp   200 321  3.602
10.1.8.2 2012-11-14 11:04:02 POST /myApp/go.jsp    200 432  3.577
10.1.8.2 2012-11-14 11:04:02 GET  /myApp/map.jsp   200 754  3.599
10.5.8.4 2012-11-14 11:04:02 POST /myApp/put.jsp   200 100  3.602
10.6.8.6 2012-11-14 11:04:02 POST /myApp/put.jsp   200 184  3.588
10.3.8.9 2012-11-14 11:04:02 POST /myApp/put.jsp   200 5433 3.591
10.2.8.9 2012-11-14 11:04:02 GET  /myApp/home.jsp  200 4031 0.039
```

The access.log file can be used in a troubleshooting process to analyze if the whole Managed Server is slow or only a particular request is taking more time than usual.

Always compare a problematic scenario to an error-free scenario when troubleshooting a WebLogic Managed Server. Compare the heap usage, count the number of requests, and watch the time taken.

There's more...

The access.log file can be customized with WLST.

Adding the time taken field using WLST

Carry out the following steps to add the time taken field:

1. Log in as a wls user to shell and start WLST:

   ```
   [wls@prod01]$ $WL_HOME/common/bin/wlst.sh
   ```

2. Connect to the Administration Server using wlsadmin as the user, <pwd> as the password, and t3://adminhost.domain.local:7001 as the server URL:

   ```
   wls:/offline> connect("wlsadmin","<pwd>","t3://adminhost.domain.local:7001")
   ```

3. Run the following WLST commands:

   ```
   edit()
   startEdit()

   cd('/Servers/PROD_Server01/WebServer/PROD_Server01/WebServerLog/PROD_Server01')
   cmo.setLogFileFormat('extended')
   cmo.setELFFields('c-ip date time cs-method cs-uri sc-status bytes time-taken')

   cd('/Servers/PROD_Server02/WebServer/PROD_Server02/WebServerLog/PROD_Server02')
   cmo.setLogFileFormat('extended')
   cmo.setELFFields('c-ip date time cs-method cs-uri sc-status bytes time-taken')

   cd('/Servers/PROD_Server03/WebServer/PROD_Server03/WebServerLog/PROD_Server03')
   ```

```
cmo.setLogFileFormat('extended')
cmo.setELFFields('c-ip date time cs-method cs-uri sc-status bytes
time-taken')


cd('/Servers/PROD_Server04/WebServer/PROD_Server04/WebServerLog/
PROD_Server04')
cmo.setLogFileFormat('extended')
cmo.setELFFields('c-ip date time cs-method cs-uri sc-status bytes
time-taken')


activate()
exit()
```

See also

- ▸ *Changing log levels to debug*
- ▸ *Enabling the verbose garbage collection logging*

Enabling verbose garbage collection logging

Enabling **garbage collection** (**GC**) logging can provide rich information about the behavior of the JVM. Enabling the verbose GC is an easy change and will help diagnose some possible issues in the WebLogic Server.

One of the steps in the troubleshooting process is to find out if the JVM heap utilization is adequate.

This recipe enables Oracle JRockit verbose GC logging in the WebLogic standard output logfile for the `PROD_Server01` Managed Server.

It also shows an example of a troubleshooting scenario and the analysis made with the verbose GC.

Getting ready

The verbose GC has been changed using the Administration Console, so make sure the Administration Server is running.

How to do it...

To enable the `PROD_Server01` Managed Server to log the GC times in the standard output log, follow these steps:

1. Access the Administration Console by pointing your web browser to `http://adminhost.domain.local:7001/console`.

2. Click on the **Lock & Edit** button to start a new edit session.

3. Expand the **Environment** tree on the left and then click on **Servers**.

4. Click on the **PROD_Server01** link and then click on the **Server Start** tab.

5. Add the following to the **Arguments** field and click on the **Save** button:

   `-Xverbose:memory,gc -XverboseTimeStamp`

6. Click on the **Activate Changes** button.

7. Restart `PROD_Server01`.

How it works...

The `-Xverbose:memory,gc` argument enables the verbose GC and heap memory logging.

The `-XverboseTimeStamp` attribute adds the timestamp of each entry.

The verbose GC is logged to the `PROD_Server01` standard output logfile `PROD_Server01.out` under `$DOMAIN_HOME/servers/PROD_Server01/logs`.

Each entry has the following format:

```
[memory ] [<date>] [<collection type - YC or OC> #<collection counter>]
<start>-<end>: <type> <used heap before>KB-><used heap after>KB (<heap
total>KB), <time> s, sum of pauses <pause time> ms, longest pause
<pause time> ms.
```

In this troubleshooting scenario, the verbose GC log has to be analyzed to find out if the heap was an issue during a period when the CPU and load of the host machine were very high.

The pattern shown in the following screenshot is an example of where the SAR tool displays a very high load in the host `prod01` between 08:50 A.M. and 10:50 A.M..

```
[weblogic@prod01 ~]$ sar -q
08:30:01 AM    runq-sz  plist-sz   ldavg-1   ldavg-5  ldavg-15
08:30:01 AM          4      3325      6.57      6.64      5.79
08:40:01 AM          8      3336      6.12      6.43      6.07
08:50:01 AM         17      3385     13.22     10.67      8.19
09:00:01 AM         11      3528     13.53     13.30     10.98
09:10:01 AM         17      3578     16.60     15.86     13.16
09:20:01 AM         22      3803     30.02     25.14     18.87
09:30:01 AM         29      4034     29.82     30.17     24.95
09:40:01 AM         18      4150     34.60     34.38     29.52
09:50:01 AM         19      4255     29.01     31.19     30.15
10:00:01 AM         53      4103     40.70     37.95     33.72
10:10:01 AM         32      4189     30.77     32.10     32.44
10:20:01 AM         37      4217     29.91     30.44     31.47
10:30:01 AM         26      4206     32.47     34.16     32.96
10:40:01 AM         26      4211     27.81     30.40     31.77
10:50:01 AM          1      4204      6.30      9.81     20.03
11:00:01 AM          3      4191      6.34      6.86     13.54
```

Checking the verbose GC log during the period reveals that the heap usage was a possible cause of the problem.

A verbose output pattern at 8:07 AM with a regular load in the host is shown as follows:

```
[memory ][Wed Nov 14 08:07:23 2012] [YC#812] 14913.268-14913.541: YC
7444470KB->6687193KB (8388608KB), 0.273 s, sum of pauses 272.307 ms,
longest pause 272.307 ms.
[memory ][Wed Nov 14 08:07:48 2012] [YC#813] 14937.672-14938.002: YC
7581758KB->6861173KB (8388608KB), 0.330 s, sum of pauses 329.867 ms,
longest pause 329.867 ms.
[memory ][Wed Nov 14 08:08:17 2012] [YC#814] 14967.114-14967.327: YC
7793098KB->7028158KB (8388608KB), 0.213 s, sum of pauses 212.877 ms,
longest pause 212.877 ms.
[memory ][Wed Nov 14 08:08:40 2012] [YC#815] 14990.600-14990.720: YC
7956848KB->7183819KB (8388608KB), 0.120 s, sum of pauses 119.871 ms,
longest pause 119.871 ms.
[memory ][Wed Nov 14 08:09:07 2012] [YC#816] 15017.601-15017.891: YC
8068774KB->7316184KB (8388608KB), 0.289 s, sum of pauses 289.172 ms,
longest pause 289.172 ms.
[memory ][Wed Nov 14 08:09:34 2012] [YC#817] 15044.272-15044.531: YC
8198322KB->8276054KB (8388608KB), 0.259 s, sum of pauses 258.391 ms,
longest pause 258.391 ms.
[memory ][Wed Nov 14 08:09:37 2012] [OC#55] 15044.531-15047.620: OC
8276054KB->6057336KB (8388608KB), 3.089 s, sum of pauses 2966.710 ms,
longest pause 2966.710 ms.
```

```
[memory ] [Wed Nov 14 08:09:57 2012] [YC#818] 15067.458-15067.894: YC
7322811KB->6584405KB (8388608KB), 0.436 s, sum of pauses 435.444 ms,
longest pause 435.444 ms.
[memory ] [Wed Nov 14 08:10:11 2012] [YC#819] 15081.383-15081.768: YC
7512189KB->6782798KB (8388608KB), 0.385 s, sum of pauses 384.824 ms,
longest pause 384.824 ms.
[memory ] [Wed Nov 14 08:10:24 2012] [YC#820] 15094.544-15094.880: YC
7692285KB->6943754KB (8388608KB), 0.336 s, sum of pauses 335.365 ms,
longest pause 335.365 ms.
[memory ] [Wed Nov 14 08:10:51 2012] [YC#821] 15121.342-15121.577: YC
7835691KB->7046223KB (8388608KB), 0.235 s, sum of pauses 235.032 ms,
longest pause 235.032 ms.
[memory ] [Wed Nov 14 08:11:21 2012] [YC#822] 15151.297-15151.591: YC
8017711KB->7260111KB (8388608KB), 0.293 s, sum of pauses 293.211 ms,
longest pause 293.211 ms.
[memory ] [Wed Nov 14 08:11:48 2012] [YC#823] 15178.616-15178.911: YC
8154226KB->7381651KB (8388608KB), 0.294 s, sum of pauses 294.275 ms,
longest pause 294.275 ms.
[memory ] [Wed Nov 14 08:12:06 2012] [OC#56] 15193.571-15196.865: OC
7865756KB->6253164KB (8388608KB), 3.294 s, sum of pauses 3156.793 ms,
longest pause 3156.793 ms.
```

There are six **Young Collections** (**YC**) before an **Old Collection** (**OC**) or full GC. There is an interval of about three minutes between full GCs.

The following log snippet is the verbose output pattern during the high load at 9:45 AM. Note the difference from the first snippet. There are several full GCs in the sequence (OC) that can indicate an excessive utilization of the heap:

```
[memory ] [Wed Nov 14 09:45:40 2012] [YC#5842] 20810.279-20810.310: YC
7864695KB->7858455KB (8388608KB), 0.030 s, sum of pauses 29.888 ms,
longest pause 29.888 ms.
[memory ] [Wed Nov 14 09:45:40 2012] [YC#5843] 20810.331-20810.380: YC
7867299KB->7863260KB (8388608KB), 0.049 s, sum of pauses 41.743 ms,
longest pause 41.743 ms.
[memory ] [Wed Nov 14 09:45:40 2012] [YC#5844] 20810.394-20810.447: YC
7872603KB->7866498KB (8388608KB), 0.053 s, sum of pauses 27.567 ms,
longest pause 27.567 ms.
[memory ] [Wed Nov 14 09:45:46 2012] [OC#422] 20810.448-20816.019: OC
7867363KB->7136145KB (8388608KB), 5.570 s, sum of pauses 5400.986 ms,
longest pause 5400.986 ms.
[memory ] [Wed Nov 14 09:45:51 2012] [OC#423] 20816.061-20821.829: OC
7203083KB->7145813KB (8388608KB), 5.768 s, sum of pauses 5534.001 ms,
longest pause 5534.001 ms.
[memory ] [Wed Nov 14 09:45:57 2012] [OC#424] 20821.988-20827.727: OC
7179027KB->7148829KB (8388608KB), 5.739 s, sum of pauses 5533.360 ms,
longest pause 5533.360 ms.
[memory ] [Wed Nov 14 09:46:03 2012] [OC#425] 20827.738-20833.656: OC
```

```
7184774KB->7152045KB (8388608KB), 5.918 s, sum of pauses 5759.204 ms,
longest pause 5759.204 ms.
[memory ] [Wed Nov 14 09:46:09 2012] [OC#426] 20833.656-20839.466: OC
7192291KB->7155809KB (8388608KB), 5.809 s, sum of pauses 5648.369 ms,
longest pause 5648.369 ms.
```

The heap free is at 15 percent after the first full GC at 09:45:46 AM (OC #422). The time spent is about 5.5 seconds. Just after it, another full GC is triggered at 09:45:51 AM (OC #423). Again, the heap free is about 15 percent and the time spent is 5.7 seconds, and another full GC is triggered. This pattern continues, indicating that the JVM is spending almost all the CPU time on garbage collections; so, the machine high load is probably a consequence of the GC threads working in a non-stop fashion, trying to free the heap memory.

Excessive utilization of the heap can be the consequence of a peak load in the WebLogic Managed Server. Too many threads are executing at the same time, so too many objects are live in the heap. The problem may be the consequence of a heap size being too small or the concurrency being too high. Raise the heap size according to the footprint needed or limit the threads' concurrency. Adding more Managed Servers to the cluster is also an option.

 Try to find a heap size that has at least 30-40 percent of the heap free after a full GC during a peak load test.

The high heap usage can also be the result of a memory leak. Memory leaks are usually caused by application bugs that can lead to a continuous rise of the heap utilization until an **Out of Memory (OOM)** occurs.

 The verbose GC has a little-to-none overhead and can be used in production environments.

The GC analysis can also be made using a graphical tool, such as the Monitoring Dashboard or the JRockit Mission Control. For troubleshooting purposes, the verbose GC is very precise and does not need the JVM to be up and running since the information is already written in the logfile.

There's more...

The verbose GC can be enabled at runtime with the `jrcmd` command.

Enabling the verbose GC with jrcmd

The verbose GC can be enabled without restarting the JVM using the `jrcmd` command-line tool.

1. Find the `<PID>` value of the `PROD_Server01` Managed Server process:

   ```
   [wls@prod01]$ ps aux | grep PROD_Server01 | grep -v grep | awk
   '{print $2}'
   <PID>
   ```

2. Issue a `jrcmd` command using `<PID>` as an argument:

   ```
   [wls@prod01]$ /oracle/jvm/bin/jrcmd <PID> verbosity set=gc,memory
   ```

See also

- ▸ *Changing log levels to debug*
- ▸ *Including the time taken in access.log*

Taking thread dumps

The thread dump is a well-known feature of the Java Virtual Machine. It is a snapshot of the JVM that helps the WebLogic administrator analyze which Java method the Java threads were executing in at the exact moment the snapshot was taken. As in the rest of the book, the JVM used in this recipe is Oracle JRockit JVM.

In a hypothetic scenario, the WebLogic Administrator received several e-mails from the configured WLDF alerts from the previous chapter, indicating that the `QueueLength` value is growing up in the `PROD_Server01` Managed Server. The requests are probably piling up.

In this recipe, thread dumps of `PROD_Server01` will be taken to analyze the problematic scenario.

Getting ready

The thread dump can be taken from the Administration Console from the shell using the `jrcmd` command-line tool or from the JRockit Mission Control.

How to do it...

Get the thread dump from the Administration Console:

1. Access the Administration Console by pointing your web browser to `http://adminhost.domain.local:7001/console`.

2. Expand the **Environment** tree on the left and then click on **Servers**.

3. Click on the **PROD_Server01** link; click on the **Monitoring** tab and then click on the **Threads** tab.

4. Click on the **Dump Thread Stacks** button.

The thread dump will be displayed on the screen.

The thread dump can also be taken from the shell by using the `jrcmd` command-line tool or by issuing the command `kill -3` to `<PID>`.

1. Find the `<PID>` value of the **PROD_Server01** Managed Server process:

    ```
    [wls@prod01]$ ps aux | grep PROD_Server01 | grep -v grep | awk
    '{print $2}'
    <PID>
    ```

2. Issue a `jrcmd` command using `<PID>` as an argument:

    ```
    [wls@prod01]$ /oracle/jvm/bin/jrcmd <PID> print_threads > some_
    log_file
    ```

3. Alternatively, you can also run the `kill -3` command using `<PID>` as an argument:

    ```
    [wls@prod01]$ kill -3 <PID>
    ```

How it works...

The `jrcmd` command-line tool is redirecting the output to `some_log_file` defined in the command line, so the thread dump will be written there. The thread dump taken by using the `kill` command is written to the standard output logfile of the `PROD_Server01` Managed Server.

Before starting to analyze the thread dumps, use the procedure from the last recipe and monitor the heap usage. When the JVM is spending too much CPU time on garbage collections, the incoming requests can pile up as well, raising the `QueueLength` attribute of the thread pool.

The thread dump is one of the most guaranteed methods of troubleshooting a Managed Server. Normally, you need to observe only the threads from the self-tuning thread pool. The thread stack trace from the self-tuning thread pool can have the [ACTIVE], [STANDBY], and [STUCK] flags, and it has the following pattern:

```
"[ACTIVE] ExecuteThread: '0' for queue: 'weblogic.kernel.Default
(self-tuning)'" id=39 idx=0x80 tid=4952 prio=5 alive, waiting, native_
blocked, daemon
    -- Waiting for notification on: weblogic/work/
ExecuteThread@0xf06a43b0
    [...]
    at weblogic/work/ExecuteThread.run()
```

Take some thread dumps in a sequence with a short interval between them. There is no specific formula for how many thread dumps to take or which interval to use. Sometimes, only one thread dump is sufficient.

A thread dump analysis requires certain knowledge of Java coding, but it is the most important tool to identify what is going on inside WebLogic.

In this scenario, the sequence of thread dumps reveals that almost all threads are stopped at the following stack:

```
"[ACTIVE] ExecuteThread: '10' for queue: 'weblogic.kernel.Default
(self-tuning)'" id=166 idx=0x2a4 tid=25647 prio=1 alive, in native,
daemon
    at jrockit/net/SocketNativeIO.readBytesPinned()
    [...]
    at oracle/jdbc/driver/OraclePreparedStatement.execute()
    [...]
    at oracle/jdbc/driver/OraclePreparedStatementWrapper.execute()
    at weblogic/jdbc/wrapper/PreparedStatement.execute()
    at com/myapp/db/DBUtil.executeQuery()
    [...]
    at weblogic/work/ExecuteThread.execute()
    at weblogic/work/ExecuteThread.run()
```

The important Java methods to observe are `com.myapp.db.DBUtil.executeQuery()` and `oracle.jdbc.driver.OraclePreparedStatement.execute()`. The application is probably executing some function in the database, and all the threads are waiting for the response, piling up the requests. In this specific case, it is possible that the problem is coming from a slow database or from a large query that is not using any indexes, or even from some sort of database lock. The thread dump can point to the right direction and, in this scenario, further investigation will be needed in the application code and the database.

> The `[STUCK]` flag means the thread is processing a request for a longer time than has been configured in the **Max Stuck Thread Time** field of the **Overload** configuration page for a Managed Server. The default configured time is `600s`. In conjunction with the other parameters and Node Manager, it is possible to configure the Managed Server to automatically restart when a maximum number of stuck threads is reached. This configuration was set in *Chapter 2, High Availability with WebLogic Clusters*, and may be useful in some scenarios, but you may lose the opportunity to troubleshoot if the Managed Server restarts automatically. `[ACTIVE]` and `[STANDBY]` are status flags related to the self-tuning thread pool and do not indicate if the thread is processing a request.

See also

▸ *Enabling the JRockit Mission Control Flight Recorder*

▸ *Analyzing a heap dump*

Enabling the JRockit Mission Control Flight Recorder

Mission Control is a monitoring and troubleshooting application provided with Oracle JRockit.

Besides the Management Console covered in *Chapter 5, Monitoring WebLogic Server 12c*, Oracle JRockit also provides an important feature called the **Flight Recorder**. The Flight Recorder registers the JVM's metrics and events, garbage collection behavior, thread contention, locking, and other information, according to the configuration template you use. The default template has a very low overhead and can be used in production environments.

This recipe will enable the Flight Recorder to store a flight recorder file (`.jfr` extension) for the Managed Servers `PROD_Server01`, `PROD_Server02`, `PROD_Server03`, and `PROD_Server04` with the default template configuration. The recording will be configured to store the last 24 hours of events or the maximum of a 100 MB file.

Getting ready

There is no need to start Oracle JRockit Mission Control to configure the Flight Recorder. It is enabled by changing parameters using the Administration Console. So make sure the Administration Server is running.

How to do it...

To enable the Managed Servers to record the Flight Recorder's events, follow these steps:

1. Access the Administration Console by pointing your web browser to `http://adminhost.domain.local:7001/console`.

2. Click on the **Lock & Edit** button to start a new edit session.

3. Expand the **Environment** tree on the left and then click on **Servers**.

4. Click on the **PROD_Server01** link and then click on the **Server Start** tab.

5. Add the following line of code to the **Arguments** field and click on the **Save** button:

```
-XX:FlightRecorderOptions=defaultrecording=true,disk=true,
repository=./jfr/PROD_Server01,maxage=1440m,size=100m
```

6. Click on the **Activate Changes** button.

7. Restart `PROD_Server01`.

8. Repeat the previous steps for the Managed Servers `PROD_Server02`, `PROD_Server03`, and `PROD_Server04`, and define the corresponding path for the `repository=./jfr/PROD_ServerXX` repository parameter of each server.

How it works...

The `repository=./jfr/PROD_ServerXX` parameter sets the file location of the recordings. In this case, it will save the recording to the `$DOMAIN_HOME/jfr/PROD_ServerXX` directory. The directory will be created automatically if it does not exist.

The Flight Recorder is enabled and configured to store the last 24 hours of events, or until the file size reaches 100 MB. The objective is to record the previous events like an airplane's black box.

There are many settings you can change for the Flight Recorder. The parameters can be altered to save the events during the entire life cycle of the JVM. Change the `maxage` and `size` parameters to 0 as shown in the following line of code:

```
-XX:FlightRecorderOptions=defaultrecording=true,disk=true,
repository=./jfr/PROD_Server0X,maxage=0,size=0
```

For every new recording, a new directory with the pattern `$DOMAIN_HOME/jrf/<SERVER_NAME>/YYYY_MM_DD_HH_MM_SS_PID` is created. `YYYY` stands for the year, `MM` stands for the month, `DD` for the day, `HH` for the hour, `SS` for the second, and `PID` is the process ID of the WebLogic Managed Server.

The file has a similar pattern `YYYY_MM_DD_HH_MM_SS_PID.jfr` and it must be opened in the JRockit Mission Control to be analyzed. The content of the Mission Control Management Console is mostly the same, but it can include more information depending on the configuration template used to save the `.jfr` file.

See also

▸ *Analyzing a heap dump*

Analyzing a heap dump

A heap dump is another important feature of the Java Virtual Machine. It contains a memory dump of all the current live Java objects of the heap.

The heap dump is useful in problematic situations, such as in a memory leak condition in a WebLogic Server where the heap usage grows until the JVM crashes by **Out of Memory** (**OOM**), or when the heap utilization is so high that the Managed Server hangs and stops responding. Both scenarios can use a heap dump to discover the offender objects in the heap.

This recipe will display how to take a heap dump from a Managed Server in the HPROF format. HPROF is a binary file that stores the heap and CPU profiles of the JVM. For demonstration purposes, the heap dump was taken from a JVM configured to a small heap with a maximum size of 256 MB (`-Xmx256mb`).

Getting ready

The heap dump can be taken from the shell using the `jrcmd` command-line tool or from the Mission Control.

The heap dump will be analyzed with the **Eclipse Memory Analyzer** (**MAT**), so download and install it from `http://www.eclipse.com/mat`.

How to do it...

1. Log in to the shell and use the JRCMD tool.

2. Find the `<PID>` value of the `PROD_Server01` Managed Server process:

   ```
   [wls@prod01]$ ps aux | grep PROD_Server01 | grep -v grep | awk '{print $2}'
   <PID>
   ```

3. Issue a `jrcmd` command using `<PID>` as an argument:

   ```
   [wls@prod01]$ /oracle/jvm/bin/jrcmd <PID> hprofdump
   <PID>:
   Wrote dump to heapdump_<date>.hprof
   ```

Analyze the heap dump with MAT.

1. Open MAT by executing the file `MemoryAnalyzer.exe`.

Name ▲	Size	Type
configuration		File Folder
features		File Folder
p2		File Folder
plugins		File Folder
readme		File Folder
.eclipseproduct	1 KB	ECLIPSEPRODUCT File
artifacts.xml	33 KB	XML Document
eclipsec.exe	24 KB	Application
epl-v10.html	17 KB	HTML Document
MemoryAnalyzer.exe	52 KB	Application
MemoryAnalyzer.ini	1 KB	Configuration Settings
notice.html	9 KB	HTML Document
ParseHeapDump.bat	1 KB	MS-DOS Batch File
workspace		File Folder

2. Open the **File** menu and select the **Open Heap Dump** menu option. Choose the heap dump file `heapdump_<date>.hprof`.

3. Select the **Leak Suspects Report** option from the **Getting Started Wizard** screen and click on the **Finish** button.

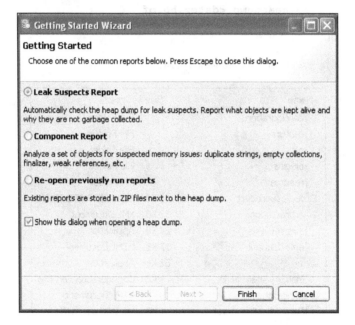

4. Watch out for the suspects that are using a large amount of memory.

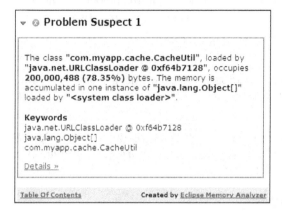

How it works...

The `jrcmd` command-line tool issues a command to the JVM to generate the heap dump.

The heap dump file is written to the `$DOMAIN_HOME` root directory with a filename of the pattern, `heapdump_<date>.hprof`.

The JVM runs a full GC before saving the heap dump, so the size of the file is the size of the live Java objects. If a heap is reaching 3 GB of utilization after a full GC, the size of the file will be 3 GB.

In this recipe, the heap dump was opened and analyzed by using the Eclipse Memory Analyzer application. The analysis indicated the `com.myapp.cache.CacheUtil` class is an offender, occupying about 80 percent of the total heap size. The following screenshot displays an ArrayList named `CACHE_LIST`; it is the variable of the `com.myapp.cache.CacheUtil` class and consumes 200 MB of the 256 MB configured for the heap.

Class Name	Retained Heap
⇄ <Regex>	<Numeric>
⊟ ☐ com.myapp.cache.CacheUtil @ 0xf05aa940	16
⊟ ☐ <class> class com.myapp.cache.CacheUtil @ 0xf05897b0	200,000,488
⊟ ■ CACHE_LIST java.util.ArrayList @ 0xf05aa948	200,000,464
⊞ ☐ elementData java.lang.Object[25] @ 0xfef0ddb8	200,000,440
⊞ ☐ <class> class java.util.ArrayList @ 0xf64af4e0 System Class	8
∑ Total: 2 entries	
⊞ ☐ <classloader> java.net.URLClassLoader @ 0xf64b7128	3,792
⊞ ☐ <class> class java.lang.Class @ 0xf64b10e0 Native Stack	56
⊞ ☐ instance com.myapp.cache.CacheUtil @ 0xf05aa940	16
⊞ ☐ <super> class java.lang.Object @ 0xf64b0310 Native Stack	0
∑ Total: 5 entries	

The heap dump analysis indicates which part of the Java code may be the offender. In this case, the Java code must be revised to fix the problem or the heap size must be adjusted to fit the number of objects needed in this array. Use the solution that meets the application requirements.

 The offender Java code may belong to an internal WebLogic class. In this case, open a service request in Oracle Support.

There are several profiling tools to analyze a heap dump. The **Eclipse Memory Analyzer—MAT** (`http://www.eclipse.org/mat`) and the **YourKit Java Profiler** (`http://www.yourkit.com`) are excellent known options.

There's more...

The heap dump can be configured to be generated automatically in certain conditions.

Generating the heap dump automatically on OOM conditions

The heap dump can be generated automatically when an out of memory condition is reached.

1. Access the Administration Console by pointing your web browser to `http://adminhost.domain.local:7001/console`.

2. Click on the **Lock & Edit** button to start a new edit session.

3. Expand the **Environment** tree on the left and then click on **Servers**.

4. Click on the **PROD_Server01** link then click on the **Server Start** tab.

5. Add the following to the **Arguments** field and click on the **Save** button:

   ```
   -XX:+HeapDumpOnOutOfMemoryError
   ```

6. Click on the **Activate Changes** button.

7. Restart `PROD_Server01`.

8. Repeat the previous steps for the Managed Servers `PROD_Server02`, `PROD_Server03`, and `PROD_Server04`.

9. The heap dump file that is generated follows the same pattern when generated from the `jrcmd` tool.

Recovering the WebLogic admin password

The WebLogic Administrator username and password are used to start up the WebLogic Server instances. They are stored encrypted in the `boot.properties` file.

This recipe will provide the steps to recover the username and password from the `boot.properties` file of the `PROD_DOMAIN` domain.

Getting ready

The recovery will use WLST to decrypt the `boot.properties` file.

How to do it...

Carry out the following steps to recover the WebLogic Admin password:

1. Log in as the `wls` user to shell and set the domain environment variables for the domain you want to recover:

   ```
   [wls@prod01]$ cd $DOMAIN_HOME/bin
   [wls@prod01]$ . ./setDomainEnv.sh
   ```

2. Start WLST:

   ```
   [wls@prod01]$ $WL_HOME/common/bin/wlst.sh
   ```

3. Run the following WLST commands to display the username and password:

   ```
   from weblogic.security.internal import BootProperties
   BootProperties.load("/oracle/Middleware/user_projects/domains/
   PROD_DOMAIN/servers/PROD_AdminServer/security/boot.properties",
   false)
   prop = BootProperties.getBootProperties()
   print "username: " + prop.getOneClient()
   print "password: " + prop.getTwoClient()
   ```

   The username and password will be displayed on the screen.

How it works...

The script reads the `boot.properties` file, decrypts it, and displays the username and password provided.

The script points to the `boot.properties` file located in the `security` folder of the `PROD_AdminServer`. You can point to any `security` folder that contains the `boot.properties` file of the other Managed Servers.

It is important to set the domain environments first, otherwise the script will not be able to find the `SerializedSystemIni.dat` file, which is the seed used by the domain to encrypt and decrypt.

See also

▸ *Recovering a data source password*

Recovering the data source password

The same way that the WebLogic Administrator password is recoverable, the data source password can be retrieved as well.

In this recipe, the `ds-nonXA` data source with the JNDI name `jdbc/non-XA` will be used to retrieve the password.

Getting ready

The encrypted password must be retrieved from the JDBC configuration files in the `$DOMAIN_HOME/config/jdbc` directory. To decrypt the password, use WLST.

How to do it...

Carry out the following steps to recover the data source password:

1. Log in as a `wls` user to shell and open the `$DOMAIN_HOME/config/config.xml` file to get the JDBC configuration filename.

   [wls@prod01]$ cd $DOMAIN_HOME/config

   [wls@prod01]$ vi config.xml

2. Locate the `<jdbc-system-resource>` tag of the `ds-nonXA` data source and get the descriptor filename.

   ```
   <jdbc-system-resource>
     <name>ds-nonXA</name>
     <target></target>
         <descriptor-file-name>jdbc/ds-nonXA-jdbc.xml</descriptor-file-name>
   </jdbc-system-resource>
   ```

3. Open the JDBC file:

   [wls@prod01]$ vi jdbc/ds-nonXA-jdbc.xml

4. Locate the `<password-encrypted>` tag and copy the password.

   ```
   <password-encrypted>{AES}PASSWORD_ENCRYPTED</password-encrypted>
   ```

5. Start WLST using the following command:

```
[wls@prod01]$ $WL_HOME/common/bin/wlst.sh
```

6. Set the copied password to the `passwd` variable, set the full path of the `$DOMAIN_HOME/security` in the `secPath` variable, and run the following WLST commands to display the password:

```
from weblogic.security.internal import *

from weblogic.security.internal.encryption import *

passwd = "{AES}PASSWORD_ENCRYPTED"

secPath = "/oracle/Middleware/user_projects/domains/PROD_DOMAIN/
security"

encService = SerializedSystemIni.getEncryptionService(secPath)

coeService = ClearOrEncryptedService(encService)

print "password: " + coeService.decrypt(passwd)
```

7. The password will be displayed on the screen:

```
wls:/offline> password: dbpwd
```

How it works...

This recipe displayed a simple procedure to get the encrypted password stored in the JDBC configuration file and use it in the WLST script file.

There is no need to set the domain environment variables this time since the script receives the full path to the `SerializedSystemIni.dat` file.

See also

▸ *Recovering the WebLogic admin password*

7
Stability and Performance

In this chapter we will cover the following recipes:

- ▶ Limiting the log disk usage
- ▶ Rotating the STDOUT logfile
- ▶ Turning off the domain logging
- ▶ Enabling Linux HugePages
- ▶ Configuring the transaction (JTA) timeouts
- ▶ Choosing the JRockit garbage collection mode
- ▶ Tuning thread concurrency with default work managers
- ▶ Tuning the application thread concurrency with custom work managers
- ▶ Limiting the JMS Queue consumers

Introduction

This chapter is about WebLogic Server stability and performance, but most of the recipes are focused on stability.

For the WebLogic Administrator, stability should come first in the priority list of objectives. It is improbable that an unstable system achieves sufficient performance.

This chapter provides simple but effective small tunings, targeting a stable and predictable production environment.

In most cases, the performance should suffice if the environment is very stable, with predictable behavior and common bottlenecks removed.

Limiting the log disk usage

WebLogic Server 12c fixes a file size limit of 5 MB for the domain, server, and HTTP logs. It also sets `100` as the maximum number of rotated files for the domain and server logs. The HTTP `access.log` file does not have a default limit of rotated files. This is the default configuration for WebLogic Server 12c domains running in the production mode.

In this recipe, the logging subsystem will be configured, so that all the `PROD_DOMAIN` domain logfiles usage never surpasses a known disk size usage.

Getting ready

The logging subsystem is configured by using the Administration Console, so make sure the Administration Server is running.

How to do it...

Carry out the following steps to limit the log disk usage:

1. Access the Administration Console with your web browser at `http://adminhost.domain.local:7001/console`.

2. Click on the **Lock & Edit** button to start a new edit session.

3. Expand the **Environment** tree to the left and then click on **Servers**.

4. Click on the **PROD_Server01** link. Click on the **Logging** tab and then click on the **General** tab.

5. Type `50000` in the **Rotation file size** text field.

6. Make sure that the **Limit number of retained files** checkbox is checked.

7. Type `20` in the **Files to retain** text field.

8. Check the **Rotate log file on startup** checkbox.

9. Click on the **Save** button and then click on the **Advanced** link to open the advanced options.

10. Check the **Redirect stdout logging enabled** checkbox.

11. Check the **Redirect stderr logging enabled** checkbox.

12. Change the **Severity Level** of the **Standard out** drop-down menu to **Off**.

13. Click on the **Save** button.

14. Click on the **HTTP** tab.

15. Type `50000` in the **Rotation file size** text field.

16. Make sure that the **Limit number of retained files** checkbox is checked.

17. Type `20` in the **Files to retain** text field.

18. Check the **Rotate log file on startup** checkbox.

19. Click on the **Save** button.

20. Repeat the previous steps for the `PROD_Server02`, `PROD_Server03` and `PROD_Server04` Managed Servers and the `PROD_AdminServer` Administration Server.

21. Click on the **PROD_DOMAIN** link on the left-hand side navigation tree and then click on the **Logging** tab.

22. Type `50000` in the **Rotation file size** text field.

23. Make sure that the **Limit number of retained files** checkbox is checked.

24. Type `20` in the **Files to retain** text field.

25. Check the **Rotate log file on startup** checkbox and click on the **Save** button.

26. Click on the **Activate Changes** button to finish.

27. Restart the entire `PROD_DOMAIN` domain.

How it works...

In production environments, predictability must be a priority when setting up WebLogic. This configuration brings a fixed known value to the logging disk usage of the entire domain.

WebLogic Instance/DOMAIN	Server log	HTTP log
`PROD_AdminServer`	10 MB * 50 MB = 500 MB	10 MB * 50 MB = 500 MB
`PROD_Server01`	500 MB	500 MB
`PROD_Server02`	500 MB	500 MB
`PROD_Server03`	500 MB	500 MB
`PROD_Server04`	500 MB	500 MB
`PROD_DOMAIN` log	500 MB	
Total	6 MB * 500 MB = 3 GB	5 MB * 500 MB = 2.5 GB

WebLogic Server does not provide an out of the box configuration to rotate the standard output log (`$DOMAIN_HOME/servers/PROD_ServerXX/PROD_ServerXX.out`). As a workaround, `STDOUT` and `STDERR` from the `PROD_ServerXX.out` file were redirected to the server log and disabled. This configuration maintains the information of the `PROD_ServerXX.out` file in the `PROD_ServerXX.log` file.

All -Xverbose JRockit loggings are not redirected to the server logfile and still written to the PROD_ServerXX.out file.

Rotating the STDOUT log will be explained further on this chapter.

There's more...

The log disk usage can be limited with WLST.

Limiting the log disk usage by using WLST

1. Log in as the wls user to shell and start WLST:

   [wls@prod01] $ $WL_HOME/common/bin/wlst.sh

2. Connect to the Administration Server using wlsadmin as the user, \<pwd\> as the password, and t3://adminhost.domain.local:7001 as the server URL:

   wls:/offline> connect("wlsadmin","\<pwd\>","t3://adminhost.domain.local:7001")

3. Run the following WLST commands:

   edit()

   startEdit()

   cd('/Log/PROD_DOMAIN')

   cmo.setRotateLogOnStartup(true)

   cmo.setFileMinSize(50000)

   cmo.setNumberOfFilesLimited(true)

   cmo.setFileCount(20)

   cd('/Servers/PROD_Server01/Log/PROD_Server01')

   cmo.setRotateLogOnStartup(true)

   cmo.setFileMinSize(50000)

   cmo.setNumberOfFilesLimited(true)

   cmo.setFileCount(20)

   cmo.setRedirectStdoutToServerLogEnabled(true)

   cmo.setRedirectStderrToServerLogEnabled(true)

   cmo.setStdoutSeverity('Off')

   cd('/Servers/PROD_Server01/WebServer/PROD_Server01/WebServerLog/PROD_Server01')

```
cmo.setRotateLogOnStartup(true)
cmo.setFileMinSize(50000)
cmo.setNumberOfFilesLimited(true)
cmo.setFileCount(20)


cd('/Servers/PROD_Server02/Log/PROD_Server02')
cmo.setRotateLogOnStartup(true)
cmo.setFileMinSize(50000)
cmo.setNumberOfFilesLimited(true)
cmo.setFileCount(20)
cmo.setRedirectStdoutToServerLogEnabled(true)
cmo.setRedirectStderrToServerLogEnabled(true)
cmo.setStdoutSeverity('Off')
cd('/Servers/PROD_Server02/WebServer/PROD_Server02/WebServerLog/
PROD_Server02')
cmo.setRotateLogOnStartup(true)
cmo.setFileMinSize(50000)
cmo.setNumberOfFilesLimited(true)
cmo.setFileCount(20)


cd('/Servers/PROD_Server03/Log/PROD_Server03')
cmo.setRotateLogOnStartup(true)
cmo.setFileMinSize(50000)
cmo.setNumberOfFilesLimited(true)
cmo.setFileCount(20)
cmo.setRedirectStdoutToServerLogEnabled(true)
cmo.setRedirectStderrToServerLogEnabled(true)
cmo.setStdoutSeverity('Off')
cd('/Servers/PROD_Server03/WebServer/PROD_Server03/WebServerLog/
PROD_Server03')
cmo.setRotateLogOnStartup(true)
cmo.setFileMinSize(50000)
cmo.setNumberOfFilesLimited(true)
cmo.setFileCount(20)


cd('/Servers/PROD_Server04/Log/PROD_Server04')
```

```
cmo.setRotateLogOnStartup(true)
cmo.setFileMinSize(50000)
cmo.setNumberOfFilesLimited(true)
cmo.setFileCount(20)
cmo.setRedirectStdoutToServerLogEnabled(true)
cmo.setRedirectStderrToServerLogEnabled(true)
cmo.setStdoutSeverity('Off')
cd('/Servers/PROD_Server04/WebServer/PROD_Server04/WebServerLog/
PROD_Server04')
cmo.setRotateLogOnStartup(true)
cmo.setFileMinSize(50000)
cmo.setNumberOfFilesLimited(true)
cmo.setFileCount(20)

activate()
exit()
```

See also

> ▸ *Rotating the STDOUT logfile*
> ▸ *Turning off the domain logging*

Rotating the STDOUT logfile

Oracle WebLogic Server 12c does not provide an out of the box configuration to rotate the STDOUT and STDERR logfiles in runtime (.out file). In the previous recipe, as a workaround, it was redirected to the server logfile and disabled.

Fortunately in Linux, the included logrotate command-line tool can do the job.

In this recipe, the logrotate will be configured to run hourly and rotate all .out files from the PROD_DOMAIN WebLogic instances larger than 50 MB. It will rotate to the limit of 20 files, repeating the configuration of the server logfiles in the previous recipe.

Getting ready

The logrotate settings must be configured in the machine shell. To do this log in to the prod01 machine.

How to do it...

Carry out the following steps to rotate the .out file:

1. Log in as a wls user to shell and create a new file wls-stdout-logrotate.conf and save it to the $DOMAIN_HOME folder:

   ```
   [wls@prod01]$ cd /oracle/Middleware/user_projects/domains/PROD_DOMAIN

   [wls@prod01]$ vi wls-stdout-logrotate.conf
   ```

2. Add the following lines to the file:

   ```
   # WebLogic STDOUT logrotate for PROD_DOMAIN
   /oracle/Middleware/user_projects/domains/PROD_DOMAIN/servers/PROD_*/logs/*.out {
        rotate 20
        size 50M
        copytruncate
        nocompress
        missingok
        nodateext
        noolddir
        create 0640 wls wls
   }
   ```

3. Type :ws! to save the file and exit.

4. Change to root user and create the wls-stdout-logrotate file to add new entry to the hourly crontab:

   ```
   [root@prod01]# vi /etc/cron.hourly/wls-stdout-logrotate
   ```

5. Add the following lines to the script:

   ```
   #!/bin/sh

   sudo /usr/sbin/logrotate /oracle/Middleware/user_projects/domains/PROD_DOMAIN/wls-stdout-logrotate.conf
   RETCODE=$?
   if [ $RETCODE != 0 ]; then
      /usr/bin/logger -t logrotate "WLS STDOUT logrotate finished abnormally with code [$RETCODE]"
   fi
   exit 0
   ```

6. Type `:ws!` to save the file and exit.

7. Change the file permissions:

    `[root@prod01]# chmod 755 /etc/cron.hourly/wls-stdout-logrotate`

8. Repeat the previous steps for all machines in the `PROD_DOMAIN`.

How it works...

The `logrotate` settings will be read from the `wls-stdout-logrotate.conf` configuration file. The file was saved in the root directory of the WebLogic domain, but it can be saved anywhere.

A crontab job was added to run hourly in the form of a script. This configuration must be executed by the `root` user.

When the crontab job runs, it checks for all `.out files` that matches the path `$OMAIN_HOME/servers/PROD_*/logs/*.out`. If the file size is over 50 MB, the job will copy the file content to a new one (`PROD_Server01.out.1`) and then truncate the original file.

The `copytruncate` parameter guarantees that the rotation works properly since WebLogic keeps the stream to the `.out` file open.

 When the STDOUT logfile reaches the file size limit of 2 GB in 32-bit environments, the WebLogic Server instance can hang. Rotating the STDOUT can prevent this situation from happening.

See also

▶ *Limiting the logging disk usage*

▶ *Turning off the domain logging*

Turning off domain logging

The WebLogic Domain's log concentrates all the WebLogic Managed Server loggings in one single log managed by the Administration Server.

The domain log can become a bottleneck and affect the performance in certain scenarios with a very large domain with several Managed Servers.

In this recipe, the log will be turned off for the `PROD_DOMAIN` domain.

Getting ready

The log levels will be changed using the Administration Console, so make sure the Administration Server is running.

How to do it...

Carry out the following steps to turn off the domain logging:

1. Access the Administration Console by pointing your web browser to
   `http://adminhost.domain.local:7001/console`.
2. Click on the **Lock & Edit** button to start a new edit session.
3. Click on the **PROD_DOMAIN** link on the navigation tree to the left and then click on the **Logging** tab.
4. Change **Severity level** of the **Domain log broadcaster** drop-down menu to **Off**, as shown in the following screenshot:

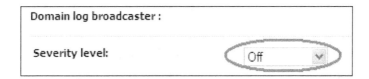

5. Click on the **Save** button.
6. Repeat the preceding steps for all Managed Servers in the PROD_DOMAIN domain.
7. Click on the **Activate Changes** button.

How it works...

Disabling the domain log can lighten the communication between the Managed Servers and the Administration Server.

It is a recommended setting in very busy WebLogic environments since the information logged already exists on each of the Managed Servers.

There's more...

The domain log can also be disabled through WLST.

Disabling the domain log by using WLST

Carry out the following steps:

1. Log in as `wls` user to shell and start WLST:

   [wls@prod01]$ $WL_HOME/common/bin/wlst.sh

2. Connect to the Administration Server using `wlsadmin` as the user, `<pwd>` as the password, and `t3://adminhost.domain.local:7001` as the server URL:

   wls:/offline> connect("wlsadmin","<pwd>","t3://adminhost.domain.local:7001")

3. Run the following WLST commands:

   ```
   edit()
   startEdit()

   cd('/Servers/PROD_Server01/Log/PROD_Server01')
   cmo.setDomainLogBroadcastSeverity('Off')


   cd('/Servers/PROD_Server01/Log/PROD_Server02')
   cmo.setDomainLogBroadcastSeverity('Off')


   cd('/Servers/PROD_Server01/Log/PROD_Server03')
   cmo.setDomainLogBroadcastSeverity('Off')


   cd('/Servers/PROD_Server01/Log/PROD_Server04')
   cmo.setDomainLogBroadcastSeverity('Off')

   save()
   activate()
   exit()
   ```

See also

▶ *Limiting the log disk usage*
▶ *Rotating the STDOUT logfile*

Enabling Linux HugePages

Enabling Linux HugePages can improve the performance of the Oracle JRockit JVM and have several advantages over the default page size of 4 KB in Linux.

In this recipe, the HugePages will be enabled on all machines in the PROD_DOMAIN domain. A new JVM parameter will be added to the Managed Servers so the JVM makes use of the HugePages.

prod01 hosts the **PROD_Server01** and **PROD_Server02** Managed Servers. Since each instance is configured with a heap size of 2 GB, reserving 4 GB for HugePages in **prod01** should be enough.

Getting ready

Before configuring the Linux HugePages, shut down all WebLogic Servers in the domain. Also stop the Administration Console instance and the Node Manager.

How to do it...

To enable the Linux HugePages, you must log in as root user:

1. Log in as root user to the shell and execute the following commands to check the HugePages configuration:

    ```
    [root@prod01]$ cat /proc/meminfo | grep Huge
    HugePages_Total:      0
    HugePages_Free:       0
    HugePages_Rsvd:       0
    Hugepagesize:      2048 kB
    ```

2. Create a mount point of type hugetlbfs:

    ```
    [root@prod01]$ mkdir /mnt/hugepages
    [root@prod01]$ chmod -R 777 /mnt/hugepages
    [root@prod01]$ mount -t hugetlbfs nodev /mnt/hugepages
    ```

3. Add the following mount point to the /etc/fstab:

    ```
    [root@prod01]$ vi /etc/fstab
    ```

4. Add the following line:

    ```
    hugetlbfs  /mnt/hugepages  hugetlbfs  rw,mode=0777  0 0
    ```

5. Enter `:ws!` to save the file and exit.

6. Edit the `sysctl.conf` file under `/etc/`:

   [root@prod01]$ vi /etc/sysctl.conf

7. Reserve `2048` HugePages by adding the following line:

   vm.nr_hugepages = 2048

8. Enter `:ws!` to save the file and exit.

9. Execute the following command to make the changes effective:

   [root@prod01]# sysctl -p

10. Verify the change:

    ```
    [root@prod01]$ cat /proc/meminfo | grep Huge
    HugePages_Total:   2048
    HugePages_Free:    2048
    HugePages_Rsvd:       0
    Hugepagesize:      2048 kB
    ```

11. Restart the host if the HugePages could not be allocated.

12. Repeat the preceding steps on all machines in the `PROD_DOMAIN`.

To enable the Managed Servers to make use of the HugePages, follow the ensuing steps:

1. Access the Administration Console by pointing your web browser to `http://adminhost.domain.local:7001/console`.

2. Click on the **Lock & Edit** button to start a new edit session.

3. Expand the **Environment** tree to the left and then click on **Servers**.

4. Click on the **PROD_Server01** link and then click on the **Server Start** tab.

5. Add the following to the **Arguments** field and click on the **Save** button:

   `-XX:+UseLargePagesForHeap`

6. Click on the **Activate Changes** button.

7. Restart **PROD_Server01**.

8. Repeat the preceding steps for **PROD_Server02, PROD_Server03,** and **PROD_Server04**.

How it works...

The first thing to do is to estimate how much memory should be reserved as HugePages. Sum all heap sizes of the JVMs in the machine. In our case, we have 2 JVMs with 2 GB each so a total of 4 GB should be reserved in HugePages.

To calculate how many pages, get the memory needed and divide by the page size. The formula is *sum of JVM heaps / page size*.

The memory needed is 4 GB (4096 MB) and the page size is 2 MB (Hugepagesize is 2048 KB). The number of HugePages is *4096/2 = 2048*.

This 4 GB of reserved HugePages will be pre-allocated and cannot be used by other applications, even when the JVMs are not running, so be sure to do the sizing properly.

 It is a common mistake to reserve a large amount of memory in HugePages and the host starts to swap. Remember to leave enough memory for the other applications and the operating system. Avoid the swapping at all costs.

If you have the `-Xverbose:gc,memory` enabled, you can check if the JVM is using the HugePages properly in the STDOUT logfile.

```
[INFO ][memory ] Using 2MB pages for Java heap.
```

With the `PROD_Server01` started, checking the `/proc/meminfo` should also reveal that HugePages are in use.

```
[wls@prod01]$ cat /proc/meminfo | grep Huge
HugePages_Total:   2048
HugePages_Free:    1024
HugePages_Rsvd:       0
Hugepagesize:      2048 kB
```

Using HugePages provides some significant advantages:

▸ Because of the larger page size, the page table will be smaller in size. With HugePages, a 10 GB heap size should use only 5120 page entries despite the 2621440 page entries present when using the default 4 KB page size. This minimizes the CPU cost and the page table memory usage.

▸ A performance boost in memory operations because the TLB cache works more efficiently, with more cache hits.

▸ The memory reserved for HugePages will never swap to disk.

▸ It forces a more controlled memory usage of the heap sizes.

Configuring the transaction (JTA) timeouts

In production environments, slowness in a legacy or external system (a database or web service for example) can lead to a scenario where all WebLogic threads and resources become busy waiting for response. The slowness can pile up the requests, generating a hang scenario in WebLogic.

In this recipe, the timeouts will be configured for the PROD_DOMAIN, including the domain JTA timeout and a hypothetic XA resource, such as the XA data source ds-XA, that points to an Oracle Database. The recipe will use a timeout of 600 seconds as base.

Getting ready

The timeouts will be configured by using the Administration Console, so make sure the Administration Server is running.

How to do it...

Carry out the following steps to configure the timeouts:

1. Access the Administration Console with your web browser at http://adminhost. domain.local:7001/console.

2. Click on the **Lock & Edit** button to start a new edit session.

3. Click on the **PROD_DOMAIN** link on the left-hand side navigation menu, and then click on the **JTA** tab to open the **JTA** page under **Domain | Configuration**.

4. Type 600 in the **Timeout seconds** text field (as shown in the following screenshot) and click on the **Save** button.

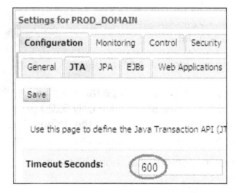

5. Expand the **Services** tree to the left and then click on **Data Sources**.

6. Click on the **ds-XA** data source then the **Transaction** tab to navigate to **Configuration | Transaction**.

7. Check the **Set XA Transaction Timeout** checkbox and enter 620 in the **XA Transaction Timeout** text field, as shown in the following screenshot:

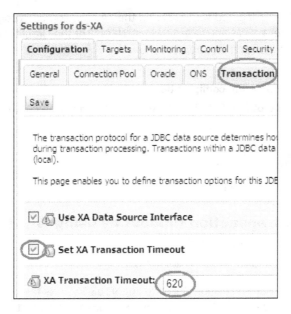

8. Click on the **Save** button.

9. Click on the **Activate Changes** button to finish.

How it works...

The timeout settings are important configurations to prevent a hang scenario, freeing WebLogic resources that are busy for a longer time than expected. The inverse situation can also occur where a request can naturally take a long time to process and a timeout error is thrown unnecessarily.

 Ensure that the timeout is set according to the system and application requirements.

The WebLogic applications usually make use of the **Java Transaction API** (**JTA**) standards to control the transaction processes. It allows multiple resources (XA) to participate in the same transaction. The timeout configurations must be set correctly; otherwise, the timeout exception will not be properly handled by the application when invoked.

As a rule of thumb, the **Transaction Manager** (**TM**) should have a smaller timeout value than the XA resources it calls. When the timeout is reached for the TM, the TM should properly handle all resources, rolling back all resource transactions. If a resource times out by itself, the TM probably won't handle the error properly.

In this recipe, the JTA is configured with 600 and the XA data source is configured with 620. In this case, the parameter DISTRIBUTED_LOCK_TIMEOUT of the Oracle Database should also be set with a higher value, such as 1000 seconds.

> **Comparing configurations**
>
> JTA (600) < Data Source XA (620) < Oracle Database (1000).

There's more...

The timeouts can be configured through WLST.

Configuring the transaction timeout by using WLST

1. Log in as wls user to shell and start WLST:

    ```
    [wls@prod01]$ $WL_HOME/common/bin/wlst.sh
    ```

2. Connect to the Administration Server using wlsadmin as the user, <pwd> as the password and t3://adminhost.domain.local:7001 as the server URL:

    ```
    wls:/offline> connect("wlsadmin","<pwd>","t3://adminhost.domain.
    local:7001")
    ```

3. Run the following WLST commands:

    ```
    edit()
    startEdit()


    cd('/JTA/PROD_DOMAIN')
    cmo.setTimeoutSeconds(600)


    cd('/JDBCSystemResources/ds-XA/JDBCResource/ds-XA/JDBCXAParams/ds-
    XA')
    cmo.setXaTransactionTimeout(620)
    cmo.setXaSetTransactionTimeout(true)


    activate()
    exit()
    ```

Choosing the JRockit garbage collection mode

Some WebLogic Administrators consider JVM tuning as the top tuning recommendation for WebLogic. But nowadays, with the newer JVM releases, just setting -Xms and -Xmx arguments and leaving the GC with default throughput GC mode, should be fine for most of the WebLogic applications. Since R28, the Oracle JRockit behaves very well out of the box and, in the majority of the cases, more advanced JVM tunings are not necessary.

There are some situations where a specific WebLogic application could not wait for a full GC that lasts more than a few seconds. In this recipe, the GC mode will be changed to the pausetime mode for this particular application.

Getting ready

A JVM startup argument will be added, by using the Administration Console, so make sure the Administration Server is running.

How to do it...

To change the JVM garbage collection mode:

1. Access the Administration Console by pointing your web browser to `http://adminhost.domain.local:7001/console`.
2. Click on the **Lock & Edit** button to start a new edit session.
3. Expand the **Environment** tree to the left and then click on **Servers**.
4. Click on the **PROD_Server01** link and then click on the **Server Start** tab.
5. Add the following to the **Arguments** field and click on the **Save** button:

   `-Xgc:pausetime`

6. Click on the **Activate Changes** button.
7. Restart **PROD_Server01**.
8. Repeat the preceding steps for Managed Servers **PROD_Server02**, **PROD_Server03**, and **PROD_Server04**.

How it works...

The following graph displays the results of two different tests with the response times of the exactly same application. The only difference between the results is the GC mode:

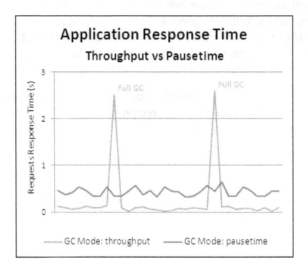

The blue line shows the default throughput mode. It has very low application response times for most of the test (average of 100 ms), but returns a higher response time when the GC is triggered. Note that the graph is from the application response time and not from the GC pause time. The throughput mode tries to leave the JVM running without any interference. Then, when needed, execute the GC as fast as possible by running it in parallel and using all the CPUs available; on the start up, the JVM checks how many CPU cores the machine has and starts the same number of GC threads. Although the JVM lets the application run at full speed when the GC is not needed, it will "stop the world" when full GC is invoked.

The red line shows the pausetime GC mode behavior. The application is not sensitive to full GC as the throughput mode, keeping the time consistent during all times. On the other hand, the responses get a much higher average time (400 ms) in comparison to the blue line. Since the JVM focuses on keeping the GC pausetime low, it keeps the GC running concurrent to the application, sharing CPU cycles and increasing the response time.

 Although the default throughput mode should be fine to almost all scenarios, some application requirements can't handle the response time variations. The graph comparison image is also an example. Test the application and choose the GC mode that best suits your needs.

Tuning thread concurrency with the default work manager

In production environments, keeping the computer resources such as memory, processes, connections, and threads under control is essential to maintain a stable and predictable system.

For a WebLogic Administrator focused on stability, the top tuning recommendation for WebLogic should be controlling the thread concurrency and resources usage.

In this recipe, the default work manager will be created to override the default settings with a new maximum thread constraint named `defaultMaxThreads` and configured with 50, targeting it to the cluster, `PROD_Cluster`.

Getting ready

The work manager will be created in the Administration Console.

How to do it...

Create the `defaultMaxThreads` maximum threads constraint and the `default` work manager in the Administration Console by following the ensuing steps:

1. Access the Administration Console by pointing your web browser to `http://adminhost.domain.local:7001/console`.

2. Click on the **Lock & Edit** button to start a new edit session.

3. Expand the **Environment** tree to the left and then click on **Work Managers**.

4. Click on the **New** button then select the **Maximum Threads Constraint** radio button. Click on the **Next** button.

5. Enter `defaultMaxThreads` in the **Name** text field and `50` in the **Count** text field. Click on the **Next** button.

6. Select the **All servers in the cluster** radio button from the **PROD_Cluster** option and click on the **Finish** button.

7. Click on the **New** button again and select the **Work Manager** radio button. Click on the **Next** button.

8. Enter `default` in the **Name** text field (as shown in the following screenshot) and click on the **Next** button.

9. Select the **All servers in the cluster** radio button from the **PROD_Cluster** option and click on the **Finish** button.

10. Click on the newly created **default** work manager and select the `defaultMaxThreads` option from the **Maximum Threads Constraint** drop-down menu. Check the **Ignore Stuck Threads** checkbox (as shown in the following screenshot) and click on the **Save** button.

11. Click on the **Activate Changes** button to finish.

How it works...

The Oracle WebLogic Server is a multithreaded application server. In a very simplistic way, it is a thread pool that receives and dispatches the incoming requests to be processed by the execution threads.

The WebLogic thread pool is called **Self-tuning Thread Pool**. It adjusts itself automatically trying to maximize the throughput by increasing and decreasing the number of active threads in the pool. The Self-tuning Thread Pool feature was introduced in WebLogic Server Version 9 and is, at the same time, one of its greatest features and one of the greatest weaknesses of the WebLogic Server.

In production environments, some scenarios of peak time or large bursts of incoming requests can fool the Self-tuning Thread Pool to grow too much, reaching some hundred threads. The default maximum size the Self-tuning Thread Pool can have is 400 threads and, with this size, it is unlikely that the WebLogic Server would handle all the concurrent incoming requests, probably leading the system to a hang situation.

The following graph illustrates a scenario where a WebLogic Managed Server hangs after it reaches a concurrency of 100 simultaneous requests being processed. The response time increases until the WebLogic Managed Server hangs:

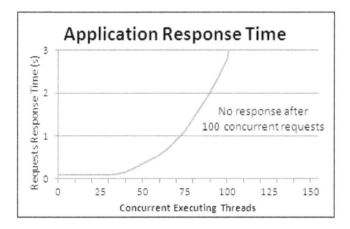

Designing a clustered architecture of small boxes, with low concurrency and low number of threads running in each Managed Server will normally get better stability and performance than a single, larger instance with a lot of threads.

A single thread consumes memory and resources, so the WebLogic Administrator must be aware of the Self-tuning Thread Pool behavior. In some scenarios, it must have the concurrency limited in order to protect WebLogic from peak times and incoming burst requests.

In this recipe, the default work manager was created to override the default configuration, limiting the concurrency of all applications deployed. The default work manager handles the application requests when no other work manager is defined. The work manager constraints are valid per WebLogic Server, so this configuration limits the **PROD_Server01**, **PROD_Server02**, **PROD_Server03**, and **PROD_Server04** to execute a maximum of 50 concurrent and simultaneous threads in each; or 200 concurrent threads, if counting the whole **PROD_Cluster** (50 threads * 4 instances).

At peak time, when the default work manager already has 50 threads executing on a Managed Server, the next request will be queued in the priority queue and wait until a thread is free. This configuration avoids the Self-tuning Thread Pool increasing the number of threads to a point that the WebLogic cannot handle the concurrency. On the other side, it also adds the possibility of queuing some of the requests, with a possible impact in the response time.

The following graph illustrates the protected WebLogic. Even though it's receiving more than 50 incoming requests, the Managed Server processes only 50 simultaneously, maintaining the SLA.

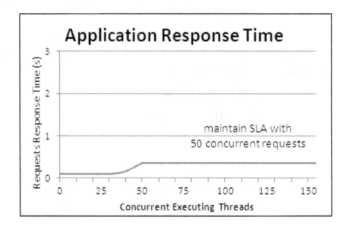

There's more...

The default work manager can be created through WLST.

Creating the default work manager by using WLST

Carry out the following steps:

1. Log in as `wls` user to shell and start WLST:

   `[wls@prod01]$ $WL_HOME/common/bin/wlst.sh`

2. Connect to the Administration Server using `wlsadmin` as the user, `<pwd>` as the password and `t3://adminhost.domain.local:7001` as the server URL:

   `wls:/offline> connect("wlsadmin","<pwd>","t3://adminhost.domain.local:7001")`

3. Run the following WLST commands:

```
edit()
startEdit()


cd('/SelfTuning/PROD_DOMAIN')
cmo.createMaxThreadsConstraint('defaultMaxThreadsConstraint')
cd('/SelfTuning/PROD_DOMAIN/MaxThreadsConstraints/
defaultMaxThreadsConstraint')
set('Targets',jarray.array([ObjectName('com.bea:Name=PROD_
Cluster,Type=Cluster')], ObjectName))
cmo.setCount(50)
cmo.unSet('ConnectionPoolName')


cd('/SelfTuning/PROD_DOMAIN')
cmo.createWorkManager('default')


cd('/SelfTuning/PROD_DOMAIN/WorkManagers/default')
set('Targets',jarray.array([ObjectName('com.bea:Name=PROD_
Cluster,Type=Cluster')], ObjectName))
cmo.setMaxThreadsConstraint(getMBean('/SelfTuning/PROD_DOMAIN/
MaxThreadsConstraints/defaultMaxThreadsConstraint'))
cmo.setIgnoreStuckThreads(true)
set('Targets',jarray.array([ObjectName('com.bea:Name=PROD_
Cluster,Type=Cluster')], ObjectName))


activate()
exit()
```

See also

▸ *Tuning application thread concurrency with custom work managers*

Tuning the application thread concurrency with custom work managers

In the previous recipe, the `default` work manager was created to limit the concurrency of all applications deployed in the **PROD_Cluster** cluster.

In this recipe, a new custom work manager `myWebServiceWM` will be created, with a maximum thread constraint named `myWebServiceMaxThreads`, configured with 20, and a capacity constraint of 20 as well.

The `myWebServiceWM` will be associated with the `myWebService.war` application so only the concurrency for the requests of this application will be limited to 20 threads per Managed Server.

Getting ready

The work manager will be defined in the Administration Console. The application also must update a descriptor in order to be associated with the new work manager.

How to do it...

First create the `myWebServiceMaxThreads` maximum threads constraint and the `myWebServiceWM` work manager in the Administration Console:

1. Access the Administration Console with your web browser at `http://adminhost.domain.local:7001/console`.

2. Click on the **Lock & Edit** button to start a new edit session.

3. Expand the **Environment** tree on the left and then click on **Work Managers**.

4. Click on the **New** button then select the **Maximum Threads Constraint** radio button. Click on the **Next** button.

5. Type `myWebServiceMaxThreads` in the **Name** text field and `20` in the **Count** text field. Click on the **Next** button.

6. Select the `All servers in the cluster` radio button from the **PROD_Cluster** option and click on the **Finish** button.

7. Click on the **New** button and select the **Capacity Constraint** radio button.

8. Type `myWebServiceCapacityConstraint` in the **Name** field and `20` in the **Count** field. Click on the **Next** button.

9. Select the **All servers in the cluster** radio button from the **PROD_Cluster** option and click on the **Finish** button.

10. Click on the **New** button again and select the **Work Manager** radio button. Click on the **Next** button.

11. Type `myWebServiceWM` in the **Name** text field and click on the **Next** button.

12. Select the **All servers in the cluster** radio button from the **PROD_Cluster** option and click on the **Finish** button.

13. Click on the newly created **myWebServiceWM** work manager. Select the `myWebServiceMaxThreads` option from the **Maximum Threads Constraint** drop-down menu and the `myWebServiceCapacityConstraint` option from the **Capacity Constraint** drop-down menu. Check the **Ignore Stuck Threads** checkbox (as shown in the following screenshot) and click on the **Save** button.

14. Click on the **Activate Changes** button to finish.

Now associate the `myWebServiceWM` work manager to be used by the `myWebService.war` application, by editing the file descriptor, `WEB-INF/weblogic.xml`:

1. Edit the file `WEB-INF/weblogic.xml` and add the tag `<wl-dispatch-policy>`:

```
<weblogic-web-app>
  <session-descriptor>
  ...
  </session-descriptor>
        <wl-dispatch-policy>myWebServiceWM</wl-dispatch-policy>
</weblogic-web-app>
```

2. Save and repack the `myWebService.war` application.

3. Redeploy the `myWebService.war` application.

How it works...

The custom work manager works the same way as the default work manager, but is limited to handle only the `myWebService.war` application requests.

In this recipe, a capacity constraint was also added to the work manager. The capacity constraint is the sum of the concurrent executing threads (limited by max threads constraint) and the queued requests. Since the `myWebServiceWM` is configured with the capacity constraint and max threads constraint with the same value of 20, the work manager won't allow any requests to be queued in the instance.

This application exposes only stateless web services, so there is no need for session affinity. The requests can be load balanced in a round-robin fashion. When one WebLogic Server instance reaches 20 concurrent requests, the next request will fail over to the next WebLogic instance of the cluster. In practice, when the instance is overloaded with the defined max threads running, it returns the HTTP Code 503. The recognizes the 503 code and fails over the request to the next instance, which is transparent to the caller.

> The HTTP request failover is controlled by the WebLogic plug-in, so it's mandatory to use the Apache/OHS with the plug-in when configuring work managers.

The WebLogic plug-in is covered in *Chapter 2, High Availability with WebLogic Clusters*.

> It is a common mistake to suppose that the WebLogic Plug-ins 1.1 failover works only when the `IDEMPOTENT` parameter is `true`. In fact, the parameter affects only the requests that were accepted by the WebLogic instance. Even when setting the `IDEMPOTENT` to `false`, the failover still works if the plug-in cannot connect to a WebLogic Instance (connect failover) or when it receives an HTTP 503 (overload failover). It is also recommended to set the `IDEMPOTENT` to `false` since it can inadvertently duplicate requests.

There's more...

The custom work manager can be created through WLST.

Creating the custom work manager by using WLST

Carry out the following steps:

1. Log in as the `wls` user to shell and start WLST:

   ```
   [wls@prod01]$ $WL_HOME/common/bin/wlst.sh
   ```

2. Connect to the Administration Server using `wlsadmin` as the user, `<pwd>` as the password and `t3://adminhost.domain.local:7001` as the server URL:

   ```
   wls:/offline> connect("wlsadmin","<pwd>","t3://adminhost.domain.
   local:7001")
   ```

3. Run the following WLST commands:

   ```
   edit()
   startEdit()

   cmo.createWorkManager('myWebServiceWM')

   cd('/SelfTuning/PROD_DOMAIN/WorkManagers/myWebServiceWM')
   set('Targets',jarray.array([ObjectName('com.bea:Name=PROD_
   Cluster,Type=Cluster')], ObjectName))

   cd('/SelfTuning/PROD_DOMAIN')
   cmo.createMaxThreadsConstraint('myWebServiceMaxThreads')
   cd('/SelfTuning/PROD_DOMAIN/MaxThreadsConstraints/
   myWebServiceMaxThreads')
   set('Targets',jarray.array([ObjectName('com.bea:Name=PROD_
   Cluster,Type=Cluster')], ObjectName))
   cmo.setCount(20)
   cmo.unSet('ConnectionPoolName')

   cd('/SelfTuning/PROD_DOMAIN')
   cmo.createCapacity('myWebServiceCapacityConstraint')
   cd('/SelfTuning/PROD_DOMAIN/Capacities/
   myWebServiceCapacityConstraint')
   set('Targets',jarray.array([ObjectName('com.bea:Name=PROD_
   Cluster,Type=Cluster')], ObjectName))
   cmo.setCount(20)

   cd('/SelfTuning/PROD_DOMAIN/WorkManagers/myWebServiceWM')
   cmo.setMaxThreadsConstraint(getMBean('/SelfTuning/PROD_DOMAIN/
   MaxThreadsConstraints/myWebServiceMaxThreads'))
   ```

```
cmo.setCapacity(getMBean('/SelfTuning/PROD_DOMAIN/Capacities/
myWebServiceCapacityConstraint'))

cmo.setIgnoreStuckThreads(true)


activate()

exit()
```

See also

▶ *Tuning thread concurrency with the default work manager*

▶ *Limiting the JMS Queue consumers*

Limiting the JMS Queue consumers

By default, an MDB (message driven bean) uses up to 16 threads per WebLogic Server instance to consume a JMS Queue destination.

In this recipe, an MDB QueueMDB from the hypothetical JMSApp application will be configured to use only one thread to consume the JMS Queue. This will be done by creating a new work manager jmsAppWM with a maximum thread constraint jmsAppMaxThreads with the value 1 and update the MDB descriptor to associate the new work manager.

Getting ready

The work manager will be defined in the Administration Console. The MDB descriptor must also update a descriptor in order to be associated with the new work manager.

How to do it...

First, create the jmsAppMaxThreads maximum threads constraint and the jmsAppWM work manager in the Administration Console:

1. Access the Administration Console by pointing your web browser to `http://adminhost.domain.local:7001/console`.

2. Click on the **Lock & Edit** button to start a new edit session.

3. Expand the **Environment** tree to the left and then click on **Work Managers**.

4. Click on the **New** button and then select the **Maximum Threads Constraint** radio button. Click on the **Next** button.

5. Type `jmsAppMaxThreads` in the **Name** text field and `1` in the **Count** text field. Click on the **Next** button.

6. Select the **All servers in the cluster** radio button from the **PROD_Cluster** option and click on the **Finish** button.

7. Click on the **New** button again and select the **Work Manager** radio button. Click on the **Next** button.

8. Type `jmsAppWM` in the **Name** text field and click on the **Next** button.

9. Select the **All servers in the cluster** radio button from the **PROD_Cluster** option and click on the **Finish** button.

10. Click on the newly created **jmsAppWM** work manager. Select the `jmsAppMaxThreads` option from the **Maximum Threads Constraint** drop-down menu. Check the **Ignore Stuck Threads** checkbox and click on the **Save** button.

11. Click on the **Activate Changes** button to finish.

Now associate the `jmsAppWM` work manager to be used by the `JMSApp` application, by editing the file descriptor `META-INF/weblogic-ejb-jar.xml`:

1. Edit the file `META-INF/weblogic-ejb-jar.xml` and add the tag `<dispatch-policy>`:

```
<weblogic-enterprise-bean>
  <ejb-name>QueueMDB</ejb-name>
  <message-driven-descriptor>
  . . .
  </message-driven-descriptor>
<dispatch-policy>jmsAppWM</dispatch-policy>
</weblogic-enterprise-bean>
```

2. Save and repack the `JMSApp` application.

3. Redeploy the `JMSApp` application.

How it works...

The `QueueMDB` now consumes the JMS Queue with a maximum of 1 thread instead of 16.

Controlling the JMS Queue consumers is important to prevent too much concurrency in the environments with a lot of JMS Queues. In a scenario where a hypothetic application uses 20 JMS Queues and there is a large backlog of messages in them, WebLogic can use up to 320 threads (20 Queues * 16 consumer threads).

The primary objective of controlling the thread concurrency is to avoid scenarios that can lead to an overloaded WebLogic, affecting the service level and availability.

See also

▸ *Tuning thread concurrency with the default work manager*

▸ *Tuning application thread concurrency with custom work managers*

8
Security

In this chapter, we will cover the following recipes:

- ▸ Setting up SSL for production environments
- ▸ Creating a new SQL authentication provider
- ▸ Assigning a user to a group
- ▸ Securing a web application with basic authentication
- ▸ Enabling the Administration Port

Introduction

To properly secure a production WebLogic domain, the hardware and host machines must be physically safe, and operating system and filesystem access must be restricted. Network access must be protected from unwanted traffic by means of a firewall, and communication must be encrypted to protect information.

The security subject in Oracle WebLogic Server 12c includes so many aspects and features that a whole book could be written about it.

WebLogic Server includes the WebLogic Security Service, a set of configurations and tools to secure the WebLogic domain and its resources.

As this is an administration cookbook, this chapter focuses on some security administration tasks, such as setting up an authentication provider and enabling **Secure Sockets Layer** (**SSL**).

Setting up SSL for production environments

WebLogic Server 12*c* supports SSL to add security and encryption to the data transmitted over the network.

In this recipe, SSL will be enabled in the `PROD_AdminServer` instance of the `PROD_DOMAIN` domain.

A new identity keystore and a new trusted keystore will be created to store the new certificate. The WebLogic Server instances and the Node Manager will be configured to enable the SSL protocol and use the custom keystores.

Getting ready

The keystores are created with the `keytool` command-line utility, and we will demonstrate signing a certificate with the `CertGen` Java utility. `keytool` comes as standard with the Java distribution, and `CertGen` is part of the WebLogic Server. Both utilities run from the command line, so log in to the Linux shell.

How to do it...

Create the identity keystore `PRODIdentity.jks` on the `prod01` machine:

1. Log in to shell as the user `wls`, and create a new folder named `/oracle/Middleware/user_projects/domains/PROD_DOMAIN/keystores`:

   [wls@prod01]$ mkdir /oracle/Middleware/user_projects/domains/PROD_DOMAIN/keystores

2. Set the `PROD_DOMAIN` environment variables with the `setDomainEnv.sh` script and create the keystore:

   [wls@prod01]$ cd /oracle/Middleware/user_projects/domains/PROD_DOMAIN/bin

   [wls@prod01]$ . ./setDomainEnv.sh

   [wls@prod01]$ cd keystores

   [wls@prod01]$ keytool -genkeypair -alias prodcert -keyalg RSA -keysize 1024 -dname "CN=*.domain.local,OU=MyOrganization,O=MyCompany,L=MyCity,S=MyState,C=US" -keystore PRODIdentity.jks

3. Type and confirm the password for the keystore, and then type `<ENTER>` to use the same password for `prodcert`:

   Enter keystore password: <Type a new password>

   Re-enter new password: <Re-type the password>

   Enter key password for <prodcert>

```
(RETURN if same as keystore password): <ENTER>
```

Generate a new CSR using `PRODIdentity.jks`:

1. Execute the `keytool` utility to generate the CSR.

    ```
    [wls@prod01]$ keytool -certreq -v -alias prodcert -file PRODCert.
    csr -keystore PRODIdentity.jks
    ```

2. Type the password when required:

    ```
    Enter keystore password: <Type the password>

    Certification request stored in file <PRODCert.csr>

    Submit this to your CA
    ```

Sign the CSR and import it into the identity keystore:

1. Submit `PRODCert.csr` to the Certificate Authority of your choice to get the digital certificate and its private key. For demonstration purposes, this recipe will use the `CertGen` utility to create and sign the certificate from the CSR. `CertGen` uses the WebLogic Demo CA (`CertGenCA.der`):

    ```
    [wls@prod01]$ java utils.CertGen -keyfile PRODCertPrivateKey
    -keyfilepass password -certfile PRODCert -cn "*.domain.local"

    Generating a certificate with common name *.domain.local and key
    strength 1024

    /oracle/Middleware/wlserver_12.1/server/lib/CertGenCA.der file and
    key from /oracle/Middleware/wlserver_12.1/server/lib/CertGenCAKey.
    der file
    ```

2. Import the server certificate and private keys to the `PRODIdentity.jks` keystore:

    ```
    [wls@prod01]$ java utils.ImportPrivateKey -keystore PRODIdentity.
    jks -keyfile PRODCertPrivateKey.pem -keyfilepass password
    -certfile PRODCert.pem -storepass password -alias prodcert
    ```

Create the custom trust keystore `PRODTrust.jks` on the `prod01` machine:

1. Create the `PRODTrust.jks` keystore by making a copy from the Standard Java Trust.

    ```
    [wls@prod01]$ cp /oracle/jvm/jre/lib/security/cacerts ./PRODTrust.
    jks
    ```

2. Change the default `cacerts` password. The default is `changeit`. Change it to a new one:

    ```
    [wls@prod01]$ keytool -storepasswd -keystore PRODTrust.jks

    Enter keystore password: changeit
    New keystore password: <Type the new password>
    ```

```
Re-enter new keystore password: <Re-type the new password>
```

3. In previous steps, the WebLogic Demo CA (`CertGenCA.der`) was used to sign the certificate, so it will be imported to the trust keystore. In production, import the CA certificate from your trusted CA vendor.

```
[wls@prod01]$ keytool -import -v -trustcacerts -alias rootCA
-file /oracle/Middleware/wlserver_12.1/server/lib/CertGenCA.der
-keystore PRODTrust.jks
```

Distribute the `keystore` folder to all machines on the `PROD_DOMAIN` domain:

1. Copy the `keystore` folder to the `prod02` machine:

```
[wls@prod01]$ scp -r /oracle/Middleware/user_projects/domains/
PROD_DOMAIN/keystores prod02:/oracle/Middleware/user_projects/
domains/PROD_DOMAIN/
```

Change the Node Manager in the `prod01` and `prod02` machines to use the custom keystores and the new certificate:

1. Edit the `nodemanager.properties` file:

```
[wls@prod01]$ vi $WL_HOME/common/nodemanager/nodemanager.
properties
```

2. Add the following lines to the file:

```
KeyStores=CustomIdentityAndCustomTrust
CustomIdentityKeyStoreFileName=/oracle/Middleware/user_projects/
domains/PROD_DOMAIN/keystores/PRODIdentity.jks
CustomIdentityKeyStorePassPhrase=password
CustomIdentityAlias=prodcert
CustomIdentityPrivateKeyPassPhrase=password
```

3. Enter `:ws!` to save and exit.

4. Repeat the `nodemanager.properties` configurations for the `prod02` machine.

5. Restart the Node Manager.

Assign WebLogic Server instances to use the custom keystores and the certificate:

1. Access the Administration Console by pointing your web browser to `http://adminhost.domain.local:7001/console`.

2. Click on the **[+] Environment** sign from the navigation box to the left and then click on the **Servers** link.

3. Click on the **PROD_AdminServer** link.

4. Click on the **Keystores** tab and then click on the **Change** button from the **Keystores** option As shown in the following screenshot:

5. Select the **Custom Identity and Custom Trust** option from the **Keystores** drop-down menu and click on the **Save** button.

6. Enter `./keystores/PRODIdentity.jks` in the **Custom Identity Keystore** text field. Then, enter `jks` in the **Custom Identity Keystore Type** text field. Enter the password chosen earlier in **Custom Identity Keystore Passphrase** and **Confirm Custom Identity Keystore Passphrase.**

7. Enter `./keystores/PRODTrust.jks` in the **Custom Trust Keystore** text field. Then, enter `jks` in the **Custom Trust Keystore Type** text field. Enter the password chosen earlier in **Custom Trust Keystore Passphrase** and **Confirm Custom Trust Keystore Passphrase**. Click on the **Save** button.

8. Click on the **SSL** tab and type `prodcert` in the **Private Key Alias** text field. Enter the password chosen earlier in **Private Key Passphrase** and **Confirm Private Key Passphrase**. Select the **Custom Hostname Verifier** option from the **Hostname Verification** drop-down menu and enter `weblogic.security.utils.SSLWLSWildcardHostnameVerifier` in the **Custom Hostname Verifier** text field. Click on the **Save** button.

9. Click on the **General** tab and check the **SSL Listen Port Enabled** checkbox As shown in the following screenshot:

10. Enter `7002` in the **SSL Listen Port** text field and click on the **Save** button.

11. Repeat the preceding steps for the PROD_Server01, PROD_Server02, PROD_Server03, and PROD_Server04 instances, using 9001, 9002, 9003, and 9004 in the **SSL Listen Port** text fields, respectively.

12. Click on the **Activate Changes** button.

13. Restart the Administration Server and the Managed Servers.

How it works...

Two new custom keystores were created. The identity keystore, PRODIdentity.jks, was created to store the certificate and its private key. The trust keystore, PRODTrust.jks, was created to store the root CA certificate.

 This recipe used the CertGen Java utility to sign the certificate using the WebLogic Demo CA, but in production, you should obtain the digital certificate from a trusted Certificate Authority such as Symantec, Comodo, GoDaddy, and GlobalSign.

All WebLogic Server instances were configured to use the custom identity and trust keystores and stop using the default DemoIdentity.jks and DemoTrust.jks keystores. The Node Manager was also configured to use the custom keystores and the new certificate.

The SSL protocol was then enabled in the PROD_AdminServer and PROD_Server01, PROD_Server02, PROD_Server03, and PROD_Server04 Managed Servers.

This recipe used only one certificate for the WebLogic server instances and the Node Managers. The certificate was signed with CN=*.domain.local, meaning it should be valid to any host with the domain.local address. This is possible by enabling the weblogic.security.utils.SSLWLSWildcardHostnameVerifier class of the Custom HostName Verification namespace.

See also

▸ *Enabling the Administration Port*

Creating a new SQL authentication provider

New domains in WebLogic Server 12c are created with the default authentication provider called DefaultAuthenticator. DefaultAuthenticator authenticates the users and groups stored in the internal LDAP mechanism on the WebLogic Server. The internal LDAP runs embedded with the WebLogic Server Instance. The Administration Server runs the master LDAP and the Managed Servers run the LDAP as replicas.

It is possible to use the internal LDAP to store and authenticate the users and groups in production, but the WebLogic administrator can add more robust types of authentication providers such as, a database, Active Directory, and external LDAP, among many others.

In this recipe, a new SQL authentication provider named PRODSQLProvider will be configured and added to the PROD_DOMAIN domain to store and handle the users and groups in an Oracle database.

A new data source, ds-Provider, will be created. The database runs at the dbhost hostname and listens to the port 1521. The listener accepts requests to the service name dbservice. The database username is dbuser, and the password is dbpwd.

Getting ready

Unfortunately, WebLogic Server 12c does not provide an out of the box database script to create the tables needed to store the users and groups, so you must run the script provided to create the tables and insert the default groups.

How to do it...

Create the tables needed in your database:

1. Run the following script to create the tables in your Oracle database:

```
CREATE TABLE USERS
  (
      U_NAME          VARCHAR(200) NOT NULL,
      U_PASSWORD      VARCHAR(50) NOT NULL,
      U_DESCRIPTION VARCHAR(1000)
  );
ALTER TABLE USERS
  ADD CONSTRAINT PK_USERS PRIMARY KEY (U_NAME);
CREATE TABLE GROUPS
  (
      G_NAME          VARCHAR(200) NOT NULL,
      G_DESCRIPTION VARCHAR(1000) NULL
  );
ALTER TABLE GROUPS
  ADD CONSTRAINT PK_GROUPS PRIMARY KEY (G_NAME);
CREATE TABLE GROUPMEMBERS
  (
      G_NAME   VARCHAR(200) NOT NULL,
      G_MEMBER VARCHAR(200) NOT NULL
  );
ALTER TABLE GROUPMEMBERS
```

```
   ADD CONSTRAINT PK_GROUPMEMS PRIMARY KEY ( G_NAME, G_MEMBER );
ALTER TABLE GROUPMEMBERS
   ADD CONSTRAINT FK1_GROUPMEMBERS FOREIGN KEY ( G_NAME )
REFERENCES GROUPS (
   G_NAME) ON DELETE CASCADE;
```

2. Populate the tables with the default WebLogic groups:

```
INSERT INTO GROUPS (G_NAME,G_DESCRIPTION) VALUES ('AdminChannelUse
rs','AdminChannelUsers can access the admin channel.');
INSERT INTO GROUPS (G_NAME,G_DESCRIPTION) VALUES ('Administrators
','Administrators can view and modify all resource attributes and
start and stop servers.');
INSERT INTO GROUPS (G_NAME,G_DESCRIPTION) VALUES
('AppTesters','AppTesters group.');
INSERT INTO GROUPS (G_NAME,G_DESCRIPTION) VALUES ('CrossDomainCon
nectors','CrossDomainConnectors can make inter-domain calls from
foreign domains.');
INSERT INTO GROUPS (G_NAME,G_DESCRIPTION) VALUES
('Deployers','Deployers can view all resource attributes and
deploy applications.');
INSERT INTO GROUPS (G_NAME,G_DESCRIPTION) VALUES
('Monitors','Monitors can view and modify all resource attributes
and perform operations not restricted by roles.');
INSERT INTO GROUPS (G_NAME,G_DESCRIPTION) VALUES
('Operators','Operators can view and modify all resource
attributes and perform server lifecycle operations.');
INSERT INTO GROUPS (G_NAME,G_DESCRIPTION) VALUES
('OracleSystemGroup','Oracle application software system group.');

COMMIT;
```

Access the Administration Console to create the new data source ds-Provider:

1. Access the Administration Console by pointing your web browser to
   http://adminhost.domain.local:7001/console.

2. Click on the **Lock & Edit** button to start a new edit session.

3. Expand the **Services** tree to the left, and then click on **Data Sources**.

4. Click on the **New** button and then click on **Generic Data Source**.

5. Enter ds-Provider in the **Name** field and jdbc/ds-Provider in the **JNDI Name**
   field. Leave the **Database Type** drop-down menu with the **Oracle** option selected.
   Click on the **Next** button.

6. Choose *Oracle's Driver (Thin) for Service connections;
   Versions:9.0.1 and later from the **Database Driver** drop-down menu.
   Click on the **Next** button.

7. Leave **Transaction Options** with the default values and click on the **Next** button.

8. On the **Connection Properties** page, enter dbservice in the **Database Name** field, dbhost in the **Host Name** field, and 1521 in the **Port** field. Fill the **Database User Name**, **Password**, and **Confirm Password** fields with dbuser and dbpwd. Click on the **Next** button.

9. Click on the **Next** button on the **Test Database Connection** page.

10. Select the **PROD_AdminServer** checkbox and the **All servers in the cluster** radio button from the **PROD_Cluster** cluster. Click on the **Finish** button.

11. Click on the **Activate Changes** button.

Create a new security provider, PRODSQLProvider:

1. Click on the **Lock & Edit** button to start a new edit session.

2. Click on the **Security Realms** option (shown in the following screenshot) in the left-hand navigation box and then click on the **myrealm** link.

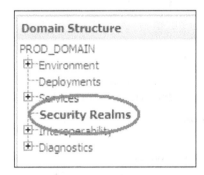

3. On the **Settings for myrealm** page, click on the **Providers** tab.

4. Click on the **New** button on the **Authentication Providers** page.

5. Enter PRODSQLProvider in the **Name** text field and choose SQLAuthenticator in the **Type** drop-down menu. Click on the **OK** button.

6. Click on **PRODSQLProvider** and then click on the **Provider Specific** tab.

7. Enter `ds-Provider` in the **Data Source Name** text field (as shown in the following screenshot) and click on the **Save** button. Leave all other options at their default values.

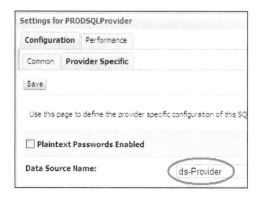

8. Click on the **Activate Changes** button.
9. Restart all instances of `PROD_DOMAIN`.

Create a new user, `wlsadmin`, for your new provider:

1. Access the Administration Console again by pointing your web browser to `http://adminhost.domain.local:7001/console`.
2. Click on the **Security Realms** option in the left-hand navigation box, and then click on the **myrealm** link.
3. Click on the **Users and Groups** tab.
4. On the **Users** page, click on the **New** button.
5. Enter `wlsadmin` in the **Name** text field, choose the `PRODSQLProvider` from the **Provider** drop-down menu, and enter `wlspwd123` in the **Password** and **Confirm Password** text fields. Click on the **OK** button, as shown in the following screenshot:

6. Click on the previously created **wlsadmin** user for **PRODSQLProvider** and click on the **Groups** tab.

7. Associate the **Administrators** group with the user by selecting the **Administrators** checkbox in the **Available:** table and then clicking on the **>** button (as shown in the following screenshot). Click on the **Save** button.

Assign **PRODSQLProvider** as the first provider and leave **DefaultAuthenticator** as the second provider. To do this, follow the steps mentioned below:

1. Click on the **Lock & Edit** button to start a new edit session.
2. Click on the **Security Realms** option in the left-hand navigation box and then click on the **myrealm** link.
3. On the **Settings for myrealm** page, click on the **Providers** tab.
4. Click on the **Reorder** button.
5. Select the **PRODSQLProvider** checkbox in the **Available** table and click on the upper arrow on the right to move **PRODSQLProvider** to the top of the list (as shown in the following screenshot). Click on the **OK** button.

6. Click on **PRODSLQProvider** again. Change the **Control Flag** drop-down menu to **SUFFICENT**. Click on the **Save** button.
7. Go back to the **Providers** page and click on **DefaultAuthenticator**. Change the **Control Flag** drop-down menu selection to **SUFFICENT**. Click on the **Save** button.
8. Click on the **Activate Changes** button.
9. Shut down the Administration Server and all instances of the PROD_DOMAIN.

Change the boot.properties file of the Administration Server to look up for the user PRODSQLProvider wlsadmin by following these steps:

1. Go to the Administration Server root folder:

   [wls@prod01]$ cd $DOMAIN_HOME/servers/PROD_AdminServer/security

2. Recreate the boot.properties file to match the wlsadmin user created:

   **[wls@prod01]$ echo -ne "username=wlsadmin\npassword=wlspwd123" >
   boot.properties**

   [wls@prod01]$ cat boot.properties

```
username=wlsadmin
password=wlspwd123
```

3. Start the Administration Server.

How it works...

The first step created the tables in the database to store the user and group data.

 It is necessary to insert the provided groups into the new provider to maintain consistency with the default global roles in the WebLogic Server.

We created the provider PRODSQLProvider with the default values, including the use of encrypted passwords only. We created the data source ds-Provider and associated it with the provider to handle the database connection.

We changed the order of the providers such that PRODSQLProvider is placed before the DefaultAuthenticator provider. With both providers configured with the SUFFICIENT control flag, WebLogic will try to authenticate first on PRODSQLProvider; if authentication fails, it will try on DefaultAuthenticator. A possible alternative configuration is to delete DefaultAuthenticator and leave only PRODSQLProvider with the REQUIRED control flag.

 It's an option to leave DefaultAuthenticator as a second provider in case of a database outage.

We also changed the boot.properties file to match a username and password from the new database authentication provider.

See also

▸ _Securing a web application with basic authentication_

Assigning a user to a group

In this recipe, a new group called myAuthGroup will be created and a new user, authUser, will be created and assigned to this group. PRODSQLProvider will be used.

Getting ready

The change will be made by using the Administration Console, so make sure the Administration Server is running.

How to do it...

Create a new group, `myAuthGroup`, and a new user, `authUser`, for `PRODSQLProvider`:

1. Access the Administration Console again by pointing your web browser to `http://adminhost.domain.local:7001/console`.

2. Click on the **Security Realms** option in the left-hand navigation box, and then click on the **myrealm** link.

3. Click on the **Users and Groups** tab.

4. Click on the **Groups** tab and click on the **New** button.

5. Enter `myAuthGroup` in the **Name** text field and choose **PRODSQLProvider** from the **Provider** drop-down menu. Click on the **OK** button.

6. Click on the **Users** tab and then on the **New** button.

7. Enter `authUser` in the **Name** text field, choose **PRODSQLProvider** from the **Provider** drop-down menu, and enter `authpwd123` in the **Password** and **Confirm Password** text fields. Click on the **OK** button.

8. Click on the **authUser** user for **PRODSQLProvider** and click on the **Groups** tab.

9. Associate the **myAuthGroup** group with the user by checking the **myAuthGroup** checkbox in the **Available** table and then clicking on the **>** button. Click on the **Save** button.

See also

▶ *Securing a web application with basic authentication*

Securing a web application with basic authentication

WebLogic Security services allow the WebLogic Administrator to add declarative security roles and policies to WebLogic resources such as web applications, EJBs, and other resources without making changes to the source code or to the file descriptors of the application.

In this recipe, a hypothetical `myAuthApp.war` web application will be deployed and configured to be accessed only by the users from the `PRODSQLProvider` that are members of the group `myAuthGroup`.

Getting ready

An application file named `myAuthApp.war` will be deployed and configured using the Administration Console, so make sure the Administration Server is running.

How to do it...

Deploy `myAuthApp.war` to `PROD_Cluster`:

1. Create a new application installation directory using the syntax: `/oracle/applicat ions/<environment>/<application>/<version>`:

   ```
   [wls@prod01]$ mkdir -p /oracle/applications/prod/myAuthApp/v1
   [wls@prod01]$ cd /oracle/applications/prod/myAuthApp/v1
   ```

2. Create two directories using the following commands:

   ```
   [wls@prod01]$ mkdir app
   [wls@prod01]$ mkdir plan
   ```

3. Copy the `myAuthApp.war` file to the `app` directory.

4. Access the Administration Console at `http://adminhost.domain.local:7001/console`.

5. Click on the **Lock & Edit** button to start a new edit session.

6. Navigate to the **Deployments** page by clicking on the link in the **Domain Structure** on the left-hand side navigation table.

7. Click on the **Install** button to install a new application.

8. Type the path `/oracle/applications/prod/myAuthApp/v1/app` and click on **Next**.

9. Select `myAuthApp.war` from the list and click on **Next**.

10. Select **Install this deployment as an application** and click on **Next**.

11. Select the **All servers from the cluster** radio button from the **PROD_Cluster** cluster and click on **Next**.

12. Select the **Custom Roles and Policies: Use only roles and policies that are defined in the Administration Console** radio button from the **Security** tab and click on the **Finish** button.

13. A new deployment plan file called `Plan.xml` will automatically be created in `/oracle/applications/prod/myAuthApp/v1/plan`.

14. Click on the **Activate Changes** button to apply the changes.

Apply security to `myAuthApp.war` by following these steps:

1. Click on the **myAuthApp** link from the **Deployments** page.

2. Open the **Security** tab and then click on the **Policies** tab from the **Application Scope**. Click on the **Add Condition** button, as shown in the following screenshot:

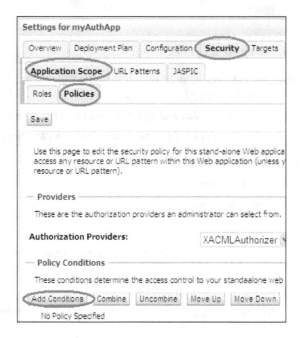

3. Choose the **Group** option from the **Predicate List** drop-down menu and click on the **Next** button.

4. Enter `myAuthGroup` in the **Group Argument Name** text field and click on the **Add** button (see the following screenshot) to add it to the list below. Click on the **Finish** button.

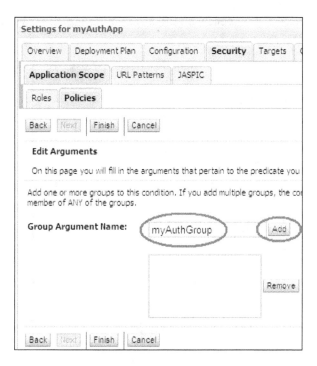

5. Click on the **Save** button on the **Policies** page to finish.

How it works...

The myAuthApp.war application can now be accessed only by users that match the
security policy. In this case, the security policy checks whether the user belongs to the
group myAuthGroup.

 To add the declarative security roles and policies, the application must be
deployed with the **Custom Roles and Policies** option enabled.

When a user tries to access the application URI at /myAuthApp, the browser returns a basic authentication window:

To access the application, enter a username, such as authUser, which we created in the previous recipe. authUser is a member of the myAuthGroup group, which is permitted to access the application. Try accessing the application as a user that does not match the policy, and the application will return a HTTP 401 Unauthorized error.

See also

> ▸ *Creating a New SQL authentication provider*
> ▸ *Assigning a user to a group*

Enabling the Administration Port

The Administration Port is a domain wide configuration that segregates all administrative traffic from the application traffic.

In this recipe, the Administration Port will be enabled in the PROD_Domain domain.

Getting ready

The Administration Port requires all WebLogic Server instances, including the Administration Server and the Managed Server, to already be configured to use SSL.

How to do it...

To enable the Administration Port, access the Administration Console:

1. Access the Administration Console by pointing your web browser to
   `http://adminhost.domain.local:7001/console`.

2. Click on the **Lock & Edit** button to start a new edit session.

3. Click on the **PROD_DOMAIN** link on the left-hand side navigation tree.

4. Check the **Enable Administration Port** checkbox and enter `17002` in
   the **Administrative Port** text field (as shown in the following screenshot).
   Click on the **Save** button.

5. Click on **Activate Changes** to finish.

6. The Administration Console now is accessible only from the URL
   `https://adminhost.domain.local:17002/console`.

How it works...

With the Administration Port enabled, the WebLogic Server creates a new internal network administrative channel that is now used to transfer administrative data between the Administration Server and the Managed Servers.

The Administration Port also allows the segregation of application and administrative traffic through different channels.

Enabling the Administration Port forces every WebLogic instance in the domain to listen for the port defined (17002, in this recipe). Make sure there won't be any port binding conflicts by assigning different IP addresses to each Managed Server.

There's more...

The Administrative Port can also be enabled through WLST.

Enabling the Administration Port by using WLST

1. Log in to the shell as the user `wls` and start WLST:

   `[wls@prod01]$ $WL_HOME/common/bin/wlst.sh`

2. Connect to the Administration Server using `wlsadmin` as the user, `<pwd>` as the password, and `t3://adminhost.domain.local:7001` as the server URL:

   `wls:/offline> connect("wlsadmin","<pwd>","t3://adminhost.domain.`
   `local:7001")`

3. Run the following WLST commands:

   `edit()`

   `startEdit()`

   `cmo.setAdministrationPortEnabled(true)`

   `cmo.setAdministrationPort(17002)`

   `activate()`

   `exit()`

See also

► *Setting up SSL for production environments*

Index

Symbols

[STUCK] flag 200
-XverboseTimeStamp attribute 193

A

access.log file 189, 191
Activate Changes button 140, 181
Activate Changes option 19
Administration Console
  about 18, 158
  active changes 19
  changes making, WLST used 19-21
  changes, protecting 21-23
  changes protecting, WLST used 23
  content, adding 28
  customizing 24-26
  extending 24-26
  extension, removing from 28
  other modifications 27
  pages, adding 28
  saving 18
  tables, customizing 158-160
  thread dumps, getting from 198-200
  used, for creating file stores 107-109
  used, for creating JDBC stores 112, 113
  used, for creating JMS module 122, 123
  used, for enabling Administration Port 259
Administration Port
  about 258
  enabling 259, 260
  enabling, Administration Console used 259
  enabling, WLST used 260
Administration Server
  about 15, 73

Administration Console application,
  accessing 17
boot.properties file, creating 16, 17
files, copying to machine 74
Listen Address value, changing 73
starting, in background 17
starting, in prod02 machine 74
starting, steps for 15, 16
start script, changing 76
stop script, changing 76
Apache HTTP Server
  installing, for Web tier 56, 57
  installing, steps for 57-60
Apache HTTP Server 2.2.x
  about 60
  URL, for downloading 57
application
  deploying, steps for 35, 36
  deploying, weblogic.Deployer tool used 36
  deploying, WLST used 37
Application archived file (EAR)
  deploying, steps for 35
application thread concurrency
  tuning, with custom work managers 234, 235
authUser 258

B

Balance HTTP Requests
  loading to WebLogic cluster, Web Server
    Plug-in used 60-62
BIG-IP F5
  URL 61
boot.properties file 252
  creating 16, 17

C

CertGen 242
Clear Statement Cache operation 93
cluster. *See* WebLogic cluster
Cluster Address configuration 51
cluster channel
  defining, WLST used 70-72
cluster communications
  Multicast, using for 54, 55
  Unicast, using for 52, 53
cluster parameters
  changing 49, 50
cluster settings
  changing, WLST used 51
collected metrics 178
connection factory
  about 136
  creating, WLST used 130, 132
Consensus option 143
consumers
  for JMSAppQueue queue, resuming 132, 133
  of JMSAppQueue queue, resuming 133
  pausing, WLST used 134
  resuming, WLST used 135
CrashRecoveryEnabled parameter 48, 50
CSR
  generating, PRODIdentity.jks used 243

D

Database Name field 82
Data Source Name text field 250
data source password
  recovering 208, 209
data source tuning
  setting 94-96
  WLST used 96
DefaultAuthenticator provider 253
distributed queue
  about 127
  creating, steps for 128-130
  creating, WLST used 130-132
domain logging
  disabling, WLST used 220
  turning off 218, 219

E

Eclipse Memory Analyzer. *See* MAT
EmailAlertModule WLDF module, creating 167, 168
ENABLE=BROKEN parameter 99
Enterprise Java Beans (EJB) 51

F

Failover algorithm 87
FAILOVER=OFF parameter 99
Failover Request if Busy option 98
Fast Application Notification (FAN) 90
file stores
  creating 106, 107
  creating, Administration Console used 107-109
  creating, WLST used 109
Flight Recorder 200
fully qualified domain name (FQDN) 9

G

GC
  enabling, with jrcmd 197
  logging, enabling 192-196
GridLink data source
  advantages, over multi data source 90
  creating 88, 89
  creating, steps for 89
  creating, WLST used 90
group
  user, assigning 253, 254

H

HA Strategy, multi data source
  configuring 87
  defining 86
HA WebLogic cluster parameters
  configuring 48, 49, 50
heap dump
  about 202
  analyzing 203-206
  automatic generation, on OOM conditions 206
httpd-weblogic.conf file 64

U

Unicast
used, for cluster communications 52, 53
unpack command 13
user
assigning, to group 253, 254

V

verbose garbage collection (GC). *See* **GC**
Virtual IP addresses (VIP) 46

W

watches and notifications
creating, for WLDF module 169, 170
web application
securing, with basic authentication 254-258
Web Application (WAR) 35
WebLogic Admin password
recovering 206, 207
WebLogic cluster
about 39, 40, 138
Balance HTTP Requests loading to, Web
Server Plug-in used 60-62
creating 40-43
creating, WLST used 44
requests, proxying to 65, 66
WebLogic configuration 185, 186
weblogic.Deployer tool
used, for deploying application 36
WebLogic Diagnostic Framework. *See* **WLDF**
WebLogic domain
about 8, 9
creating, steps for 9-11
files, distributing to remote machines 12, 13
files, manual distribution 13
WebLogic Managed Server
starting 32
starting, Node Manager used 32, 33
starting, with provided shell script 33, 34
starting, WLST used 32, 33
stopping 32
stopping, Node Manager used 32, 33
stopping, with provided shell script 33, 34
stopping, WLST used 32, 33

WebLogic plug-in
configuring 62-64
WebLogic Security 254, 256
WebLogic Server 5, 241
WebLogic Server 12c
installing 6
installing, requisites for 6
installing, steps for 7, 8
Web Server Plug-in
Balance HTTP Requests, loading to WebLogic
cluster 60-62
Web tier
Apache HTTP Server, installing 56, 57
WLDF
about 166
EmailAlertMailSession mail session, creating
167
EmailAlertModule WLDF module, creating
167, 168
Harvester, creating 182
module, creating 182
watches and notifications, creating 169, 170
WLST
log levels, changing 188, 189
used, for adding time taken field 191, 192
used, for changing cluster settings 51
used, for changing Listen Address value 47
used, for changing multi data source
algorithm type 88
used, for changing server affinity 138
used, for configuring messaging bridge 148-
151
used, for configuring Multicast 56
used, for configuring timeouts 226
used, for creating connection factory 130,
132
used, for creating custom work manager 237
used, for creating default work manager 232,
233
used, for creating distributed queue 130-132
used, for creating file stores 109
used, for creating GridLink data source 90
used, for creating JDBC data source 79, 80
used, for creating JDBC stores 113-116
used, for creating JMS module 123
used, for creating JMS servers 119
used, for creating JMS servers with JDBC

X

Y

Thank you for buying
Oracle WebLogic Server 12c Advanced
Administration Cookbook

About Packt Publishing

Packt, pronounced 'packed', published its first book "*Mastering phpMyAdmin for Effective MySQL Management*" in April 2004 and subsequently continued to specialize in publishing highly focused books on specific technologies and solutions.

Our books and publications share the experiences of your fellow IT professionals in adapting and customizing today's systems, applications, and frameworks. Our solution-based books give you the knowledge and power to customize the software and technologies you're using to get the job done. Packt books are more specific and less general than the IT books you have seen in the past. Our unique business model allows us to bring you more focused information, giving you more of what you need to know, and less of what you don't.

Packt is a modern, yet unique publishing company, which focuses on producing quality, cutting-edge books for communities of developers, administrators, and newbies alike. For more information, please visit our website: www.PacktPub.com.

About Packt Enterprise

In 2010, Packt launched two new brands, Packt Enterprise and Packt Open Source, in order to continue its focus on specialization. This book is part of the Packt Enterprise brand, home to books published on enterprise software – software created by major vendors, including (but not limited to) IBM, Microsoft and Oracle, often for use in other corporations. Its titles will offer information relevant to a range of users of this software, including administrators, developers, architects, and end users.

Writing for Packt

We welcome all inquiries from people who are interested in authoring. Book proposals should be sent to author@packtpub.com. If your book idea is still at an early stage and you would like to discuss it first before writing a formal book proposal, contact us; one of our commissioning editors will get in touch with you.

We're not just looking for published authors; if you have strong technical skills but no writing experience, our experienced editors can help you develop a writing career, or simply get some additional reward for your expertise.

Oracle Weblogic Server 11gR1 PS2: Administration Essentials

ISBN: 978-1-84968-302-9   Paperback: 304 pages

Install, configure, deploy and administer Java EE applications with Oracle WebLogic Server

1. A practical book with step-by-step instructions for admins in real-time company environments

2. Create, commit, undo, and monitor a change session using the Administration Console

3. Create basic automated tooling with WLST

Oracle WebLogic Server 12c: First Look

ISBN: 978-1-84968-718-8   Paperback: 144 pages

A sneak peek at Oracle's recently launched WebLogic 12c, guiding you through new features and techniques.

1. A concise and practical first look to immediately get you started with Oracle Weblogic 12c

2. Understand the position and use of Oracle WebLogic 12c in Exalogic and the Cloud

Please check **www.PacktPub.com** for information on our titles

Instant Securing WebLogic Server 12c

ISBN: 978-1-84968-778-2   Paperback: 100 pages

Learn to develop, administer and troubleshoot your WebLogic Server

1. Discover Authentication providers

2. Configure security for WebLogic applications and develop your own security providers

3. Step by step guide to administer and configure WebLogic security providers

4. Quick guide to security configuration in WebLogic realm

Oracle Enterprise Manager Grid Control 11g R1: Business Service Management

ISBN: 978-1-84968-216-9   Paperback: 360 pages

Build enterprise-ready business applications with Silverlight

1. Govern Business Service Management using Oracle Enterprise Manager 11gR1

2. Discover the evolution of enterprise IT infrastructure and the modeling paradigms to manage it

3. Use and apply various techniques in modeling complex data centers using Oracle Enterprise Manager

4. Model and define various composite targets such as Groups, Systems, and Services

Please check **www.PacktPub.com** for information on our titles